D1161535

THE NEW DEAL
AND
FOREIGN TRADE

THE MACMILLAN COMPANY
NEW YORK · BOSTON · CHICAGO · DALLAS
ATLANTA · SAN FRANCISCO

MACMILLAN & CO., LIMITED
LONDON · BOMBAY · CALCUTTA
MELBOURNE

THE MACMILLAN COMPANY
OF CANADA, LIMITED
TORONTO

THE NEW DEAL AND FOREIGN TRADE

By

ALONZO E. TAYLOR

Director, Food Research Institute,
Stanford University, California

New York

THE MACMILLAN COMPANY

1935

Set up and printed.
Published, July, 1935.

SET UP BY BROWN BROTHERS LINOTYPERS
PRINTED IN THE UNITED STATES OF AMERICA
BY THE FERRIS PRINTING COMPANY

PREFACE

THE problem of foreign trade now looms large on the political horizon. At the peak of trade activity in 1929, the monetary value of the exports of goods of reporting countries had an estimated value equivalent to about 35 billion gold dollars. These goods represented an undetermined fraction of the total volume of goods produced within all countries. Incomplete as is our information on foreign trade, it is much more complete than our information on domestic production. For a country like the United States, it may be stated that the goods exported in 1929 represented, let us say, 10 per cent of the total production of all goods. For some countries, the proportion of domestic production passing to export is much larger. Suppose for illustration we assume that the goods represented in the 35 billion dollars' worth of exports were about a sixth of the total production of goods in the world. With a population estimate for the world of 1.8 billion people, this might suggest that the average annual per capita production of goods in the world amounted to the equivalent of the small sum of about 115 dollars (pre-devaluation gold), of which about 19 dollars represented goods which had moved to consumers through the channels of foreign trade. The figures are merely illustrative and imply nothing, but might be used as basis for inquiry into trend. Is the proportion of export goods to total goods to be expected to rise or decline in the future?

The total volume of production is more important than the volume or proportion passing to export. Material civilization depends on continuing development of the arts of production, continuing enlargement in the outturn of production, and continuing expansion of the radius and extent of consumption. The stream of goods must lengthen, widen, and deepen. The improvements in production and the elevation of the standard of living do not occur simultaneously in all countries nor to the same extent, even from the uneven base lines. But with full allowance for all irregularity and lag, progress in material civilization depends on expansion of production. We think too much of prices, too little of volume of goods. Services of course are forms of goods.

The world faces the problem of recovery from an unprecedented depression. This is first a local problem in every country. In each country, more or less, recovery of domestic production, internal utilization and export revolve about five more or less separate questions, on the assumption that what appears to be a relative overproduction of certain materials during recent years has, in fact, been a relative underconsumption.

(1) By what methods, to what extent, and under what political institutions are countries to expand volume of production and reduce cost of production?

(2) How are countries to determine the real internal values of their more or less depreciated currencies and revalue them to arrive at what they regard as equitable domestic relations between capital and labor, investment and debt, extraction and processing?

(3) How are countries to determine the foreign exchange values of their internally revalued currencies, i.e., the purchasing power abroad, the new relations of the revalued currencies in countries trading with one another?

(4) What are the outlets in foreign countries for the goods already producible in many countries in excess of domestic requirements, as the expression of natural resources and existing processes of production?

(5) Under continuing developments in the arts of production, utilization, and substitution, what are the new relations of comparative costs of production in different surplus-producing countries and the comparative costs of consumption in the different importing countries?

If one could answer these questions, one could try to forecast the trend of volume of outturn of all goods in the world, and the proportion which would be distributed through international commerce. Whether this proportion would exceed, merely equal, or be less than the proportion in 1909-13 or in 1925-29, is not predictable. Some internationalists of strong convictions seem to infer that the trend ought to be in the direction of a continuing enlargement of the proportion of world production passing into international trade. Some nationalists of strong convictions seem to infer that the trend ought to be in the direction of a continuing contraction of the proportion of world production passing into international trade. The forthright internationalist and the outright nationalist both make assumptions in respect of circumstances which they range under the term "comparative costs"; these, however, include different concepts of standards of living and of mobility of labor and capital as well as of goods and services. Both nationalist and internationalist unconsciously impose on the general trend of the future the implications of particular experiences in the past. Both nationalists and internationalists predicate increase in world production of goods and services, let us say at the continuing rate of 3-4 per cent per annum; their difference in view concerns the proportion that is to go to export.

Important questions arise involving larger areas than individual countries. What is the future of intra-continental foreign trade, contrasted with inter-continental foreign trade? With changes in boundaries emerge different relations of foreign commerce, of which eastern Asia will offer the next illustration. Is the foreign trade of Europe destined to continue to decline relatively? Those who speak of "free trade" usually mean free (or freer) movement of goods from country to country. They may also include in free trade the free movement of services and of capital, which of course are merely a form of movement of goods. But the expression "free trade" does not usually include free movement in monetary metals, and certainly it does not include free trade in labor, i.e., unrestricted immigration. Therefore any conceivable state of free trade in the modern world implies only a limited form of free trade. If we had no import tariff duties, the movement of goods between countries would be increased. But to assume that in each country, taking any common year as a base line, the foreign trade would be enlarged proportionally by a more or less uniform horizontal elevation, is certainly fallacious: the enlarged movement of goods under free trade would be greatly altered in geographical relations, there might be more inter-continental trade and less intra-continental trade, less movement of goods into and out of Europe, and more movement of goods into and out of Asia. A revived foreign commerce will not be the *status quo ante bellum* plus enlargement; it will be a different commerce, both in character of goods and in regional distribution.

Three things, separate but interconnected, are evident in a general decline of foreign trade such as now persists in the world. (1) The gross volume of goods is reduced; the reductions fall differently on different categories, and indeed an occasional commodity may be exported in enlarged amount. (2) The gross value of goods moving in foreign trade is reduced; again the reductions fall differently on different categories, and an occasional commodity may display a rise in price. (3) The proportions of different goods in the gross total are altered; some decline in export movement more than others and an occasional commodity may flow outward in enlarged amount. Now, a considerable amount of faulty discussion on recovery of foreign trade is based upon disregard of these circumstances. To a rather surprising extent, in the expectation of recovery of world trade is implied the naïve assumption of direct reversal back to the pre-depression situation. Quite generally, it seems to be realized that in the decline of production in this depression the output of consumption goods, broadly speaking, has been lowered 25-30 per cent, while the outturn of capital goods has been lowered 70-75 per cent. This deviation holds of course, generally speaking, in foreign trade. In the meantime, cost structures have been altered within countries and changes have occurred in the available array of goods and services; with recovery, the expanding foreign commerce will be influenced by such changes. Therefore, while one may hope for a total restoration of world trade in terms of comparable monetary units or in terms of amounts, the recovery cannot be merely the reversion of the decline, since the development of new resources and the perfection of new methods must make that impossible. Similarly, whatever the degree of recovery in volume and value, the categories of goods in foreign trade is certain to be significantly changed.

Similarly, individual countries envisage their recovery from the depression predominatingly in terms of revival of export trade. We read that the decline in living standards in Germany can only be arrested through recovery of a predicated foreign commerce. We read that Britain has recovered as far as is possible on domestic grounds and further recovery rests on revival of foreign commerce. Clearly such statements rest on terms of domestic population rather than on terms of foreign trade. But is there such a thing as a per capita rank in foreign commerce, quite irrespective of the gross volume of said commerce?

At present there is no real "trial and error" in foreign commerce. There can be no real "trial and error" in the absence of at least tentative solution of the five questions stated above. In the absence, however, of conditions indispensable to a real test, by "trial and error," of the trend of relation of total production to international trade, the exigencies of war losses, of post-war deterioration and of demoralization proceeding from the depression have led a large number of the countries of the world (perhaps now a majority of them) to sponsor and adopt the revival of an old method of exchange of goods. This is direct trade between two countries, which in its latest political version is represented by bilateral trade agreements, more or less channelized. The system of direct trade between countries was outgrown during the progress of the industrial revolution in the last century and replaced by the system of multangular, or multilateral, trade. It is now revived, not as an old tool adaptable to present circumstances, but by implication as a new tool designed to fit unprecedented circumstances in the world.

It is evident that this political development has sprung largely from the exigencies of producers of primary materials. During the century before the World War, the producers of primary materials in the world played, in a way, a passive rôle. The initiative in trade lay largely on the processing side. The processor was essentially the servant of the consumer. Now the producers of primary materials—whether as major activities in the extractive countries or as minor activities in the processing countries—are for the time being in political control. The doctrine of the development of foreign commerce through bilateral trade agreements is one result of this situation. The Reciprocal Tariff Act is the direct expression of American participation in the movement. It is not an accident, nor yet an incident, that American agriculture seeks to assume leadership in American foreign trade policy. It is very much the same in most countries. Agriculture, more than mining, lumbering, and the other extractive industries, seeks to impose its control on processing factors and on the distributive services. Instead of meeting demand, agriculture now tries to control supply and regulate distribution. Whether this is a short-term phase of a changing long-term movement or a definitive shift in the balance of economic and political forces, we may expect to find revealed in the occurrences of the next few years.

This book is openly but respectfully critical. In the social as well as in the physical sciences, it is proper to criticise what is regarded as error without putting an asserted truth in the place of the error criticised. It is in medicine, for example, an ethical duty to denounce a false cure, without trying to set up a true cure. It is scientific duty for a meteorologist to combat a false system of forecasting rainfall, even if he has no proposed method of forecasting to suggest. The right and duty of criticism are not to be abridged by the inability of the critic to prepare and offer an alternative. Progress in society is not advanced ready-made in that fashion. But in fact, for the problem of foreign trade, the alternative exists in historical experiences since the industrial revolution. The reader should begin with the realization that the theory of foreign commerce proclaimed in the New Deal was not originated in this country and is not new. It is a revival of ancient doctrine under stress of economic exigencies and is more or less rampant abroad, having appeared in various versions under several garbs in many foreign countries since the war. Therefore, advocates and critics of the New Deal in foreign commerce must look backward as well as forward.

Every author faces one dilemma in a technical presentation. In the interest of widespread appreciation, broad statements are attractive. But broad statements are usually inaccurate in the technical sense. If, on the other hand, all statements are conditioned and qualified so as to be minutely accurate, the text becomes unattractive. The author has sought to follow a middle course, probably with less success than is hoped for. The questions on review are large; only when the issues are reviewed in correct perspective does the panorama become clear. Yet in the nature of the numerous commodity relations, the details must be preserved.

CONTENTS

CHAPTER		PAGE
	Preface	v
	Introduction	1
I.	The Case Stated	11
II.	Hypothesis of Planned Adjustment of Supply to Demand	31
III.	Gross Extent of Planned Contraction and Adjustment Contemplated	47
IV.	Acreage Contraction Considered in Detail	56
V.	Population Influences	86
VI.	Foreign Need of American Farm Products versus American Need of Agricultural Exports	98
VII.	Balance of Merchandise Trade before and since the War	115
VIII.	Raising the Passive Balance of Merchandise Trade	153
IX.	Bilateral Trade Treaties	178
X.	Considerations on the Side of Foreign Countries	226
XI.	Organization Involved in the Three Plans	262
XII.	Summarized Criticism	275
	Index	297

THE NEW DEAL AND FOREIGN TRADE

INTRODUCTION

The Honorable Henry A. Wallace, Secretary of Agriculture, has prepared for the Foreign Policy Association of New York and the World Peace Foundation of Boston, as a *World Affairs Pamphlet*, a statement of policy in international trade, under the title *America Must Choose*. This was issued in February 1934. The same general views were presented in the issue of *Foreign Affairs*, for January 1934, under the title "American Agriculture and World Markets." It seems warranted to infer that in principle *America Must Choose* and "American Agriculture and World Markets" embody the policy of the Administration of President Roosevelt. Our political history contains instances of disavowal by the President, as administration policy, of formal declarations by a member of his Cabinet. In the present instance, however, we take it that the Secretary of Agriculture speaks with the authority and voice of the administration. The Secretary of Agriculture, not the Secretary of State, for the time being at least, seems to be the spearhead of the foreign trade policy of the New Deal.

Prior to his entrance into the Cabinet, Henry A. Wallace was the editor of *Wallace's Farmer*, in which position he was preceded by his father, Henry C. Wallace, who was Secretary of Agriculture during the Harding Administration. Before him was Henry Wallace, an outstanding personality, whose editorial activities and leadership in rural affairs in Iowa extended back before the 'nineties. Henry A. Wallace appeared directly after the war as a writer on farm economics, in a book on *Agricultural Prices,* issued in 1920. He is a recognized authority on corn. Therefore in an unique sense the present Secretary of Agriculture represents the culmination of a half-century of technical, social, and political activities of a family on behalf of agriculture in the corn belt. In 1932 Henry A. Wallace deserted the Republican party for the New Deal. In the main building of the Department of Agriculture in Washington is a beautiful mural painting by Gilbert White, of which the dominant note is contentment. To bring contentment to the American farmer is the laudable ambition of Henry A. Wallace.

It is further of particular significance that the two mentioned formal statements on foreign trade policy were issued not in the American rural press, nor in the metropolitan press, nor yet through domestic political channels; they were really addressed to foreign audiences. The *World Affairs Pamphlets,* issued by the Foreign Policy Association of New York and the World Peace Foundation of Boston, have indeed the purpose of informing an educated American audience. But with due respect to these organizations, the *World Affairs Pamphlets* cannot be regarded as addressed to the average citizen; they are not fitted to familiarize educated but insular Americans with the international point of view. These pamphlets, we feel sure, will find abroad a more responsive audience than in this country; abroad certainly they will be read by officials, by politicians in controlling positions, by professional students of economics and of history, and by specialists in agriculture and commerce. The enunciated policies are designed as policies for all countries. Under these circumstances, we regard the proposals advanced by the Secretary of Agriculture, under the title *America Must Choose,* to represent rather an advance notice to foreigners than a lesson to Americans.

Secretary Wallace has since addressed the American public. A short popular statement appeared in the *New York Times* of August 19, 1934, under the title "A Charted Course toward Stable Prosperity," in which particular attention was given to the agricultural surplus in the light of drought and other transient influences. In October 1934 appeared a book with the engaging title of *New Frontiers*.[1] In this presentation more particular attention is given to technical phases of the domestic problems revolving about surpluses of farm products. In a particular sense *New Frontiers* complements *America Must Choose* and we take it this was a planned order of presentation, with declarations adressed respectively to foreign and domestic audiences. *New Frontiers* is composed in a more provocative and less tolerant vein than *America Must Choose;* for illustration, in the first chapter, the conservatives of our generations are referred to as "Bourbons" and "troglodytes," a journalistic satire which Secretary Wallace did not employ in *America Must Choose.* Numerous quotations from these two publications will be given below, with page references.

The Secretary of Agriculture was born in 1888 and stands, therefore, in early middle life. He has a strongly religious nature and is prone to promote political and social "reforms" with the internal ardor and external forcefulness of a crusader. The two named publications, broad in outline and almost devoid of technical data, deserve to be called bold rather than comprehensive. We take it that the policy originated with the Secretary of Agriculture, not in the technical staff of the Department of Agriculture. Indeed, premonitions of the policy are to be found in editorials of Henry A. Wallace in *Wallaces' Farmer.* The present views of the Secretary were clearly forecast in a review by him of the author's book on *Corn and Hog Surplus of the Corn Belt*

[1] Henry A. Wallace, *New Frontiers* (New York, Reynal and Hitchcock, 1934).

which appeared in the July 1932 issue of the *Journal of Farm Economics*.

Secretary Wallace, is, of course, not the first to have posed the question of the effect upon our agriculture of the shift from net-debtor to net-creditor position; nor of the consequent effect on industry and agriculture of the imperative need of debtors to make their payments, if at all, in goods and services. That dilemma was innate in the "equalization fee" and "export debenture"; the net-creditor position of the country stood as a specter behind the Federal Farm Board of the Hoover Administration. But here we find an ingeniously candid consideration. Secretary Wallace is the first official of Cabinet rank definitely to set up as major objective the shift from active to passive balance of merchandise trade. The "planned middle course" must stand or fall with the success or failure of development of a heavy passive balance in our foreign commerce.[1]

There is ground to suspect that in the present Cabinet continues to exist a respectful and respectable schism in foreign trade policy. Since the early days of the Harding Administration there has been divergence over foreign policy between the Department of State and the Departments of Agriculture and Commerce, differences related largely to the growing importance of invisible foreign trade. Henry A. Wallace and Cordell Hull are alike in several characteristics: they are impersonal, austere, and ethically minded. Secretary Hull has an outstanding capacity for poise and self-

[1] In explanation of an old terminology, an active, positive or favorable balance of international trade is one where exports of goods preponderate over imports; a passive, negative or unfavorable balance is one where imports of goods predominate over exports. The expressions favorable and unfavorable date back to mercantilism, carry misleading connotations and ought to be dropped. Throughout this book we shall use the term *active balance of trade* to indicate for a country an excess of goods exported over goods imported and *passive balance of trade* to indicate for a country an excess of goods imported over goods exported, in values with quantities disregarded. For further detail, see note on pages 115-6.

restraint under stress, as was illustrated in London and Montevideo. Secretary Wallace has the crusader's spirit, which may be found later to be more appropriate on domestic than on foreign fields. We suspect they think alike on long-term international policies, but have not the same ideas on the technique of international relations. We take it that Secretary Wallace believes in putting his cards on the table first, or at least making the bid and taking the lead; Secretary Hull quite probably prefers to have the other country expose its hand and make the bid. We infer that Secretary Wallace inclines to the use of quotas, to which Secretary Hull is presumably averse. If one defines four factors as necessary for successful foreign policy—*good intentions, discriminating intelligence, reliable mechanism,* and *sustaining discipline*—we surmise that Secretary Hull and his entourage have the advantage over Secretary Wallace and his entourage in all but the first of the four. The Department of State has the advantage of being in the traditional and continuing position of confidence of foreign countries. As we shall see, the new foreign trade policy is to be effectuated through treaties. In a treaty negotiation, it is the Department of State which sits in the drafting room, contrasts past with future, and holds the scales of alternatives in equity. Therefore, in the final analysis, the negotiated bilateral trade agreements are likely to follow more the views of the Department of State than those of the Department of Agriculture.[1] As

[1] Indications of divergence of views in respect not of objective but of procedure will be shown by comparing *America Must Choose, New Frontiers,* and "Fundamental Concepts of Foreign Trade," by George N. Peek, reprinted in *Vital Speeches,* January 28, 1935, I, 260, with the address of Secretary Hull delivered before the American Farm Bureau Federation at Nashville, Tennessee, on December 10, 1934, an address by Assistant Secretary of State Sayre on the "Menace of Economic Nationalism," before the New York Academy of Political Science on November 7, 1934, and an address on "International Aspects of National Planning," delivered before the National Rural Forum in Washington, on November 18, 1934, by Wallace McClure, assistant to Assistant Secretary Sayre. See also the radio address of Secretary Hull on Saturday, March 23, 1925. See especially the

guardian of urban industries, we suspect that the Secretary of Commerce will be found most often in virtual alignment with the Secretary of State. We surmise that when it gets right down to treaty-making, the grapes gathered by the Secretaries of Agriculture and Commerce will be sorted, pressed, fermented, clarified, and bottled by the Secretary of State.

Secretary Wallace lacks extensive personal experience abroad; his observations therefore tend to be telescopic rather than microscopic. This may be a political advantage, but has the danger of picturing a European landscape as a reflection of American scenery. The problem is larger than the scope of the Agricultural Adjustment Act; it is not invidious to suggest that it will last longer than the term of Secretary Wallace.

In the course of a Lincoln Day address, delivered on February 13, 1933, in New York City, the then President Hoover made the following statement:

"The American people will soon be at the fork of three roads. The first is the highway of cooperation among nations, thereby to remove the obstructions to world consumption and rising prices. This road leads to real stability, to expanding standards of living, to a resumption of the march of progress by all peoples. It is today the immediate road to relief of agriculture and unemployment, not alone for us but for the entire world.

"The second road is to rely upon our high degree of national self-containment, to increase our tariffs, to create quotas and discriminations, and to engage in definite methods of curtailment of production of agricultural and other products and thus to secure a larger measure of economic isolation from world influences. It would be a long road of readjustments into unknown and uncertain fields. But it may be necessary if the first way out is closed

---

addresses of Secretary Hull and Assistant Secretary Sayre before the Chamber of Commerce of the United States at the latest annual meeting in Washington in the spring of 1935. The divergence really centers on the respective advantages of direct and multangular foreign trade, stipulated quotas, and most-favored-nation treatment.

to us. Some measures may be necessary pending cooperative conclusions with other nations.

"The third road is that we inflate our currency, consequently abandon the gold standard, and with our depreciated currency attempt to enter a world economic war, with the certainty that it leads to complete destruction, both at home and abroad."

It will be observed that the first "road" of ex-President Hoover corresponds with the "internationalism" of Secretary Wallace; the second "road" of ex-President Hoover corresponds with the "nationalism" of Secretary Wallace. The third "road" of ex-President Hoover was not a compromise, or middle course, between the first two, but instead a forecast of the economic deterioration which would follow a general depreciation of currencies.

America Must Choose, in the nature of the address, has brevity instead of amplification, declaration more than persuasion. The Secretary is in the position of the Irishman: "I'm not arguin', I'm tellin' you." It may perhaps be suggested respectfully that the writings of Secretary Wallace, like those of most reformers, illustrate the tactics of Robert Owen: "Never argue, repeat your assertion." At the close of the address, however, the Secretary exhorts Americans to face an open discussion of the question.

"I should like to see the campaign for a middle-ground policy conducted as a campaign of reason, with millions of personal contacts and arguments, man to man. . . . It needs study, and above all dispassionate discussion. . . . I want to see the whole question examined by our people in a new spirit." (p. 33)

Bertrand Russell, in his brilliant *Freedom versus Organization,*[1] has remarked that "Economic nationalism, the dominant force in the modern world, derives its strength from the fact that it combines the motives of self-interest, to which Marx and the Radicals appealed, with those less rational

[1] New York, W. W. Norton and Co., Inc., 1934.

motives that inspire patriotism." Secretary Wallace would surely make the rejoinder that internationalism has no less of self-interest and should have no less of real patriotism.

Here for the first time, in a veritably "grand manner," foreign trade is included in the ambit of social reform. What we buy and sell abroad is to become a part of "the co-operatively good life." Since we are to treat, and trust, our foreign neighbor as we treat, and trust, our domestic neighbor, he also must be inducted into the balanced commercial life. But on what grounds of experience is it to be regarded as practicable to plan a foreign trade as one plans a domestic economy? The Soviets have not tried it, nor the Fascists. This is indeed something new for the country to contemplate.

When one scans the century of diplomacy following the Treaty of Vienna, one comes to appreciate that fulfilment of treaties between countries hangs on four points. The first is *good intentions,* of which it used to be related in Germany that Bismarck once said no one questioned them in advance. The second is *intelligence*—realistic, historical, political, and technical intelligence. The third is *mechanism,* the possession of the appropriate instrument through which the observance of a treaty may be naturally effectuated. The fourth is *discipline,* the power to hold domestic political forces to the support of the adopted foreign plan. These reflections may appropriately be applied to the foreign trade policy of the administration.

Good intentions need to be both outgoing and incoming. Good intention leads us to seek equity for foreigners as well as advantage to us. Good intention implies effort to elevate all, not disproportionately to elevate ourselves. Good intention includes even recognition of equity between different classes in foreign countries comparable to the equity envisaged between classes in this country. This view of intentions in international trade agreements is everywhere forcefully in evidence in the writings of Secretary Wallace,—

though naturally the picture of good intention at home is more vivid than that of good intention abroad.

Intelligence implies an understanding of the internal economies, industrial and agricultural characteristics, technical information, and the psychological, racial and cultural qualities of foreign countries. Many treaties have broken down on the score of inadequate or misplaced understanding. When now the foreign trade policy of a century comes to be fundamentally altered, it is of the greatest importance that our understanding of other countries should be as comprehensive as our understanding of our own.

The mechanism of the new policy is of the greatest tactical and strategic importance. A well-intentioned treaty, based on adequate understanding, may collapse through lack of mechanism of enforcement. The mechanism ought to be such that the treaty fulfils itself, and is not enforced with the implication of coercion. The mechanism includes not only the good manners of diplomatic intercourse, but a great deal more, namely, the technique appropriate to the national characteristics and material circumstances.

Lastly, the importance of discipline behind the government is hardly to be overemphasized. Lack of discipline at home is possibly the most frequent cause of the breakdown of foreign treaties. Treaties are contracted between the executive departments of governments, with the specific approval, usually, of legislative branches of governments. Rarely are the peoples made fully to understand in advance the implications, as well as the objectives, of treaties. All too often, the peoples need to be educated up to the fulfilment of treaties after their adoption. Most treaties are fair-weather treaties; when storms arise they are wrecked. The discipline of fulfilment includes moral and intellectual elements, as well as technical appreciation. As an illustration among the purely commercial treaties, one has only to look at the position in the world of today of so-called most-favored-nation treatment, to realize the failure in country after country, through lack of internal discipline, to fulfil not merely the spirit but also the letter of treaties guaranteeing most-favored-nation treatment. Under these circumstances, it is to be regarded as an advantage that the new foreign trade policy of the United States is to be introduced gradually. We take it as prearranged that the first steps in the new policy are being taken with countries of lesser commercial importance. The administrative test of the new policy will depend on whether it is found possible, on both sides, to formulate treaties based on good intentions, developed with comprehension, supported by intelligence, maintained with adequate mechanism of fulfilment, and sustained by effective discipline within the countries of the contracting parties. In the past, foreign trade may be said to have incorporated at once the most concrete competition and the most abstract accounting. Here, in a governmental policy, is proposed the introduction into foreign commerce of "faith, hope, and charity." The new domestic policy in agriculture is the chief support of the planned program of foreign trade. While the British admit that David Lloyd-George now follows the example of President Roosevelt in calling for a New Deal, they may claim that Secretary Wallace is following the example of their Minister of Agriculture, Walter Elliot. The situation is not peculiar to Britain and America. More or less the world over agriculture has assumed leadership in foreign trade policy, and we take it for granted this will last for a decade or more. Naturally and properly, our producers and consumers will wish to know how the proposed socialization compares with the already established socializations in Russia and Italy. This unique proposal of "reform"—and the relation of "reform" to "recovery"—deserves the close and respectful attention and the objective appraisal of Americans.

CHAPTER I

THE CASE STATED

THE case of the New Dealers against American society is divided into a general case and a special case. Though it is our purpose to examine only the special case, it is in place to state the general case, since implications flow from the general to the special case. The general case is the age-old indictment based on lack of equity between men. In our capitalistic society, all persons do not enjoy the same opportunities and rewards. The national dividend is not equitably partitioned. Some of the prevailing inequities are inherent in differences in individual capacities; but many of them, perhaps most of them, are artificial, and motivated, proceeding from what Secretary Wallace calls the "rules of the game." Certain groups, holding strategic or political power, are in position to enlarge the share of the national dividend going to some and to lessen the share going to others. Ownership and management secure too much, workers too little. Creditors are favored, debtors exploited. These predicated "rules of the game" the New Dealers intend to revise in the direction of leveling opportunities and rewards to correspond to capacities. They seek a "balance" between men, between groups, between classes, between regions, between owners and workers, between country and city.

This indictment of our society, as such, is merely a revision. At frequent intervals society is, and needs to be, reindicted. The first socialism of Robert Owen was based on such a reindictment; the later communism of Karl Marx represented a more penetrating reindictment. Indeed the indictment of modern society by the New Dealers is a moderate charge. What the New Dealers hope will be their particular achievement is the advancement of solution under private ownership through cooperation between otherwise competitive groups, under governmentally directed powers within a democratic state, thus in sharp contradistinction to state socialism, the dictatorship of the proletariat, and Fascism. The New Deal thus defined is the organization of a planned society, with policies effectuated through cooperation between groups, voluntary groups within a democracy, the state exercising the ultimate function of "directing, watching, stimulating, and restraining as circumstances suggest or necessity demands," to use words of Pope Pius XI quoted by Secretary Wallace. Like words are to be found in the records of the Federal Council of the Churches of Christ in America. Every ardent social reform is likely to contain a religious appeal, as was the case with prohibition, because in most of us it is but a step from the ethical to the religious.

The following resolution, adopted by the Council at its quadrennial meeting in 1932, indicates the source from which Henry A. Wallace may in part have drawn his inspiration:

> "Practical application of the Christian principle of social well-being to the acquisition and use of wealth; subordination of speculation and the profit motive to the creative and cooperative spirit.
>
> "Social planning and control of the credit and monetary systems and the economic processes for the common good.
>
> "The right of all to the opportunity for self-maintenance; a wider and fairer distribution of wealth; a living wage as a minimum, and above this a just share for the worker in the product of industry and agriculture.

"The right of employees and employers alike to organize for collective bargaining and social action, protection of both in the exercise of this right; the obligation of both to work for the public good; encouragement of cooperatives and other organizations among farmers and other groups.

"Economic justice for the farmer in legislation, financing, agricultural transportation and the price of farm products as compared with the cost of machinery, and other commodities, which he must buy.

"Extension of the primary cultural opportunities and social services now enjoyed by urban populations to the farm family."

It is not blameworthy, but only natural, that the terminology of the New Deal in all countries should savor of Eleusinian concepts. The New Deal is a revival of the old ideal that economic democracy must rank with political democracy. No New Dealer has surpassed the declaration of Walter Rathenau that the equalization of property and the dissemination of income are prescribed both by ethics and by economics. If we agree that a social reconstruction requires intentions, intelligence, mechanism, and discipline, it seems obvious that the New Deal equals, or may excel, Communism and Fascism in intention and intelligence; but in mechanism and discipline, the planned reconstruction within a democracy stands under obvious disadvantages.

With this reference to the general case, the special indictment by Secretary Wallace may be briefly stated, though the gravamen is long. Special charges of inequality, drawn from the general indictment, are applied to the relations of agriculture and urban industry. Agriculture receives less than its due share of the national dividend, urban industry an excessive share. Services are more highly accounted than materials. The percentage of the national income going to creditors and public utility classes has been greatly increased, the percentage going to farmers has been heavily reduced. Burdens of tax and interest bear more heavily on agriculture than on industry. The farming classes find themselves unable to maintain the advancing improvement in the standard of living. Foreign trade has declined and this decline has fallen disproportionately on agriculture, both before and during the depression. Prerequisite to the restoration of American agriculture, this must recover an equitable share in the exports of the United States; there is an equitable place for American farm products in the markets of the world and the recovery of an export outlet is indispensable to the restoration of our agriculture.

The consideration of a disease, in the established custom in books, is divided into diagnosis, prognosis, and treatment. The Secretary of Agriculture has virtually followed such a sequence. Regarding the decline in export trade as an economic disease, general and not local, one may condense and interpret the presentation, with quotations from *America Must Choose*.

DIAGNOSIS

(a) Before the war the United States was a net-debtor country, on account of private investments, with the appropriate active (positive, miscalled favorable), balance of merchandise trade.

(b) On private account we became a net-creditor country after the war, through commercial investment abroad of over 17 billion dollars.

> "We went into the World War owing other nations 200 million dollars annually on interest account, and came out with other nations owing us 500 million dollars annually. . . . In the United States we have changed so suddenly from a debtor to a creditor nation that our people are only now becoming aware of the need for a definite program of long-continued action which will continue without great changes no matter which party shall be in power." (pp. 5 and 17)

(c) The export industries were greatly expanded during the war; thereafter, contraction to "normal" (that is peace-time) dimensions has been difficult both for factory and farm.

". . . To replace the 50 million lost acres of Europe, America had added 40 million acres to its tilled domain and thrown its whole farm plant into high gear.

"When the war ended, Europe no longer needed those extra 40 million hard-tilled acres of ours, or for only a little longer, at best. . . . at least 40 million acres of land, scattered all over the country, became surplus acreage very rapidly." (p. 5)

(d) To avoid drastic contraction of overextended industry and agriculture and to provide export outlets for their outturns, a policy of active foreign lending from 1919 to 1930 had the more or less subconscious effect, if not the express purpose, of facilitating the export of billions of dollars' value of goods. These artificial export outlets delayed the otherwise-to-be-expected adjustment of supply to demand, especially in agriculture.

". . . The foreign loans we made to sustain our expanded productive capacity after the war, merely concealed the true nature of our situation. When the loans ended—as they were sure to, since we refused to accept sufficient goods in payment—our artificial market for the surplus disappeared overnight." (p. 8)

(e) With the tapering-off of American foreign lending after 1929, and the consequent (though lagging) decline in foreign purchasing power for American products, unexportable and almost unsalable stocks and carry-overs began to accumulate, to some extent abroad but especially in the United States, aided by heavy production in several countries.

". . . This country has more industrial as well as more agricultural capacity than it needs for home consumption." (p. 30)

". . . In consequence we are forced to think of what we ought to do with the . . . marginal acres of plowland we are going to take out of cultivation . . . because the world no longer will pay us for the extra wheat, cotton and corn we have been growing there." (p. 4)

"When the present administration came into power on March 4, 1933, it had been for several years apparent that there is no longer an effective foreign purchasing power for our customary exportable surplus of cotton, wheat, lard and tobacco at prices high enough to assure social stability in the United States." (p. 6)

(f) At the same time (1922 and 1930) the protective tariff had been raised to such a level as to prevent foreign countries from sending in their (duty paid) goods to pay for service charges due on American foreign investments and also to cover accustomed [1] purchases of American farm products. Through the action of the high tariff, supplemented by foreign lending and other devices, we continued to exhibit the active (positive, miscalled favorable) balance of merchandise trade characteristic of a net-debtor country, instead of accepting the passive (negative, miscalled unfavorable) balance of merchandise trade characteristic of our mature position as a net-creditor country.

(g) Our active balance of merchandise trade compelled debtors to pay in gold. This accounts in part for our present large stock of monetary gold reserve, which has been still further augmented in 1934. The accumulation of gold in a few countries had an indirect deflationary influence; the weight of gold in Washington pressed down the prices on the American farm.

(h) The equilibrium between the trading countries of the world is generally dislocated, and this is ascribed (by implication) principally to economic nationalism and high tariffs. World trade measured in gold has continued annually to fall since 1932.

[1] The word "accustomed" applies more to us than to the importing countries.

(i) In short, our positions in international finance and in merchandise trade have been inconsistent and mutually incompatible. Collapse occurred on both sides, aided by general business depression throughout the world. On account especially of the abnormal trade behavior of the United States (and of Germany also), the world depression has been intensified. Within five years has occurred an unprecedented fall in gold prices of goods and of physical volumes of trade; but pronounced as was this decline in price level (of primary materials especially), it is unwarranted to term deflation the cause of the depression of production and trade. It is not to be contended that the major causes of the world depression lay in these circumstances; but collapse has been intensified and recovery is certainly retarded by them. (In general, the above-stated declarations may be said to be in harmony with the views of many "classical" economists.)

PROGNOSIS

There are at least three paths: internationalism, nationalism and a "planned middle course."

The country may decide on economic nationalism and retain the high tariff. In that case we shall have to withdraw land from cultivation, close mines and other deposits of raw materials, shut down factories, and have foreign investments reduced or canceled.

> "Under nationalism we must be prepared to make permanent the retirement of from 40 to 100 million acres of crop land. Forty million, if we take out good land; 100 million if we take out the worst." (pp. 10-11)

> "Great prosperity is possible for the United States if we follow the strictly nationalist course, but in such case we must be prepared for a fundamental planning and regimentation of agriculture and industry far beyond that which anyone has yet suggested." (p. 17)

The alternative to nationalism is internationalism—low

tariffs on protected articles and wide extension of the free list, perhaps a virtual tariff-for-revenue, with the acceptance of such added increases of imports of merchandise as would give us the heavy passive balance of merchandise trade appropriate to our net-creditor position.

". . . We cannot take the path of internationalism unless we stand ready to import nearly a billion dollars more goods than we did in 1929." (p. 1)

Such a course in favor of freer international trade involves sacrifices. Goods must be taken as debt payments. Larger markets can be secured abroad if we take the products of other countries in return for ours, and induce other countries to lower their tariffs to meet our tariff reductions.

". . . If we are going to lower tariffs radically, there may have to be some definite planning whereby certain industries or businesses will have to be retired." (p. 18)

Americans must learn to function internationally as buyers as well as sellers. We must face competitive *laissez-faire* in the outer world, as we now face it domestically behind the tariff wall. Otherwise, in the long view a continuation of industrial tariffs would imply, indeed provoke, a continuation of subsidies to agriculture, for export and perhaps on domestic prices.

"It should be recognized that our surplus problems here in the United States, and the resulting necessity of keeping parts of our factories idle and withdrawing acreage, or of widening foreign markets, or of doing these things in combination, is really part of a world surplus problem. This country has more industrial as well as more agricultural capacity than it needs for home consumption. Surplus capacity in industry shows up mainly in unemployment, rather than in a persistent accumulation of commodities; but in all branches of our economic life there is an identical tendency for production to outrun consumption. Other nations have just the same trouble, as we know from the prevalence of unemployment and dole systems throughout the world." (p. 30)

". . . Absolutely free competition, conducted nationally or on a world scale, produces unendurable overconcentrations of goods and power." (p. 14)

TREATMENT

Treatment may be directed at the basic disorder or merely at alleviation of symptoms. The Secretary of Agriculture rejects both the nationalist and the internationalist extremes. He presents what he terms "a planned middle course." A continuation of high-tariff nationalism is rejected because the contraction of agriculture thereby enforced is unacceptable to the social order. The Secretary endeavors earnestly to mediate and to partition between factory and farm the burdens of readjustment.

". . . the fact remains that the pain and distress of nationalist readjustment, and a retreat from world markets would bear down far more heavily on agriculture than on industry." (p. 10)

"If we finally go all the way toward nationalism, it may be necessary to have compulsory control of marketing, licensing of plowed land, and base and surplus quotas for every farmer for every product for each month in the year." (p. 11)

"International planning, on the other hand, would throw the greater burden of adjustment on factories rather than on farms." (p. 8)

". . . What tariffs should we lower? What goods shall we import? Which goods?" (p. 1)

". . . I cannot too sharply emphasize my conviction that internationalism must be even more carefully planned than a program of economic nationalism." (p. 2)

The specific treatment of Secretary Wallace is stated as follows:

"The planned middle course I propose as a basis for present discussion is one precisely halfway [*sic*] between these two extremes: a line of march along which we would lower tariffs enough to bring in another half-billion dollars worth of goods annually, and permanently retract of our good agricultural land some 25 million acres." (p. 27)

"To depict the pain this course would cause industry on the one hand, and agriculture on the other, would be but to restate in less demanding terms, facts and speculations developed in previous sections of this pamphlet, in respect to the price of unmodified isolation, on the one hand, and of an unmodified drive for world markets, on the other. The fact that agriculture would suffer far the more under isolation, and that industry would bear the brunt of changes necessary to widespread renewal of world trade, may here, however, be briefly reiterated; for here is a fact suggesting that a planned middle course is the fairest and wisest for all concerned." (p. 27)

"Here at home, as elsewhere, the problem fundamentally is one of deciding what this people wants to do *soon,* how much they want to accept from abroad and how much they wish to send abroad." (p. 24)

". . . If we are going to increase foreign purchasing power enough to sell abroad our normal surpluses of cotton, wheat and tobacco at a decent price, we shall have to accept nearly a billion dollars more goods from abroad than we did in 1929. We shall have to get that much more in order to service the debts that are coming to us from abroad and have enough left over to pay us a fair price for what we send abroad." (p. 18)

In *New Frontiers* the address is directed to the American public therefore it is appropriate to make supplementary quotations therefrom. The extent of the social changes envisaged by Secretary Wallace, in order to move into what is called the land of a cooperative good life, are illustrated in the following quotations:

". . . We must invent, build and put to work new social machinery. This machinery will carry out the Sermon on the Mount as well as the present social machinery carries out and intensifies the law of the jungle." (p. 11)

". . . Modern governments must of necessity consider changing the rules to make for a maximum of balance between producing and consuming forces with the minimum of disturbance to individual liberties." (p. 38)

". . . the tariff, the balance of international payments, monetary policy, subsidies, taxation, price and production policies, and railroad rate regulations" are matters whose "significance lies in the fact that by their manipulation it is possible to direct, stimulate, restrain, and balance those forces which have to do with proportioning the national income." (pp. 19-20)

"The object is a continually moving, but balanced state." (p. 47)

"The 10 million unemployed plus the 5 million living on land which can never be farmed are a continuing menace to the established industry and agriculture of the United States." (p. 244)

". . . We are trying to produce continuously a supply and demand situation which will get farmers their normal share of the national income." (p. 231)

". . . At the low point of 1933 farm prices averaged 60 per cent lower than in 1926, textiles 49 per cent, food prices 47 per cent lower, hides and leather 32 per cent lower, building materials 30 per cent, metals, chemicals and house furnishings about 29 per cent, and metal products 23 per cent lower." (p. 125)

". . . The end of the World War had left the American farmer high and dry. Along with everybody else, but ten years ahead of most of them, he was perched on the stilts of high prices, high labor costs, high land values, and high debts." (p. 142)

". . . We are committed to getting the farmer, the laborer, and the industrialist such share of the national income as will put each in a balanced relationship with the other." (p. 29)

In *New Frontiers* Secretary Wallace further develops the special analysis in greater detail, of which a number of paragraphs deserve to be quoted.

Five disintegrating, yet ultimately beneficent forces have been under way and are not yet completed. These forces are:

"1. The end of westward expansion, the gradual reduction in great population increase, and the necessity for meeting unemployment problems more consciously. There is no longer cheap land on which we can thoughtlessly place the unemployed.

"2. The rising tide of scientific investigation, inventions, and methods of mass production. This brings sudden and unexpected technological loss of employment, loss of investment and general confusion.

"3. The post-war reversal in credit balances between the United States and other nations. Eventually this makes necessary either a reduction in United States exports or an increase in United States imports.

"4. The steadily increasing concentration of industrial activity into a few great corporations. This has almost destroyed the effectiveness of the old-fashioned free-play of the market place.

"5. The decentralizing effect of a loaded freight-rate structure, shattering as a result of developing highway transportation." (p. 40)

"1. We are no longer a pioneer nation with free lands. We cannot, therefore, solve our depressions by pushing our unemployed out where land is cheap and labor is scarce.

"2. Our whole psychology has been one of producing to the limit, and postponing our consumption until some future time. As a result of our enormous natural resources, our scientific understanding and our methods of mass production we have been able to turn out an enormous quantity of goods per hour of man labor. But our economic machinery for distribution and consumption was always based on the theory of competitive scarcity. In brief, our economic machinery has not been able to keep pace with our mechanical machinery.

"3. The United States, as a result of the World War, shifted with exceeding suddenness from a debtor to a creditor nation, which has made necessary a complete shift in her attitude toward other nations at a time when, as a result of the World War, it was impossible psychologically for us to make a sufficient shift.

"4. The steadily increasing concentration of industrial activity into a few great corporations has destroyed the effectiveness of the free and open market as a device for balancing economic interests." (pp. 252-53)

"More and more people are beginning to understand that there is a relationship between the United States and the rest of the world which is in the nature of a double-entry bookkeeping or a balance sheet. If you change one side of the page there must inevitably be a change on the other side. If the United States should further build up her merchant marine and then pay foreign ships less for carrying American products, the result will be to cut down foreign purchasing power for our exports. If we insist on foreign nations paying us what they owe us at once, the result again must be reduced foreign purchasing power for our exports. The international balance sheet between the United States and the rest of the world, as expressed by imports of all kinds of goods and services on the one hand and exports of all kinds on the other, must add up to come out even. If it does not come out even the discrepancy must be made good by either short-time or long-time credit [or gold, ours]." (pp. 85-86)

"More than almost anything else, at present the different peoples of the world, and especially the American people need to understand the remorseless logic of international bookkeeping. When this logic is understood, it can then be realized that every policy, no matter what it may be, has its advantages and disadvantages. An increase in export trade must also be accompanied by an increase in import trade or by an increase in tourist expenditures in foreign countries, or by the shipment of more goods in foreign vessels, or by loaning money abroad, or by continually depreciating American currency, or by a little of any two or more of these five possibilities." (p. 86)

"It is possible to be almost as critical of the internationalists. They speak in flowing terms of how increased imports into the United States will restore the normal market for our farm products abroad. They glory in the thought that we can get along entirely without any type of regimentation if the foreign markets are thus restored. But they do not like to indicate just which goods we are going to import. They talk glibly of non-competitive goods but find it difficult to point out just how much of what particular goods should be allowed to come into the United States." (pp. 87-88)

"Moreover, the internationalists are not as a rule familiar with the fact that there has been a tremendous expansion in European agriculture as a result of the subsidies of one kind or another which the European nations have given their farmers. How rapidly can European agriculture be contracted from its high point in the early '30s in order to reestablish markets for the exporting agricultural nations?" (p. 88)

". . . More and more the nationalists and the internationalists in the United States are beginning to find fundamental facts. The nationalists are discovering that in case we go the whole route and insist on growing our own sugar, our own rubber, and eliminating all kinds of foreign imports as much as possible, it will be necessary to contract our export industries and agriculture by exceedingly resolute methods to a much smaller size. The extreme nationalists may not admit it, but it is probable that even a half-way nationalism such as is involved in maintaining the Hawley-Smoot Tariff schedule and loaning no more money abroad, means such a terrific slack in foreign purchasing power that the government for many years will have to step in and help the cotton farmers, the wheat farmers, the hog farmers and the tobacco farmers make multitudinous readjustments." (p. 87)

"The honest high-tariff nationalists are more and more beginning to understand the price that must be paid. In its extreme form the price is regimentation, altogether repugnant to democratic traditions. But if education is properly carried out by an enlightened leadership in every community, the price might not perhaps be too great. Thus far, however, many of the nationalists seem to have been possessed with a kind of emotional fury which has made it difficult for them to understand the price a thorough-going nationalism demands. They have been propagandists for the advantages of nationalism and have dodged the disadvantages." (p. 87)

"European purchasing power for our surplus is shattered. We still have great adjustments to make before we can safely face that fact." (p. 47)

"Personally, I have long favored a combination of the national and the international approach, but I recognize that this also has its peculiar difficulties. Such a course is hard to define with the necessary precision. In practice it means that the Agricultural Adjustment Administration would have to go ahead for a good many years keeping out of use perhaps 20 or 30 million acres of plow land, while the Presidential tariff powers of 1934 are being exercised as rapidly as is just and possible to restore a foreign demand for our surplus farm products." (p. 88)

"Politically, the middle course is somewhat difficult. On the one hand it exposes the Administration to the criticism of those who do not like acreage control, and on the other hand to the criticism of those who do not like low tariffs. Logically, of course, a defender of high tariffs cannot object to acreage control under the post-war situation. But actually, the high tariff people, for hell-raising purposes, often disregard the logic of their position, defending high tariffs with one breath, attacking all efforts to adjust the international economy to the fact of high tariffs with the next." (pp. 88-89)

"As the tariffs are gradually reduced, may it not be wise to work out a plan for liquidating, definitely, yet slowly, these inefficient industries?" (p. 76)

The New Democracy, written by Harold L. Ickes, Secretary of the Interior is, by hearsay and inference, taken to be the companion of *New Frontiers* in sponsorship of the New Deal. It is to be recalled that for a long time the Departments of the Interior and of Agriculture have been in conflict rather than in cooperation in their overlapping affairs. Doubtless this no longer holds under the New Deal; Secretary Wallace, by chance or intention, respects the affairs under the Department of the Interior, Secretary Ickes pays his colleague the same compliment. In *The New Democracy,* there is little discussion of agriculture, and no excursion into the field of foreign trade.

Finally, we may quote the President. In an address of the President to the NRA authorities, on March 5, 1934, stands the following:

"Economic balance is our objective. . . . We seek also balance

—that our trade with other nations be increased on both sides of the ledger."

The situation is fairly summarized as follows in *International Economic Relations:*

". . . the United States cannot continue to
(1) export manufactures;
(2) export foodstuffs and raw materials;
(3) export capital;
and at the same time
(4) refuse to accept interest either in manufactures or in foodstuffs and raw materials." [1]

In *Wallace's Farmer* of November 24, 1934, p. 1, stands the following formulation:

". . . Do we want to establish a system that will try to get incomes of $2,500 each for 20,000,000 families, instead of a system that gets incomes of $75,000 each for 36,000 families? . . . How can this goal be attained? How can the nation use federal power to do the things that cannot be done by individuals and private groups, and keep it out of the things that can be done better by individuals and private groups?"

The political influence of agrarians does not decline with their numbers. There is an old German proverb,

Hat der Bauer Geld
So hat's die ganze Welt [2]

which dates back to the time when the agrarians constituted over three-fourths of the population of the country. As a practical philosophy it still holds in the United States, where the rural-farm population is 25 per cent of the total, in California where the rural-farm population is 10 per cent of the total, and in the United Kingdom, where the farm popu-

[1] Commission of Inquiry into National Policy in International Economic Relations, *International Economic Relations* (Minneapolis, University of Minnesota Press, 1934), p. 34.
[2] When the peasant has gold, the whole world has it.

lation is under 10 per cent of the total. The primitive precept of the feudal state of society carries over because it represents the instinct of security.

In the "planned middle course"[1] are evidently four separated but co-related objectives:

(a) Twenty-five million acres of good land (or 50 million acres of poor land) are to be taken out of crop use; to compensate for the effects thereby entailed, appropriate adjustments are to be made in our rural institutions and activities.

(b) A heavy increase in import of merchandise (let us say a billion dollars in value) is to be brought about; to compensate for the effects thereby entailed, appropriate adjustments are to be made in our urban institutions and activities.

(c) The passive balance of merchandise trade in the international account of our country is to be secured by our acceptance of much increased imports of non-agricultural goods, for the three-fold purpose of (1) overcoming the present preponderance of export goods, (2) covering an added export of farm products, and (3) incorporating the sum due us annually in payment of service charges on foreign loans and investments.

(d) An additional export of farm products over the otherwise level to the extent of some 500 million dollars' value is to be secured (c-2), to be paid for out of the added imports stipulated under (b).

These changes are next to be effectuated through a series of bilateral commercial treaties, contracted with a large number of individual foreign countries, these to be coordinated to these objectives and to one another. Acreage control through cooperative effort under federal powers and expansion of export of farm products through bilateral trade

[1] We take it that the "planned middle course" of Secretary Wallace dovetails with the "third economy" of Assistant Secretary Tugwell.

agreements are the two draft horses that are to pull the farm wagon out of the mire of depression. With due respect in the use of a homely farm analogy, this rather looks like using two undersized horses to pull a big wagon out of a deep mire, assuming that the exigency of the mired wagon has not been exaggerated.

This "planned middle course," the explicit proposals and the technical implications, the short-term and long-term objectives, the circumstances and influences which favor the plan and the political and institutional difficulties that oppose it we propose to consider in what seems to us to be their order. The "planned middle course" is essentially a tariff prescription without an ingredient of monetary policy. We venture to forewarn the reader that Secretary Wallace overstresses the effects of high tariffs and understresses the effects of disordered currencies. The tariffs are indeed too high and too rigid; but the currencies are both low and unstable and the exchange relations between countries have been unprecedentedly chaotic. This is not a short-term question; it took the country two decades to get into the present dilemma and we shall not get out of it within one four-year administration. It was not left to New Dealers, nor even to Americans, to discover that a country cannot sell unless it buys.

SUMMARY

The United States had become a net-creditor country (disregarding all war debts), to the extent of more than the equivalent of ten billion dollars. This necessarily enforced the maintenance of a passive (negative, miscalled "unfavorable") balance of merchandise trade. As a direct consequence of our resources and natural genius, our country is an actual heavy exporter of farm products, industrial raw materials, and manufactures proceeding from rationalization of industry and mass production. These two major facts in our economy are incompatible. If we follow our nationalistic bent and continue the pre-existing trend toward self-containment, it will be necessary to contract agriculture to a substantial and even disastrous extent and deprive a significant proportion of our farm population of their accustomed occupation. If we embark on a new route toward internationalism, this will involve a disastrous contraction of urban industries, with consequent widespread unemployment of urban workers. The "planned middle course" of Secretary Wallace is offered as a middle-of-the-road compromise which on the one hand would entail a contraction of only 25 million acres of land in harvested crops, and on the other would necessitate an increase in import of goods only equivalent to the value of a half-billion dollars. It is postulated that this "planned middle course" would bring about a balanced economy of town and country and secure for the farm population a more equitable division of the national income. It is implied that the partition of the national dividend has no influence on the amount of it; that is, the income of the country would be at least as large under a planned economy as under private initiative. The treatment embodies a cooperative socialization of agriculture, under official planning with federal powers of support and enforcement. To this must be supplemented a regimented industry. The New Deal may be aptly defined as a special form of socialism, of which the (perhaps) unprecedented feature is the doctrine of balance between town and country. The anomalous but not unprecedented position of a Secretary of Agriculture formulating a foreign trade policy for the country is based upon the tradition that the farm is the backbone of the nation and on the assumption that the purchasing power of the fourth of the population engaged in, or attached to, agriculture is more important than the purchasing power of any other fourth of the inhabitants of our country. The future historian of this movement will capitalize the names of Elliot, Wallace, and Schacht as the virtual leaders in the promotion of planned foreign trade. In this early stage it is already clear that the propulsion of the movement comes from agriculture and the resistance from urban industry. But it may turn out that urban industry is able to make better use of the new movement than is agriculture.

CHAPTER II

HYPOTHESIS OF PLANNED ADJUSTMENT OF SUPPLY TO DEMAND

IT is predicated in the "planned middle course" of Secretary Wallace that certain circumstances in American agriculture necessitate an enlargement of export of farm products. The average export of agricultural products during the years 1931-32 to 1933-34 was less than 40 per cent of the average export during the years 1924-25 to 1928-29. It is not sought to utilize the potential capacity of our agriculture in the direction of export; but a minimum outlet is regarded as indispensable to the advantageous functioning of our agriculture and to the securing of a "decent" price.

Any far-reaching adjustment of supply to demand in agriculture involves urban industries in adjustment of supply to demand. This becomes the more imperative since the "planned middle course" includes a declared shift from active balance of merchandise trade to passive balance of merchandise trade—or, more accurately, an enlargement of the preponderance of imports of goods. Before exploring the extent of planned contraction and adjustment contemplated for agriculture, it is advantageous to contrast such adjustment, in town and country respectively.

". . . Our immediate effort is to organize American agriculture to reduce its output to domestic need, plus that amount which we can export *with profit*." (Italics ours.) (*America Must Choose*, p. 6.)

". . . We are trying to build up consumption per capita at

home, as a substitute for the continual search for new consumers abroad." (*America Must Choose,* p. 31.)

"Increased consumption so promoted does not absorb every surplus. Boom wages would not melt our total cotton or wheat supply." (*America Must Choose,* p. 31.)

The theory of adjustment of supply to demand in agriculture rests upon the analogy of doctrine and practice in industry. For both, it is assumed that the rigid mathematical law of demand may be made a rule of conduct in practical business. This analogy is to a wide extent an assumption, since in industry, as a whole, no such adjustment of supply to demand exists as seems to be predicated in the reasoning of the planning school of agriculturists.

There lies in many industries the technical possibility of adjustment of supply to demand in a more perfect sense than seems possible in most branches of agriculture. Agriculture is a seasonal occupation: the area planted depends in part upon seasonal influences; rainfall, the occurrence of frost, the invasion of pests, and the yield per acre show wide seasonal variations. Our averages of planted acreages and of yield per acre are rough approximations over a rather wide range. To a considerable extent, obviously it is true of farm production that "man proposes and God disposes." At the same time, there is scope for far more control and adjustment that is used; men may "propose" more or less, wisely or unwisely. The farmer can vary the use of fertilizer; the seed used may be high-grade or nondescript; cultivation may be well done or neglected; crops may be protected from parasites or left exposed; the harvesting may be efficiently or wastefully executed; products may be well graded or the grading neglected. When one comes to animal husbandry, there is a still larger degree of control in the hands of the proprietor, since breeding is practically by his choice. In the case of hogs, not only is it possible to control the total number of sows mated, it is possible to distribute the breeding between winter and summer farrows. There is also wide latitude in marketing; animals may be rushed to market or held back, they may be fed for fat or for lean. But the hog cycles and cattle cycles indicate that practicable adjustments are neglected.

When, crop by crop, one comes to examine the planting, development, harvesting, and distribution of each individual farm product, with respect to individually controllable or uncontrollable factors, it becomes apparent that the power of adjustment of supply to demand in the hands of an individual farmer is much larger than is commonly used, or conceded in argument. To a considerable extent, the difficulty lies not in the technical scope of adjustment; it lies more in the farmers' capacity to make decisions for adjustments—to understand how, why, and when production is to be stimulated or restrained. Farmers recall Dean Swift; they like to push, dislike to hold back. And while it is to be granted that the technical scope of adjustment of production is less in agriculture than in industry, it is also true that the demand for agricultural products is more inelastic than is the demand for industrial products; less adjustment is required, on this ground.

Some of the so-called "heavy industries," which deal with fabrication of raw materials into producers' goods, use a high degree of adjustment. These industries have records of unfilled orders, there is close control over the daily flow, the seasonal curve is well understood, the large buyers can usually be foreseen and budgeted; all in all, it is possible for a well-organized unit, even without monopoly or control, to maintain a close adjustment of supply to demand, and a fairly constant position. The inventory of raw material, of material in course of manufacture and of finished goods is usually foreseeable and controllable to a definite extent. Steel is perhaps the best illustration of such adjustment of supply to demand. In the textile industries (including silk, wool, linen, jute, cotton, and rayon) there is also a considerable capacity for adjustment—marred, however, by violent and frequent instances of overcompetition. In the case of flour milling, there is close adjustment of the grind to the flour requirements of the country. Concerns like American Radiator, General Electric, Westinghouse Electric, American Steel Foundries, General Motors, the companies building locomotives, and similar organizations base their operations closely on orders and budgeted forecasts; the inventory is never large, there is fairly close adjustment of supply to demand. In coal mining, on the other hand, there has been notorious nonadjustment of supply to demand, also in lumbering, paper making, and copper mining. Adjustment of supply to demand is more likely to occur with producers' goods than with consumers' goods, though glaring exceptions occur.

When, however, one leaves industries with large units and considers those with smaller units, the picture changes. At this point it becomes apparent that managerial decisions, more than technical considerations, influence adjustment of supply to demand. The smaller units lack the facilities for analyzing demand; they are more dependent upon the reactions of individual salesmen on prices; they rely on indexes of other operations. In many of the small units the overhead is low and they lack a compelling incentive to coordinate their activities to a selling program. There are indeed small units which manufacture months ahead of orders—make first and try to sell afterwards, as wheat growers do.

Several circumstances tend to prevent many industries from maintaining close adjustment of production to demand.

Three will be mentioned: (a) The necessity of maintaining a volume of inventory which will be large enough to cover relatively wide variations in rush orders. (b) The urge of competition. At a somewhat higher outturn, the cost of production is lower; the plant takes the chance of producing more than it can computably hope to sell, in the expectation that forced salesmanship, or the favor of the gods, can be relied upon to dispose of the outturn. In the upswing of a prosperous business, excesses are produced in the conviction that anything can be sold in any volume; in the downturn of a trade cycle, excesses are produced in the belief that by forced salesmanship and price-cutting goods can be disposed of. To an amazing extent, moderate-sized units, and sometimes large units, operate not on a basis of market analysis but on a theory of salesmanship, which amounts to mere trade promotion. (c) The volume of operation. It is in many industries more expensive to shut down than to operate at a loss (example, blast furnaces). Obsolescence of physical equipment is lower, the technical staffs and labor forces are held together; from every viewpoint of technical operation, continuance is to be preferred to suspension. It would be possible for many concerns to make in six to eight months the supply of an entire year, but it is preferable to operate through the year; in such a case when demand falls to half, it may still seem preferable to maintain for months at least an unchanged outturn. The cost account of part-time and part-volume operation (especially with principal product and important by-products), as against suspension and stand-by expenses, is worked out for many industries to the extent at least of indicating, or suggesting, that sharp adjustment of supply to demand in slack seasons is poor business. Operations are often maintained principally in support of employment of workers. It is not true that inefficient plants routinely shut down and discontinue; they are more than likely to be bought up at forced sales for far less than their real obsolete values, and at the reduced valuations kept in operation as low-cost plants.

Quite generally in the United States since the war, it has been the policy of efficient industrial plants formally and annually to budget supply on the assumption that if it is properly merchandised, it can be sold. A modern industrial plant nowadays budgets supply, demand, costs, and profits. Such a budget at the extremes is based upon adjustment of supply to demand; but within these extremes, it is founded instead upon a concept of the adjustment of demand to supply in which adjustment is always pictured upwards. Plants run for profit; but in the boom period 1925-30, an almost incredible proportion of plants enjoyed only "profitless prosperity."

It would seem quite the part of folly in industrial enterprises to pile up inventories comparable with the piling up of carry-overs of wheat. But if one will contrast the stocks of copper with the stocks of wheat in the world within the past few years, one will come to realize that there is not much difference between the two performances. And if one were to modify production in adjustment of supply to demand under guidance of world stocks, one would be forced to infer that adjustment of production to demand is as difficult in copper mining as in wheat growing. Of course, it will be said that the situation in copper is anomalous in the international sense—to which it may be fittingly rejoined that the situation in wheat is anomalous in the international sense. Contrasted with copper, the outturns of nickel and of tin have been well controlled. It took the rubber plantations years to learn how to control the tapping of trees and outturns of crude rubber; they have not yet learned to control distribution. The growers of coffee have not learned how to control this tree-crop; they have not learned how to control the mere picking of the berries, to say nothing of the marketing—unless burning raw coffee is marketing it. The experiences in whaling and sea-fishing have illustrated also the striking inability of the operating units to control the magnitude of their operations, which are essentially industrial in character. Other illustrations could be easily cited; these suffice.

All in all, it is not true that industrial production is easily adjusted to demand and is routinely so adjusted, even in an approximate sense. It is not true that agricultural production is unadjustable to demand and in practice is not adjusted at all. There is some advantage on the side of industrial production; there is, on the other hand, a possibility of adjustment in agriculture which has never been invoked. *The real difference lies less in the possibilities and instruments of adjustment than in the mental attitude towards adjustment.* No Swift ever exhorted the shoemaker to supply two pairs where one pair was worn before. Industrialists are for the most part taught to look upon adjustment as a desirable thing, unless technically too difficult or too expensive on grounds of cost. Farmers as a class have not been taught to regard adjustment as something to be worked for, even if along particular lines such adjustment happens to be easy. We question if the earlier Wallaces preached individual crop control for purposes of adjustment of supply to demand.[1] Granted, there are only thousands of industrial plants, but millions of farmers. The producer of agricultural products is far ahead of the distributor and seller of the same; the producer of industrial goods stands closer to the distributor and seller. In the technique of relationship of

[1] So far as surplus is concerned, contraction of acreage may be nullified by increase of outturn per unit of area through improvement in farm practices.

production to distribution and sale lies the difference between agriculture and industry, more than in the inherent difficulties.

In *New Frontiers* Secretary Wallace has amplified to greater extent than in *America Must Choose* a threefold adjustment of current supply to effective demand for farm products. The three (to be) controlled variables are *stabilization of export, adjustment of acreage* (up or down but usually down) and *stabilization of carry-overs.* With an undeniable dexterity in the coining of slogans, Secretary Wallace has named the stabilized carry-over a "constantly normal granary." In this notion is incorporated not the New Deal but the oldest deal in grain supplies, one more or less legendary in reference to Joseph and to the Confucians. Incidentally remarked, the experiences under the Emperors Augustus and Nerva rather shake one's confidence in the story of Joseph; and certainly the defects of the ancient and modern economies can hardly have been identical. Shall it come to pass that in respect of wheat the "constantly normal granary" of Secretary Wallace may approach the abnormal Stabilization Corporation of the Federal Farm Board? If one regards the wheat supply of North America as available to the population of this continent, two assumptions may fairly be made: first, that the best prospect for wheat price in the United States would lie in keeping our supply on the verge of imports from Canada; second, that our sense of security may be founded fairly on the inference that we would always have first call on the Canadian exports, and that a wheat crop failure in North America is unthinkable to the extent of making this continent a net importer of wheat in any year. Fairly construed, the "constantly normal granary" of Secretary Wallace is an exhibit of economic nationalism, quite like the much derided wheat expansions of the importing countries of Europe.

In the broad sense, the sharp distinction commonly drawn between adjustability of supply to demand in agriculture and industry respectively, breaks down under the analysis of the business cycle. If one will read *Business Cycles* [1] by Wesley C. Mitchell, *The Theory of Economic Development* [2] by Joseph A. Schumpeter, and the appropriate sections in *A Treatise on Money* [3] by John Maynard Keynes, one will come to realize the extraordinary lack of adjustment of supply of manufactures to demand that tend to occur, and recur, in modern industry. The shifting of proportional relations between savings and investment, the overexpansion of capital-goods plants, the excesses of outturn of producers' goods and even of consumers' durable goods, and the reversions that follow in the period of recession all testify to the inability of capitalists, bankers, and entrepreneurs to foresee trends and to make even rough adjustments of supply to demand. The abuse of savings and credit is as bad in industry as in agriculture. One may indeed go further and declare that when industry goes wrong in adjudgment of prospective demand, it tends to go further wrong than does agriculture, outside of the state of war. Industry is more vulnerable than agriculture to technological changes. The range of the swing of the pendulum of production, in relation to effective demand (outside of war), is wider in the case of industry than in the case of agriculture. Between trade cycles, industry as a whole makes adjustments better than agriculture as a whole; but over the period since our Civil War, the disequilibrium seems quite as conspicuous in

[1] New York, National Bureau of Economic Research, Inc., 1930.

[2] Cambridge, Harvard University Press, 1934.

[3] New York, Harcourt, Brace and Co., 1930. Cf. also, H. S. Ellis, *German Monetary Theory,* Harvard University Press, 1934, esp, pp. 402-412. J. Schumpeter, "The Explanation of the Business Cycle," *Economica,* 21, pp. 286-312. An illuminating review of new capital equipment is to be found in the recent *Formation of Capital,* by Harold G. Moulton (Washington, Brookings Institution, 1935).

industry as in agriculture. Whether liquidation of over-investment and reduction of costs will prove to be heavier and harder in agriculture than in industry, remains to be seen.

It is evident from numerous statements of Secretary Wallace that the policy of adjustment of supply to demand applies both to agriculture and to urban industries. The "economic balance" implies appropriate bilateral extensions and contractions in pecuniary activities. Adjustments are to occur in agriculture to take account of conditions in urban industry as well as in agriculture; correspondingly, adjustments are to occur in urban industry to take account of conditions in agriculture as well as in industry. In a sense, we take it that the projected scheme of bilateral adjustments would be directed at the elimination of submarginal operations both in town and country. Certainly we have submarginal factories, obsolescent plants and equipment; certainly we have worn-out farms and lands under cultivation that should never have been ploughed. If these could be systematically and comprehensively eliminated, the outturns of farm and factory would be obtained at reduced costs. But the general recognition of need of adjustments should not be qualified by the complacent assumption that such adjustments are more easily made in towns than on farms. Ruthless competition may eliminate submarginal operations (though in experience it often fails to do so); it may be found less easy for planning to eliminate them. Planning is indeed not recommended as a substitute for competition, but as something much better. We trust so; but the effectiveness of planning as a substitute for competition in elimination of submarginal operations, remains to be demonstrated.

A general comment seems here in order. The student of the historical development of the "planned society" cannot fail to be struck by the singular inattention usually devoted to the requirements, reactions, rights and privileges of consumers, using this term to include the users of primary materials, semi-finished materials, producers' goods, durable consumption goods, and finished consumables. The planned adjustment of supply to demand usually evinces only the producers' psychology. It does not seem to be generally appreciated by planners that while restriction in one line will (or may) benefit those engaged therein, an all-around restriction tends to lead to general impoverishment. When a program of restriction is advocated in a society with a so-called surplus economy, it may be found necessary to employ more labor on products with elastic demand and less labor on products with inelastic demand; also, improvement within agriculture by restriction may tend to make greater the adjustment necessary in other lines. Two quotations from *The Great Depression* by Lionel Robbins strike us as pertinent here:

". . . A democratic community, at any rate, will attempt to organize production to meet the preferences of consumers. It will not value branches of production as such. It will value them for the various individual satisfactions which they make possible." [1]

". . . A plan which was based upon the preferences of consumers would seek so to distribute its productive resources that the demand for all commodities was satisfied to the same level of urgency. . . .

"The requirement of a rational plan, as we have just seen, is that the factors of production (the land, capital and labor) should be so distributed between the various alternatives of production that no commodity which is produced has less value than the commodities which might have been produced had the factors of production been free for other purposes. . . . How is the planning authority to decide what distribution of resources satisfies this requirement?" [2]

[1] Lionel Robbins, *The Great Depression* (London, Macmillan, 1934), p. 148.

[2] *Ibid.*, p. 150.

Agricultural planning seems to include but few references to such considerations. Evidently, Ludwig von Mises is not a prophet to the new school of planners.

Lionel Robbins, who is an orthodox Victorian liberal, has also rather vigorous ideas on the current euphemistic usage of "planning" and "socialistic."

". . . But 'planning'—ah! magic word—who would not *plan?* . . . Yet, if planning is not a polite name for giving sectional advantages to particular industries, what does it denote but socialism—central control of the means of production? . . . There is no 'proper balance' between one industry and another in the sense of a ratio of prices which must not be changed whatever the changes in the general conditions of production." *

* "The whole notion of a proper balance between industry and industry, of which so much is heard in popular discussion of planning, etc., is relevant only to the sphere of æsthetics or military strategy, if it is not strictly related to considerations of prices and costs. Outside these spheres it is an almost perfect example of the pseudo-concept—a concept which on analysis proves to have no content of meaning." [1]

These observations are germane to the question of adjustment of supply to demand in agriculture and industry, since such adjustment must be bilateral and founded upon control of the means of production both in town and country.

What we miss especially in this foreign trade policy is the appropriate inclusion of the broad truth that the material progress of society depends on application of improved methods, lowering of costs, reduction of prices, and consequent enlargement of use with progressive improvement in the standard of living.[2] This is not specifically included in

[1] Robbins, *op. cit.*, pp. 145, 130.

[2] For a discussion on national economic planning in international economic affairs, see an interesting book by Barbara P. Wootton, *Plan or No Plan* (London, Victor Gollancz, Ltd., 1934), pp. 346-52. Cf. also J. M. Clark, *Strategic Factors in Business Cycles* (New York, National Bureau of Economic Research, 1934), especially Part V. M. Palyi, "International Aspects of Problems of Production and Trade," *American Economic Review,* March 1935, Supplement, XXV, 45-62. G. D. H. Cole, *Principles of Economic Planning* (London, Macmillan, 1935).

the concept of "balance"; yet without it, we shall have a balanced stagnation. It is true we should not have ruthless individualism or cutthroat competition; but to suppress these, one does not have to disregard the experience that costs influence prices, and prices influence costs. Whether all prices of goods and services are too high or too low is one technical question. But whether prices of individual goods and services are too high or too low in relation to each other is a totally different question, and probably the more important one.

Most social reformers have followed the rule that where there is a will there is an immediate way, and many reforms have been wrecked hunting for the unknown route. The New Dealers, true to form as reformers, assume that since they have the social conscience to envisage a balanced economy and the political power to carry through the procedures of reorganization and readjustment, they also possess the factual material indubitably requisite for the proposed changes and the intelligence to appraise this factual material and encompass the inherent difficulties. Unfortunately, the reasonably predicated factual material is not in hand, not in print. This is known to the special students of processes, prices, and profits. The annual *Yearbooks of Agriculture* and the biennial censuses of manufacture offer little of direct use in the reconstruction of our economy. A balance is sought between agriculture, urban industry, and services; also, a balance between the different branches of agriculture, between the different lines of urban industries, and between the different kinds of services. These balances cannot be established on sparse samples and crude averages. Recent special studies have clarified at once the relevancy and the limitations of our factual material.[1]

[1] R. C. Epstein and F. M. Clark, *A Source-Book for the Study of Industrial Profits* (Washington, Department of Commerce, 1932); F. C. Mills, *The Behavior of Prices* (New York, National Bureau of Economic

Adjustment of supply to demand is not the mere factor of lowering stocks on the market to influence the immediate price. The solution is dynamic rather than static. There are four continuing factors in adjustment of supply to demand: on the demand side are the consumers' needs with varying elasticities and the effective purchasing power of the country; on the supply side are the used capacity for production and the unused capacity to produce. Put in another way, the two outstanding variables are the unused capacity to produce and the unused capacity to consume. The unused capacity to produce lies more in the relation of saving to investment than in the momentary state of physical plants; it is only a step from unused investment to unused capacity to produce. Perhaps changes in volume of bank credit are more important than changes in volume of physical plant equipment. But even our actual capacity to produce is difficult of appraisal.[1]

Perhaps the best historical example of a temporary balance between town and country, rich and poor, majority and minority, is to be found in the Tokugawa Shogunate epoch in Japan, which lasted through the long interval from 1603 to 1868. The standard of living was low; but with a stationary population, without civil or foreign war, the balance between population and resources and the partition of opportunities and rewards were exceptionally equitable. It was a

---

Research, 1927), and *Economic Tendencies in the United States: Aspects of Pre-War and Post-War Changes* (New York, National Bureau of Economic Research, 1932); Simon Kuznets, *Seasonal Variations in Industry and Trade* (New York, National Bureau of Economic Research, 1933); J. M. Clark, *Strategic Factors in Business Cycles* (New York, National Bureau of Economic Research, 1934); and R. C. Epstein, *Industrial Profits in the United States* (New York, National Bureau of Economic Research, 1934).

[1] Cf. E. G. Nourse and associates, *America's Capacity to Produce* (Washington, Brookings Institution, 1934); Maurice Leven, H. G. Moulton, and Clark Warburton, *America's Capacity to Consume* (Washington, Brookings Institution, 1934); and Harold Loeb and associates, *The Chart of Plenty* (New York, Viking, 1935).

planned and managed society, a cultured feudalism. With the restoration of the Imperial government and the subsequent industrialization of the country, this balanced society was thrown into disequilibrium, with pronounced inequalities in the social and economic structure. Whether this illustration suggests that a managed society is best organized by an oligarchy need not be discussed.

SUMMARY

The current assumption is that urban industries lend themselves easily to adjustment of supply to demand and are thus usually operated, while agriculture does not lend itself to such adjustment; this is the basis of the differential treatment proposed by Secretary Wallace. The assumption is untenable except in a relatively narrow sense. Many large industrial units are operated in close adjustment of supply to demand; but other large industries are not so conducted. Many small industrial units are managed without reference to supply and demand, and in the period of prosperity that terminated in 1930, a surprising proportion of the smaller units of industry had been operating without profit. For certain agricultural crops, adjustment is very difficult; but for other crops, adjustment is easy. Animal husbandry may be regulated through control of breeding, but the cycles of hog prices and of cattle prices show that this is not done. Technological changes are more rapid in industry than in agriculture. In short, there is a difference in adjustability, but it is a difference in degree and not in kind. The major difference between industry and agriculture lies not in the practicability of adjustments but in the occupational attitude towards them. The recurring trade cycles are due in large part to mistaken programs of production, especially of capital goods and producers' goods. In short, the trade cycle is the refutation of the assumption that industry as a whole practices an effective adjustment of supply to demand.

The adjustment of supply to demand in agriculture will be found to be made more difficult if simultaneously adjustment of supply to demand is to be made in urban industries. That is, bilateral adjustment will be found more complicated and difficult than adjustment in agriculture alone. Yet bilateral adjustment is predicated. Finally, such planning takes little account of the interests and reactions of consumers. When significant adjustments are artificially imposed on different groups of producers, it may easily turn out that these are later nullified by mass reactions of consumers. This is true to some extent even in war, when a final buyer exists for all commodities. When, with more or less variable plethoras of goods, consumers decide between use, abstinence, and substitution, then the adjustments imposed on producers will fail more or less as regimentation. Every producer in whatever line and of whatever rank is a final consumer; eventually the consumers consolidate their impulses and decisions into a public policy.

Chapter III

GROSS EXTENT OF PLANNED CONTRACTION AND ADJUSTMENT CONTEMPLATED

The people seek security and stability. What will contribute to these in town and country? In the brief original statement of Secretary Wallace are few specifications. Enough, however, is offered in *New Frontiers* to make it clear that the Secretary fully appreciates that adjustments on the part of non-agriculture will need to be quite as extensive as adjustments on the part of agriculture. However, adjustment of agriculture is the direct task of the Secretary of Agriculture: adjustment in industry and commerce is merely his advisory function. The preliminary major question is to determine the gross figure for acreage contraction in crop land required to bring about a "balance" between town and country, after providing for an added export of farm products to the extent of some 500 million dollars. Such added export of farm products, together with payment of service charges on foreign debt, implies the acceptance of a passive balance of merchandise trade approximating a billion dollars. Enough acres ought to be withdrawn to correspond with this result, but no more. In the "planned middle course" the Secretary has set forth the proposal to withdraw 25 million acres of good crop land.

The proposed adjustments in agriculture involve consequences to the farm population as well as to the physical plant. The possible reduction, or dislocation, of farm population and the effects upon gainful employment in town and city are not to be evaded. The effects upon size, location, and adaptation of the physical plant of agriculture will involve large technical questions. Since the AAA policy tends (with favorable weather) to restrict output, this tends to subsidize immobility and this may have a long-term deflationary influence. On the other hand, subsidy for curtailment of crop acreage may in some regions become an incentive to marginal producers. It is trite to remark that every problem of technique and price on the farm becomes a "social" problem; [1] but the truth of this adage will become more generally appreciated in the course of a planned contraction.

Among the first of the questions of procedure to be determined is the place of the initiative and referendum in the farm program. Are the planned contraction, adjustment, and organization to be imposed (planned) from the top, along strictly technical lines? Are such plans to be submitted to farmers, for acceptance or rejection by referendum? Are farmers to have the right of a formal initiative? In short, is specific policy to be determined by mere majority or by a stated required majority of farmers, with subsequent use of federal powers? Or do farmers merely accept primarily the official programs? In *New Frontiers* Secretary Wallace makes plain the widespread cooperation sought from individual farmers; but an out-and-out declaration on initiative and referendum is not made.

On the side of the non-agricultural elements of our national life, it is important to observe that it is not merely a question of factory owners and workers versus farm owners and workers. To be considered also are the widespread "service industries"—the almost innumerable collection of

[1] England has the same problem, though the agricultural class is much smaller. Recently one of the traditional agrarian leaders of that country, Sir Daniel Hall, reminded British agriculture that it ought to organize for the service of, and not at the expense of, the other nine-tenths of the population.

services which lie between city and country, including transportation, communications, wholesale and retail distribution, banking, teaching, etc. The professions come to be included. These services are all involved, both in the contraction of agriculture and in the adjustment of the non-agricultural elements contingent on a change in our international policy. *All consumers are directly involved; everybody is included in the new "balance."* Certainly, many non-agricultural domestic activities will need to be curtailed, though a few may be expanded. It may become necessary to relocate town population as well as farm population.

It is impossible to plan foreign trade without some planning for domestic trade; we shall need to classify all activities on some *grading of more or less essential values.* Since we are to export more agricultural products, we may have to export less industrial products; since we are to import more industrial products, we may have to manufacture less industrial products. These adjustments must be reciprocal. It is quite illusory to hope that such decisions can be based on current production costs; the question is not so simple. For a few specialized or "exotic" articles it is easy to say that we should import them and not make them. It is easy to open the door to imports in order to crush exploitive monopolies, where such exist. But when substitutions are considered, even such a classification becomes complex. To go over the entire domain of imports and attempt to determine what rearrangement of tariff duties needs to be undertaken in order to receive a billion dollars' worth of stated merchandise imports more than enter on the present tariff level, is a staggering task. Equally important is the circumstance that any such plan must assume "other things equal" abroad, and also continuity or foreseeability of foreign policy. Contrasted with the problem of adjustment between the conflicting and competitive elements of the non-agricultural activities—i.e., those of three-fourths of the population—the contraction of agriculture involving one-fourth of the population would seem to be inherently the simpler task. Also the farm bloc is compact politically, and agriculture is a unity in social policy; industries are not unified and also are less coherent.

The most pertinent excerpts from *America Must Choose* are the following:

". . . In consequence we are forced to think of what we ought to do with the 43 million marginal acres of plowland we are going to take out of cultivation in 1934 because the world no longer will pay us for the extra wheat, cotton and corn we have been growing there." (p. 4)

"Theoretically, we recognize that this bringing of order out of chaos should extend as rapidly as possible into world agreements. But until such agreements can be made we must work to set our own land in order." (p. 4)

". . . Our immediate effort is to organize American agriculture to reduce its output to domestic need, plus that amount which we can export with profit." (p. 6)

". . . Furthermore, if we continue year after year with only 25 or 30 million acres of cotton in the South instead of 40 or 45 million acres, it may be necessary after a time to shift part of the southern population, and there is a question as to just what kind of activity these southern farm laborers should engage in. We will find exactly the same dilemma, although not on quite such a great scale, in the corn and wheat belts." (p. 11)

"It is evident that the chief factors in our problem are linked, and cannot be separated. First there is the retreat from excessive farm production for export. How far the retreat should go depends, of course, on the state of the demand abroad and at home." (pp. 31-32)

"By the end of 1934 we shall probably have taken 15 million acres out of cotton, 20 million acres out of corn, and about half a million acres out of tobacco. Add to that the 7½ million acres that we used to sow to wheat and now shall not, and you get a total of 43 million acres which may be no longer planted to our major export crops. Forty-three million acres is nearly one-eighth of all the crop land now harvested in the United States." (p. 7)

The specific plan set forth in *America Must Choose* is to

". . . lower tariffs enough to bring in another half-billion dollars worth of goods annually, and permanently retract of our good agricultural land some 25 million acres." (p. 27)

In the Report of the National Resources Board, dated November 15, 1934, Part II is devoted to the report of the Land Planning Committee. This is a surprisingly comprehensive technical investigation, in view of the short time available. On the basis of productivity, a tentative classification of land is given, the acreage divided into five grades, in rounded figures:

Grade 1	101	million acres
Grade 2	211	" "
Grade 3	346	" "
Grade 4	263	" "
Grade 5 (essentially non-arable)	882	" "

Various estimates of harvested crop land devoted to exports in the pre-depression years have ranged from 60 to 80 million acres; here an estimate of 63 million acres was given. This we infer has been latterly reduced to around 30 million acres.

A nation-wide survey of farms proposed for retirement yielded a figure of some 450 thousand farms, including about 75 million acres, of which about 20 million acres were in crop land, 35 million acres in pasture land, and 20 million acres in forest and wood land. In addition, some 5 million acres in crop land outside of these farms were marked for retirement as crop land. This would imply, if carried out at present, the reduction of harvested crop land from 359 to 334 million acres. On the basis of an estimate of rate of growth of population, it would be necessary, with the reduced base line, to find an additional 47 million acres of new crop land between 1930 and 1960, to cover domestic requirements and the modest increase expected in export of farm products. This new crop land, to be brought in at the average rate of less than 3 million acres a year, would be secured from plowable pasture land in farms, cut-over wood land, and land to be drained and irrigated. In summary, this would involve, between the present and 1960, the withdrawal of 80 million acres of submarginal land, of which 25 million acres are in crops, and the gradual addition of 52 million acres of new crop land. This calculation takes no account of possible revolutionary changes in accepted agricultural practice.

As shall be set forth in the discussion of the balance of trade, it will not suffice to bring in additional imports of goods to the extent of only a half-billion dollars; probably twice this much will be required if the predicated increase in exports of farm products of a half-billion dollars is to be fulfilled. To arrive at the figure of needed increase in import of goods, one must include both the service charges due us on foreign investment and debt and the stipulated increase in export of farm products. To the extent that the estimate of 25 million acres is directly contingent on the half-billion dollars of added imports, the basis of contraction of acreage may need to be revised.

These excerpts from *America Must Choose* may be reinforced by the following quotations from *New Frontiers:*

". . . Science has made it possible for American agriculture since the war to increase production 25 per cent without any increase in acreage." (p. 152)

". . . Given normal weather we have still every reason to believe that we have now an effective market for the product of only about 330,000,000 acres of the United States." (p. 237)

". . . It has been my view from the first that the surplus does not consist merely of surplus bushels and bales, but of those 50 million extra acres of plowland which has been producing stuff for sale to foreign countries. We must either keep those acres out of production, or lower tariffs sufficiently to create additional foreign purchasing power for the product of those acres." (pp. 207-08)

". . . Drop production control and restore foreign purchasing power by loaning approximately $500,000,000 annually to foreign nations." (p. 216) or—

". . . Drop production control and restore foreign purchasing power by lowering tariffs sufficiently to cause imports to exceed exports by at least $500,000,000 annually." (p. 217)

From a neutral source [1] are drawn the following quotations:

". . . The direct economic dislocations that would follow would not be spread evenly over our whole economic structure. They would strike primarily at certain kinds of manufacturing and at certain types of farming." (p. 27)

". . . A very large amount of industrial plant and equipment would have to be junked with great capital losses and destruction of wealth. Large numbers of workers would be thrown out of employment. Many fields would stand fallow and revert to grass and forest. Many farmers would have to seek other means of livelihood; with extensive unemployment already prevalent in industry, they would find this difficult. Large readjustments would have to be made; population and industry redistributed; and the proportions of agricultural, industrial, and white-collar workers changed to fit the new conditions. . . . In the period while this equilibrium was being approached economic turmoil with much suffering and destruction of human values could hardly be avoided unless the new régime were approached very gradually step by step." (p. 30)

". . . What would be most desirable of all would be to increase our imports materially while at the same time slightly

[1] Commission of Inquiry into National Policy in International Economic Relations, *International Economic Relations* (Minneapolis, University of Minnesota Press, 1934).

increasing our exports so that the surplus of our imports over our exports may be large enough to assist substantially in restoring the desired balance of our foreign accounts." (p. 33)

It is evident that in *New Frontiers* Secretary Wallace is less constrained to hold to the "precisely halfway" point of contraction, at 25 million acres. This indecision presumably arises in part from inability to select in advance the particular 25 million acres to be taken out of crop land. To a larger extent, probably, it is inherent in the extent of predicated expansion of export of farm products, which in turn depends on the extent of passive balance of merchandise trade set forth. If we are to have a passive balance of merchandise trade equivalent to a billion dollars per year (as we indicate below must be accepted), this would permit of so large an added export of farm products (a half-billion dollars' worth), as to make it feasible to contract acreage by no more (perhaps even less) than 25 million. But if, as we suspect the historically minded critic might infer, pronounced resistance may be expected to develop against heavily augmenting the passive balance of merchandise trade to, let us say, the equivalent of a billion dollars, then the added export of farm products could not be so large, unless service charges due from abroad were to go in part unpaid. Finally, it would be found hazardous to fix a preliminary total figure for maximum or minimum acreage in advance of the determination of the acreage contractions of the several crops. The incentives of farmers may be general or special, pecuniary or sentimental, positive or negative. There may be a short-term pecuniary prospect, outweighing other considerations; among better-trained farmers a long-term pecuniary prospect may outweigh other considerations. As a negative incentive, a farmer may be willing to cut down acreage in order to reduce operative costs. Farmers are individualists, even though class conscious, as the Secretary of Agriculture and the head of the AAA are fully aware. The details of contraction, however planned, would certainly be found bristling with difficulties; these we shall consider in the next section.

SUMMARY

Progress in agricultural science has brought it about that under normal weather conditions probably less than 320 million acres now need to be devoted to harvested crops to cover our domestic requirements. Since the total acreage planted to harvested crops has often been above 360 million acres, the excessive area is evident. At the current level of export of farm products, at least 50 million acres of good crop land would need to be withdrawn. Even such a withdrawal would depend for success upon what may be termed a reciprocal contraction of manufacture for export. To import annually a billion dollars more of non-agricultural goods, to export annually a half-billion more of farm products, and to contract agricultural plants and industrial plants in adjustment and adaptation thereto, would create numerous and difficult local problems. Significant shifts in population from farms in some regions and from cities in others, would seem inevitable. These adjustments could not be made on the basis of mere costs of production. The "planned middle course" of Secretary Wallace—to contract acreage of crop land by 25 million and to expand import of non-agricultural goods by 500 million dollars—would alone not represent a direct solution, since the increase in imports would need to be double that figure. It is an old device in diplomacy to emphasize difficulties in the statement of "principle" and deprecate them in the statement of "detail." The Secretary, we fear, has fallen into an old form of error: making the solution look easy by reducing the figures.

CHAPTER IV

ACREAGE CONTRACTION CONSIDERED IN DETAIL

CLASSIFICATION OF FARM LAND

LAND is not mere soil area; there are many kinds and degrees of land within a small region. And even on a small farm there may be kinds and degrees of land. In some regions, on the other hand, even large farms have a uniform kind of land. In order to picture how acreage of land in crops is to be contracted, it is best to use the classification used in the decennial census. The census classification is as follows:

ALL LAND IN FARMS

- Crop Land ....
  - Crops harvested
  - Crop failure
  - Idle or fallow
- Pasture Land ....
  - Plowable
  - Wood land
  - All Other
- Wood land not used for Pasture
- All other land in farms

The classification may be applied to each state with the reservation that the terms do not correspond exactly with the same conditions in the different states. For example, "plowable" means one thing in New England with a high precipitation of rain, and another thing in arid Arizona; "wood land" means one thing in Georgia and a different thing in California; "fallow" has a different implication in

Montana and in Ohio. But with qualification, the land in farms in each state is subject to analysis, both in respect to present use and with regard to future potential employment.

The following table presents the distribution of land in farms, as reported in the *Fifteenth Census, 1930, Agriculture,* Vol. IV, as of April 1, 1930, with use of crop acreages of 1929.

		Acres
Land in farms		986,771,016
Crop land, total		413,235,890
Crop land harvested	359,242,091	
Crop failure	12,706,583	
Idle or fallow	41,287,216	
Pasture land, total		464,154,524
Plowable pasture	109,159,914	
Wood-land pasture	85,321,900	
Other pasture	269,672,710	
Wood land not used for pasture		64,623,825
Other land in farms		44,756,777

There is an overlapping of idle and fallow land with plowable pasture land. Lying within farms, as reported in the same census, was an irrigated area of 19,547,544 acres; presumably the irrigated area was almost entirely included under crop land.

In each state, the land falling under each one of these descriptions is to be classified on the basis of inches of rainfall; seasonal curve of precipitation; maximum, minimum and mean temperature; variations in rainfall from year to year; seasonal curve of temperature; monthly and annual hours of sunshine; dates of first killing autumnal frost and of last killing spring frost; history of occurrence of droughts; chemical composition of soil, and physical nature of soil. These data are only in small part the subject of census reports; but the records of the various bureaus of the national Department of Agriculture, of the land grant colleges, of the state colleges of agriculture, and of societies giving attention to the scientific study of soil and agriculture, would enable a scientific commission to make an approximate classification of all land in farms, which would serve state by state to grade the usefulness of land.

As reported in the Fifteenth Census, around 13 per cent of crop land was not harvested; it was abandoned, lay idle or was in fallow. To allow land to lie idle means to go to weeds; but to have land in fallow has the opposite effect. Abandonment of a planted crop is most prominent in the case of winter wheat, but does occur with spring-sown cereals and with cotton, and indeed may occur with any crop injured by unusual climatic occurrences. The proportion of 13 per cent reported in the Fifteenth Census would be too high in some years and too low in other years; favorable climatic circumstances would bring about a lower figure, unfavorable weather would result in a higher figure. Certainly also high prices would tend to lower the area for land thus out of use; low prices for more than a year would tend to raise the figure. Whether the 13 per cent of the crop land reported under "crop failure," and "idle or fallow" represents an average quality, or below or above the average, is not to be stated; but the inference is that poorer land goes out first. In the case of wheat, fallow is not here practiced so extensively as in Canada; but in the semi-arid wheat regions, the wheat land in fallow is representative of the general run, being merely the portion of the wheat acreage being rotated through fallow. When cereal crops are abandoned, it is, of course, possible that climatic injuries hit the poor lands harder than the good lands, and if such is the case, then the abandoned land would be below the average. Land which is merely idle and not in fallow, or which has been abandoned, not on account of the failure of a single crop, but on account of continuing low yields or low quality, is likely to be land below the average quality.

The question of classification is of importance, because if 25 or 50 million acres are to be thrown out of active use, these would be added to the some 54 million acres of crop land already reported out of use, that is, assuming that the report of idle and fallow land in the Fifteenth Census was fairly representative of other years. To add 50 million acres taken out of crop production would thus represent doubling the amount of land which is out of active use. Applying these figures, for illustration, to the data of the Fifteenth Census report—which contained crop harvested at 359 million acres and crop failure, idle or fallow land, at 54 million acres—to take a further 50 million acres out of production would mean changing these figures respectively to 309 million and 104 million acres. This would represent a significant enlargement in the proportion of crop land out of active use, being an increase in the percentage of such land from 13 to 25 per cent.

Another question arises with reference to the subsequent classification. If the figure for crop land not in use were to rise, continuing this same illustration, from 54 to 104 million acres, some farmers would find it necessary, or advantageous, to transfer part of this land into pasture land, where it would be classified under the fraction denominated "plowable." Now as a matter of fact, this is what must occur if the contraction of the crop acreage is to be advantageously carried through; it must mean not merely crop land transferred from active use into idle or fallow land, but must involve also a transfer into grass land.

If the entire 50 million acres, continuing this same illustration, were to be thus transferred to pasture, this would involve an increase in the plowable pasture land from 109 million to 159 million acres, or an increase of one-half. However valuable this might seem to the expert in farm management from the standpoint of soil regeneration, the farmer could hardly be expected to have his pasture increased by one-half without having animals to use it. Yet this is exactly what must be contemplated, since to utilize the enlarged pasture land for raising sheep, cattle or hogs would indirectly defeat the very purpose of the contraction.

SUBMARGINAL LAND

In farming are to be found three kinds of submarginal factors. (a) The submarginal soil—as related to climate, chemical composition, and physical properties. (b) The submarginal method—the out-of-date practices in farm management, tillage, rotation, etc. (c) The submarginal farmer—a low-grade owner unable to cope with the technical problems of a farm, or an untrained tenant. These three forms of the submarginal factor interact upon one another. A piece of land may be submarginal with poor methods or under a poor farmer which would not be submarginal with good methods or under a good farmer. Experienced students of farm machinery understand the three separate kinds of submarginal operations. If one were to ask the question of the extent to which "all land in farms" in the country, namely, 986,771,016 acres, contain submarginal areas, the answer would depend not merely on the soil and climate but also on stipulated methods and competency in farming. With the proved methods of agricultural science and the competency of the top one-fourth of all farmers, an entirely different answer would be secured from the one obtained with methods and machinery already available on the farms, applied with the competency of the poorest one-fourth of farmers. In all such questions and answers, it must be clearly stated that *other things are equal and weighted*. Further, the question of price cannot be disregarded. As the price level of farm products rises, some lands called submarginal cease to be so; as the price level of farm products falls, the extent of submarginal area rises. Costs also enter. It is true of farms, as of factories, that operations become feasible with interest rate at 4 per cent that could not be undertaken with interest rate at 6 per cent. The "good" crop land referred to by Secretary Wallace means, we take it, good for the export crop; the poorest land means poor for the export crop. A board of experts could take out 50, or even 100 million acres of land and not lower the wheat, corn, or cotton crops significantly.

A classification of submarginal farm land that would have been regarded as representative and equitable in the five years before the war, would not have been regarded as representative and equitable during the years of high war prices, nor yet again during the recent years of low prices. It is necessary that these implications and qualifications of the term submarginal should be fully recognized, preliminary to any definite discussion of limitation of acreage and adjustment of supply to demand, because (more or less by common consent) what should be sought in an acreage contraction for the most part would be the elimination of submarginal lands. Perhaps, however, the inference "by common consent" is not so warranted politically as it is technically.

Also there is such a thing within a region as a natural relationship between different crops, and this affects the definition of submarginal. When through an exceptional incentive a particular crop is expanded out of all proportion to previous occurrence, the natural rotation with other crops is disturbed and the farm suffers a long-term injury in order that the farmer may take advantage of a short-term cash advance. On the other hand, the low price for a particular crop may induce undesirable changes in rotation, merely to get rid of the crop with such poor prospects. An illustration is the effect in the corn belt of the reduced demand for oats in consequence of the decline in the number of work animals. In the corn belt oats is the common rotation crop for corn; if with a low price of oats this rotation is continued, a penalty is incurred; but if to avoid this penalty a less advantageous rotation is selected, a different penalty is incurred. In other words, disadvantageous practices may be selected by farmers, or be forced on them, which have indirectly an effect commonly classed under submarginal.

RETIREMENT OF CROP LAND

The expressions employed by the Secretary to indicate the scope of retrenchment under "nationalism" ("retirement of some 50 to 100 million acres," "retirement of from 40 to 100 million acres of crop land," "Forty million, if we take out good land; 100 million if we take out the worst") reveal implications in respect of both quantities and qualities of land. At the time of the last decennial census, crop land represented 42 per cent of land in farms; if 50 million acres were subtracted from the figure for crop land, the proportion of crop land to all land in farms would be reduced to 37 per cent; with 100 million acres subtracted, this proportion would be reduced to 32 per cent. With only 25 million acres retired, the proportion of crop land to all land in farms would be 39 per cent. In the Fifteenth Census, 413,235,890 acres were reported in crop land on 6,288,648 farms, indicating an average acreage in crops per farm of 66 acres. With 25 million acres of crop land subtracted, the average crop land per farm would be 62 acres; with 50 million acres subtracted from the crop land, this average crop-land acreage per farm would be reduced to 58 acres; with removal of 100 million acres subtracted from the crop land, this average crop-land acreage per farm would be reduced to 50 acres. If acres were unity, that is, if all acres within farms had the same usefulness for the crops under consideration, such horizontal reductions would have an impressive meaning; but as is explained elsewhere, this is by no means the case, and the dynamic reduction is not parallel with the static reduction.

Hypothetical scheme of distribution of global area. It is worth while to put in tabular form the changes to be expected in classification of farm land under the three projected levels of contraction of acreage in crop land. In the following table, the classification of the census of 1930 is employed as base line. This classification is then reformulated under contraction respectively of 25, 50 and 100 million acres of crop land. This has been done in an arbitrary manner, merely to provide an illustration. In the two higher illustrations, the acreage to be subtracted has been taken from crop land harvested and redistributed as follows: 30 per cent is added to idle or fallow land, 30 per cent is added to total pasture land and thereunder to plowable pasture land; and the final 40 per cent is added to wood land not used for pasture. The effect of this segregation is to subtract the total sum in each instance from crop land harvested and transfer it to idle or fallow land, plowable pasture land, and wood land not used for pasture in the proportions of 30, 30 and 40 per cent. In the case of contraction of only 25 million acres, as provided in the "planned middle course," this is subtracted from the crop land harvested and distributed between idle and fallow land, plowable pasture and wood land not used for pasture in the proportions of 8, 8 and 9 million acres respectively. The table is as follows:

TABLE I.—CLASSIFICATION OF LAND, SUGGESTED CONTRACTIONS *
(Acres)

		Contract Harvested Crop Land		
	Census, 1930	25,000,000	50,000,000	100,000,000
Land in farms	986,771,016	986,771,016	986,771,016	986,771,016
Total crop land	413,235,890	396,235,890	378,235,890	343,235,890
Crop land harvested	359,242,091	334,242,091	309,242,091	259,242,091
Crop failure	12,706,583	12,706,583	12,706,583	12,706,583
Idle or fallow	41,287,216	49,287,216	56,287,216	71,287,216
Total pasture land	464,154,524	472,154,524	479,154,524	494,154,524
Plowable pasture	109,159,914	117,159,914	124,159,914	139,159,914
Wood-land pasture	85,321,900	85,321,900	85,321,900	85,321,900
Other pasture	269,672,710	269,672,710	269,672,710	269,672,710
Wood land, not pasture	64,623,825	73,623,825	84,623,825	104,623,825
All other land in farms	44,756,777	44,756,777	44,756,777	44,756,777

* Based on data from *Fifteenth Census of the United States, 1930, Agriculture*, I.

For the purpose of the contraction, the terms "good" and "poor" cannot be used with the connotations implied in ordinary farm practice. The term "good" means good for the particular crops which are being contracted—cotton, wheat, corn, and tobacco principally. Certain lands may be good for these export crops but not for one, or several, of many other crops. For illustration, certain lands along the foggy coast in California may be poor for wheat but good for beans. Corresponding considerations apply, of course, to poor land. For illustration, some of the semi-arid areas lying on the eastern slope of the Rocky Mountains are good land for wheat, but poor land for tobacco. Therefore the 25, 50, or 100 million acres to be taken out must have a principal reference, if not an exclusive one, to the stated surplus crops. With fertilization, otherwise poor land in some of the southeastern states becomes good land. Without question, one could remove 25 or even 50 million acres of crop land called "good" for many uses, and not restrict the average crops, under attainable conditions, of wheat, corn, and cotton. Similarly, one could remove 100 million acres of poor land, that is, poor for wheat, corn, and cotton, and thereby scarcely reduce the prospective crops at all. The words "good" and "poor," it must be emphasized, are to be applied to the particular surplus crops and not to all crops.

Technique of retirement of crop land. There are two obvious ways of guiding a program of acreage contraction. One is to take out of all use the acreage denominated as excessive and leave it to the farmers to redistribute their various crops in the smaller acreage stipulated as sufficient. Such a method has plausible local advantages, since it is left to the initiative of the individual grower to use his land in accordance with soil and climate and his inclination and technical capacity. If during the past five years the total crop acreage in the United States has been held, let us say, below 320 million acres, it seems reasonable to infer that within a few years the acreage devoted to harvested crops would have been naturally divided between the several crops in such a way as to have avoided at least the largest excesses of surplus production. Of course, much would have depended upon price levels. In the Southern states, it is conceivable that the cotton acreage might not have been much reduced; but then the South would have become a heavier importer of foodstuffs from the corn belt. Possibly no reduction might be anticipated in the case of tobacco; and certainly the acreage in citrus crops would not be lowered in such a gross contraction of the area devoted to harvested crops in the entire country. On the other hand, it seems quite likely that if the gross area devoted to harvested crops had stood below 320 million acres, we would not have had a planting of anything like 70 million acres of wheat or of 100 million acres of corn. The best wheat and corn regions would have continued to plant a large acreage; but in the less favored regions, contraction would have occurred and these areas would have become importers from other regions, or at least, would have supplied less surplus to the general stock of wheat and corn. Clearly, however, contraction of acreage within farms on individual initiative would appear to be intangible.

The other method would be to proceed cumulatively, crop by crop. Using 50 million acres, as illustration, this would involve, let us say a reduction of 10 million acres planted to wheat, 20 million acres planted to corn, 15 million acres planted to cotton, with smaller amounts of contraction allocated to tobacco, raisins, etc. This reasoning implies that the existence of a non-exportable surplus indicates an excessive predominance of the particular crop as direct expression of farmers' choice. And further, if these particular tillages were directly contracted, the particular surpluses in question would be removed without significant effect upon the raising of other crops. In other words, on this theory it is felt that instead of allowing an autonomous agriculture to make internal adjustments within a stated contraction of acreage, it is better to prescribe one by one the particular contractions, the sum of which will bring the area in harvested crops under restraint down to the denominated figure. This is the method followed in 1934: farmers were then paid "benefits" to take out of wheat, corn and cotton stipulated numbers of acres previously planted to those crops.

Of course, on both sides this is largely dialectical reasoning, because it is supported by little worth-while experience. Perhaps in a few years the numerous trials of planned agriculture in various parts of the world may establish a body of precedent. It may not be sufficient merely to withdraw land from the surplus crops (let us say wheat, cotton, and corn) and to leave it to the individual farmers what to do with the crop land thus withdrawn from active use. To reduce unexportable surpluses of cotton, wheat, and hogs by creating unexportable surpluses of other crops would be only the makeshift of a solution. It may become necessary, in the alternative disposition of the lands withdrawn from surplus crops, to exercise methods of control to prevent new surpluses of other crops. The corn surplus of Iowa is not cured by reducing the corn crop and increasing the oat crop or raising soya beans to substitute soya-bean oil for lard. The problem thus becomes much more intricate than seemed originally implied in the proposed reduction of acreage of cotton, wheat, and corn. The real objective is to have the farmer make such disposition of the retired acreage as not to contribute to other embarrassed crops; that is, the (submarginal) lands withdrawn should be taken out of crop land entirely, or an equivalent area taken out, thereby increasing by that amount the area in the farm classified as grass or wood land. Now pasture land is of two kinds: one is directly used for cash-sale animal husbandry; the other is rather a reserve or used for breeding stock. Of course, 100 acres of corn land transferred to pasture land will support fewer hogs; but the argument still holds, that to plant previous corn land with alfalfa and raise hogs on it is still partially to defeat the objective of reducing the corn acreage. The solution will vary from region to region, in accordance with the nature and extent of pasture land. But as a point of doctrine, it must be insisted on that when crop land is taken out of active use and transferred to pasture land, this pasture land is not to be placed in direct use for cash-crop animal husbandry.

There is, however, another method of treatment. In countries with limited rainfall, it is common to fallow as a rotation. Such fallowing has the effect of killing weeds, holding moisture, adapting the soil to the retention of moisture when again planted, with possibly some activation of nitrogen. If one will look over the use of wheat land in the three prairie provinces of Canada, one will observe the tendency, as a regular rotation, to have one acre of wheat land in fallow while two acres are in wheat; that is, when we say that the wheat acreage in the prairie provinces of Canada in a certain year is 20 million, the real wheat acreage is around 30 million, with 10 million in fallow and 20 million planted. Such practice of fallowing is not inherently limited to soils with deficiency rainfall; it may be applied with comparable benefit to all soils. But in the case of lands with abundant rainfall, the fallowing practice is advantageously modified by planting appropriate cover crops and plowing them under, achieving at once regeneration of the soil and extermination of weeds.

Simple fallow, or fallowing with use of cover crops, involves farm labor whose cost must be entered into the account of the particular year, though without cash return at the time. Older countries have to choose between fallowing with cover crops and the application of artificial fertilizers. In a program of acreage contraction in this country, the regeneration of the soil through fallowing with cover crops would seem to represent for many regions the best technical solution of the question.

Anyone familiar with the psychology of the farmer must recognize the inextinguishable impulse to make two plants grow where one plant grew before—and then to find an animal to be raised on the second plant. The reactions of the average farmer on utilization of feeding stuffs are based upon maximum returns irrespective of time and cost, rather than on most efficient returns of feeding stuffs in edible animal products. The natural tendency of farmers is to produce the largest steer and the fattest hog, not the highest ratio of edible beef and pork from the feeding stuffs employed. In the feeding of every domesticated animal there is a time in the life of the animal up to which the gain in growth means increasing return in edible product per unit of feedstuff; beyond this point, with increased age of the animal, the rate of return in edible products declines. In a sense, one may say that up to a certain age, the law of increasing returns applies in animal husbandry; and beyond that age, a law of decreasing returns holds. Just as illustration, it may be suggested that this optimum age for recovery of edible meat products per unit of feeding stuffs employed is about six months in the case of hogs, and a year in the case of cattle. Everywhere in the world it "goes against the grain" of even intelligent farmers to market their animals at early ages and at relatively low weights. This question was an important problem in Europe during the War. It was necessary for the governments in the belligerent countries to secure from their available feeding stuffs the maximum outturns of edible meat products. Hogs are more efficient converters than cattle; therefore, it became government policy to cut down the count of cattle absolutely and raise the count of hogs, at least relatively. Also, it became policy to slaughter cattle and hogs at earlier ages than was the custom in the countries concerned. Such early slaughter of cattle and hogs was resisted by the peasants, who maintained their erroneous views of production costs and returns against the correct views of the specialists and experts.

Now the same view of animal husbandry is likely to find expression in any attempt to reduce acreage of crops used in production of animals. The presence of the animals furnishes the pretext for raising feed crops; and the possession of the feed crops furnishes the pretext for enlarging the count of domesticated animals. There is a common rule in the corn belt called the corn-hog ratio, which purports to show the price the farmer should receive for hogs when corn has a stated price; the more or less misguided farmer assumes continuation of a favorable or unfavorable relationship and breeds accordingly. Thus, if the price of corn seems to promise a price of hogs regarded as profitable, the farmers breed more sows and produce within a year a large number of pigs, for which they usually will not receive the price expected. The cycles of hog prices are due to a considerable extent to the misinterpretation of the feeding utility of a stated corn crop at a named corn price.

It is, therefore, essential in a program of contraction of corn acreage that two things should be accomplished. *First,* the outturn of corn must be in proportion to the acreage. Nothing will be gained if (through the use of selected seed and better methods of cultivation, on land above the average because of the withdrawal of the submarginal fraction, possibly also with the aid of artificial fertilizer) the crop of corn on the contracted acreage is as large as it was on the original acreage. *Second,* when a reduction in outturn of corn is secured, the farmer must not be permitted to compensate for this by increasing the outturn of other feeding stuffs which can be substituted more or less for corn in raising an unreduced count of animals.

Only those who have traveled through Argentina appreciate how extremely efficient an animal husbandry can be maintained on pasture alone. If the American farmer, who has several alternatives at his disposal, is permitted, at the same time as he reduces his corn crop, to expand his crops of small grains, soya beans, and sorghums, the end result may be that he may have as many feed calories after contraction of corn acreage as he had before; and if he has these feed calories at his disposal, he will convert them into hogs and cattle. And since the primary purpose of the contraction of the corn supply is to contract the hog supply, the entire plan may fail, simply because the farmer accomplished through substitutes for corn what he previously accomplished through corn. The solution is to reduce the use of concentrates and enlarge the use of grass.

Retirement of crop land in bulk. From the standpoint of the historical development of American agriculture, and especially in relation to the Homestead Act and the various projects of reclamation, one must realize that much of what has come to be, or ought to be, regarded as "submarginal" land was brought under cultivation less as the expression of the pioneer spirit of individual farmers, than as the consequence of political and legislative policy. In a significant sense, much of the submarginal land was brought under cultivation in bulk, so to speak. The question naturally arises whether retirement of such submarginal land might not also be accomplished in bulk.

Two excerpts from *New Frontiers* are here appropriate.

". . . as a result of the AAA taking out of use 40,000,000 acres of crop land on 3,000,000 different farms, there was growing interest in a more permanent solution. . . . Economists pointed out that it would be much sounder to take out of use the 70,000,000 poorest acres of crop land concentrated in the submarginal areas than 40,000,000 average acres on 3,000,000 farms scattered all over the United States." (p. 241)

"Unfortunately, from the standpoint of meeting the agricultural emergency at any time in the next five years, the proposal to buy poor land is not as practical as it sounds. In the first place, people living on the poorest land do not sell much. If we bought the 100,000,000 poorest acres of farm land, we probably would not cut the crop output of the United States as much as 5 per cent." (pp. 241-42)

It would lead us too far afield to consider the reasonably appraisable prospects of the various reclamation projects; but it is to be accepted that many of these projects deserve retirement when viewed as strictly agricultural ventures and independent of the local populations around them. We have next the numerous cut-over forest areas and drained swamp lands, together representing large tracts, which were brought into active agriculture by promotion, often as state or national projects, under the lure of high prices and a supposed high rate of growth of population. Finally, lying to the east of the Rocky Mountains is a strip of high land a couple of hundred miles wide, extending from Montana into the Panhandle of Texas, much of which was denuded of its native grass and turned over to wheat culture, in large part as expression of expectations in the trend of wheat consumption of the world which are not being fulfilled. Much of this semi-arid land will raise high-grade wheat, though with low yields, under favorable conditions at low costs in good years; but drought occurs so frequently and erosion so continuously that one wonders whether the larger part of this area should not have been left in native grass and devoted to a controlled range for cattle and sheep. Beyond these three sets of large tracts, a reasonable but correct technical classification, state by state, would develop a gross figure for acreage of "submarginal" lands which are now included under "crop land." [1]

It would be necessary to approach the question of bulk retirement of such land with great caution because this would involve the transfer of the contiguous population. We have no experience in the transfer of farmers, and the townsmen of villages directly dependent upon them, to distant points for settlement. Secretary Wallace refers to the possibility of relocating millions of superfluous cotton growers. Europe has a large experience, which flowed out of the World War—such as the bilateral repatriation of the peasants of Turkey and Greece. All experience indicates that such compulsory relocation of population is attended with intensive, extensive, and unfortunate social reactions; that is, not merely an occupational relocation is involved; it is still more a social reorganization.

There must further be a program of disposition of the submarginal areas retired in bulk. These would need to be reincorporated into the public domain; this would represent in a sense a reversal of the division of public land under the Homestead Act. Not only must such land withdrawn from crop use be returned to the public domain, the grass must be restored, trees or brush planted, erosion checked, and water stored and distributed with the object of restoration of the land to its primitive state. These would represent large undertakings. It is easy to convert a new country to an unsuccessful agriculture; it is very difficult to reverse the mistake and reconstitute the primitive country. And yet this seems necessary—the reconstitution of the primitive

[1] It is little consolation that other countries, for illustration Australia, have also had poor results in their public land policies.

country is quite as important as the removal of the submarginal land from the classification of "crop land" and the transfer of the population to more advantageous localities. All in all, the restoration of submarginal land *in bulk* to the public domain, while logical on technical and historical grounds, is likely to be found socially and politically difficult unless carefully planned and accompanied by a campaign of public enlightenment.

Retirement of acreage by states. In any program of contraction of acreage, a difficulty arises in the undertaking to apply the contraction by states, depending on whether the individual states are surplus states or deficiency states. For example, if we assume that the per capita use of wheat is uniform throughout the United States, then it follows that we have eighteen wheat-surplus states with a population of 26.2 million in 1930, and thirty wheat-deficiency states with a population of 96.6 million in 1930. The wheat-deficiency states may be divided into two groups; those which could readily raise more wheat and thus need to ship in less from the surplus states; and those in which the agricultures are such as not to make it expedient to expand the production of wheat. The states of the last group are few, in relation to their populations. The growers of wheat in the wheat-deficiency states tend to obtain a certain price advantage over the growers of wheat in the wheat-surplus states. In the wheat-deficiency states the growers have the advantage of the inbound freight charge from the wheat-surplus states, and possibly something more; thus the price of flour in Maine is higher than the price of flour in Kansas.

When now one considers the place of wheat in the agriculture of the wheat-deficiency states, it becomes clear that in many of these states the incentive to comply with an announced contraction of acreage is lacking, or at least weak. For example, in Pennsylvania wheat plays a major part in a complex rotation in a highly developed form of intensive agriculture. It may fairly be said that wheat is there not raised as a cash crop primarily; it is indeed often said that the straw is worth more than the grain. The wheats of Pennsylvania are mostly nondescript soft red-winter varieties; they are used to a large extent for feed for poultry and when ground in the local mills are usually mixed with hard wheat brought from a distance. Now to impose on the wheat growers of Pennsylvania a contraction of wheat acreage means a disruption of rotation, a loss of straw and of chicken feed, and a loss of filler wheat in the mixtures ground in the local flour mills. But local wheat means little directly to the cash income of the Pennsylvania farmer, and indirectly infringes but little on the market outlet of the wheat-surplus states. On behalf of many of the wheat-deficiency states, plausible arguments, based on considerations of farm management, may be advanced against the application of a horizontal reduction of wheat acreage applied to all states.[1]

Consider further the situation with corn. Here again we have heavy corn-surplus states; some states produce only a little more, or a little less, than they need; and some states produce far less than they require. The price of corn in the corn-deficiency states tends to be notably higher than in the corn-surplus states, presumably by something more than the freight, at least up to the extent of a certain volume. The corn-deficiency states are usually also hog-deficiency states. Corn is shipped from the corn-surplus states into the corn-deficiency states, either directly in the form of grain (or its milled products), or indirectly in the form of pork, lard, and beef. The animal products derived from corn in the corn belt tend to be priced higher in the deficiency states than in the corn belt. Green ham and bacon, for illustration, are

[1] In Georgia the Governor has advised farmers to plant more wheat.

shipped in carload lots from Omaha to California to be cured under California trade-marks: the packing-house price of these products in California stands above the packing-house price of the cured products in the corn belt.

Now the farmers in the corn-deficiency states find on their farms a convenient and remunerative place for a certain number of hogs. Indeed in many of the corn-deficiency states conditions exist which in themselves present attractive opportunities for hog raising. For example, in many of the far Western states where corn does not thrive, it is practicable to raise hogs on alfalfa and barley principally, just as is done in many parts of northern Europe. These farmers would find it an advantage to have the acreage of corn reduced in the corn belt and the number of hogs there correspondingly lowered. But in other sections of the country, where hogs are finished on corn shipped in from the corn-surplus area, farmers would regard a contraction of corn acreage as an injury, since it would raise the price of a major feeding stuff. The man who buys feeder hogs to be finished on corn he raises or buys is in a different position from the man who finishes on his own corn the hogs he raises. Under some circumstances therefore, it might seem as though it were the part of equity not to apply a contraction of corn acreage alike to both corn-surplus and corn-deficiency states, but instead to apply such contraction predominantly if not entirely to the corn belt.

In the broad sense the differences in conditions and incentives to be noted between different countries are found to exist to some extent between different states in this country. Contraction will not reduce crops directly, in all states alike, or benefit all alike. Further, a national prevision must be exercised, a safe level of supply must be maintained to safeguard dealers, millers and consumers. This safeguard Secretary Wallace calls the "normal granary," [1] a prevision that probably evolved from the 1934 drought.

The Land Planning Committee of the National Resources Board has made a survey of submarginal land in farms, out of which has evolved a "demonstrational program" for the retirement of poor land from cultivation. The farms in the list are individual selections. The following table illustrates the proposal:

Number of farms	454,200
Total acres	75,345,200
Acres crop land	20,163,400
Acres pasture	34,883,500
Acres wood land, farmsteads, etc.	20,298,300

It will be observed that each average farm, with an area of 166 acres, had only 44 acres in harvested crop land. Of these farms, no less than 248,200 were in Southern states; but they contained only 19,453,700 acres, or 78 acres per average farm, and each farm contained an average of only 19 acres of crop land. On the other hand, 26,000 farms on the Great Plains contained over 1,000 acres each on the average. Especially noteworthy is the large amount of land not in crop use recommended for withdrawal with the submarginal crop land, unquestionably a sound procedure. In addition, some 5 million acres of crop land lying in other farms were regarded as fit for retirement. In a sense, this comprehensive plan is a combination of withdrawal by states, contraction in bulk, and retirement of selected parcels

[1] Secretary Wallace has developed into an adept slogan-coiner. His "ever-normal granary" or "ever-constant granary" enjoys a precedent of sorts in the legend of Joseph; but the poetic phrase is quite likely to turn out to be the poetry of the Lorelei. In any event, it takes courage to use the need of a granary in China to illustrate the need of a granary in the United States. Secretary Wallace suggests that with an "ever-normal granary" the government-owned product should be used, instead of cash, to pay benefit payments the following year to those farmers who cooperate in a reduction control program. "For my part, I am convinced that the concept of an ever-normal granary cannot be satisfactorily administered unless those in positions of power determinedly hold to the concept of a harmonious continuing balance. . . ." (*New Frontiers,* p. 236.)

within farms. This long-term plan has no resemblance to the present scheme of contraction of acreage of specified crops, under cash payment for compliance with the year-by-year program of acreage contraction. Inherently sound technically, the practicability of such a contraction depends on availability of funds and of methods of inducing present owners to sell the specified farms.

EFFECT OF ACREAGE CONTRACTION ON FARM MANAGEMENT

It was the peculiar misfortune of agriculture that fall in price due to improvement in technique coincided with industrial depression and with fall in price due to the influence of deflation. The effect of contraction of acreage in harvested crops on the farm family, the equipment, and the overhead expenses, are therefore important points in internal farm management. Using the illustration given above, the land in crops on the average farm would be reduced from 66 acres to 62 acres with contraction of 25 million acres, to 58 acres with contraction of 50 million acres, and to 50 acres with contraction of 100 million acres. In net effect, the intensive fraction of the farm is contracted, the extensive and the resting fractions of the farms are expanded. Within a farm the area in crop land and the area outside of crop land have entirely different short-term and long-term meanings, since gross income, year after year, is related mostly to the area in crop land. At the time of the Fifteenth Census, per average acre reported in crop land there were available farm implements and machinery to the reported value of $7.99; if the area in crop land were contracted by 25 million acres, the average value per acre of available farm implements and machinery would rise to $8.51; if the area in crop land were contracted by 50 million acres, the average value per acre of available farm implements and machinery would rise to $9.09; if the contraction in crop land were 100 million acres, the average value per acre of available farm implements and machinery would rise to $10.54. That is, equipment in implements and machinery remaining constant (since the farmer could not sell it), with contracting acreage in crop land, a redundant equipment emerges.

The same consideration applies to other items in the overhead. With contracting acreage in crop lands, other things equal, the average farmer will need to employ fewer sons and hire less farm labor. This suggests creating an unemployment of farmers' sons and other farm workers, which would still not be alleviated if the farmers were to attempt by seed selection and improved mechanization to increase the yield per acre on the contracted acreage. Farm debt remaining unchanged, an enlarged burden falls on each acre of crop land with contraction of the same; the overhead and annual interest per acre of crop land rise. This tends to intensification of tillage. Farm taxes remaining unchanged, the tax burden per acre of crop land rises with contraction of the area of crop land. This increase of overhead items per area of crop land suggests the analogous picture of an industrial plant which shifts the proportion between active part and idle part in accordance with level of operation, gross income being secured on the active part and obsolescence written against the inactive part. With low prices, farmers tend to expand crops to enlarge the gross income to meet fixed expenses: with high prices they try to expand crops to cash in as net income. Both procedures tend to be opposed to the objective of acreage contraction.[1]

[1] An excellent idea of the thinking of the Department of Agriculture on adjustment is to be found in the following addresses of H. R. Tolley, Assistant Administrator and Director of the Program Planning Division, Agricultural Adjustment Administration: *The Problem of Long-Time Agricultural Adjustment; Land Use and Human Welfare; Land Use in Relation to Agricultural Adjustment;* and *The Adjustment Program to Follow 1935.* These have been issued by the AAA.

ADAPTATION THROUGH CHANGES IN THE DIET

Up to the present, the adjustment of production to effective demand has been explored on the assumption that acreage contraction is inevitable, that some land now in crops must be taken out of crops. There is, however, another possibility: namely, the use of land might be shifted from high returns of food calories per acre to low returns per acre. To accomplish this two major changes are available, but the steps would undoubtedly be termed "backward" by American farmers.

The first possible change would be to shift the American diet from pork to beef; for example, increase the per capita intake of beef by 30 pounds per year and reduce that of pork by the same amount.[1] Cattle are much less efficient than hogs as converters of feed nutrients into meat. In consequence, it takes a much larger acreage, even with present methods of feeding both classes, to make 100 pounds of beef than 100 pounds of pork. This fundamental difference between the two animals was the reason during the war why European countries on both sides of the conflict repressed beef production and favored pork production, in order to secure a larger outturn of meat from a limited supply of feeding stuffs. Possibly if such a question were put to a referendum in the corn belt, the majority of farmers might prefer a shift from hogs to cattle over a contraction of acreage.

Secondly, contraction of acreage could be avoided if the animals were fed, especially finished, less on concentrates and more on grass. A larger acreage is required to bring hogs and cattle to marketable weight on grass than with the use of grains. Of course, someone will protest that this is

[1] This would imply a shift from something like 50 pounds of beef and 70 pounds of pork to 80 pounds of beef and 40 pounds of pork.

inefficient from the standpoint of the definition of outturn per area; but we are considering a contraction, and this might for some regions be the best form of contraction. In Argentina, cattle are raised almost entirely on pasture, and the large shipments of excellent refrigerated beef sent to European markets come from such animals. Also, the milk supply of Argentina comes largely from grass and not from concentrates. The outturn per cow per year is lower than with the use of concentrates, but there is reason to infer that milk secured from exclusive pasture feeding is richer in vitamins and calcium than milk secured with the use of concentrates. Baby-beef cannot be produced after this fashion; the animals must be allowed to develop slowly, best up to at least three years of age. Of the expanding effect on acreage requirement to cover the needs of a stated number of animals, there can be no question.

These suggestions are probably too hypothetical to be taken seriously; but it would not be difficult to show that if a goodly shift in the diet were made from pork to beef and thereafter cattle and hogs raised less on grain and more on grass, the 25-million contraction of acreage postulated by Secretary Wallace in the "planned middle course" would not need to be put into effect.

Still another possibility exists, a comprehensive shifting in the diet from concentrated foodstuffs high in calories to foodstuffs low in calories, with a heavy increase in the per capita poundage intake per year. This could be accomplished by drastically lowering the intakes of cereals, dried legumes, sugar, fats and oils, and increasing the intakes of fresh or canned fruits and vegetables. Such a regimentation would be the converse of that employed by the European combatants during the war. Such a shift in the diet could not be secured merely on recommendation from Washington, nor yet through price changes. It would need to be secured through a regimentation. After this fashion, contraction of acreage planted to harvested crops would be evaded. There are signs that the Department of Agriculture is thinking in this direction, though the Secretary has not yet sponsored the policy officially.[1] Such a proposal would greatly disturb practices of food processors and shift regional tillages. Certainly it would provoke with consumers what might be described as a war of the roughages. Strange as it may seem in the corn and hog belt, the New Dealers may yet turn out to be vegetarians.

APPLICATION TO PRESENT ACREAGE OF CROP LAND

According to the Secretary of Agriculture, with the advent of the present administration in March, 1933,

> ". . . more than 40 million acres of American soil were producing material which could not be consumed within the country. . . ." (*America Must Choose,* p. 6.)

This "*material*" unconsumable within the country and unsalable abroad (at "decent" prices) on free and open markets, without subsidy by the producing country, is assumed to have been a major factor in the decline of the price level of agricultural products. The figure for 40 million really ought to be expanded to 50 million, since in consequence of more detailed estimates elsewhere applied to cotton, wheat, corn, and tobacco alone, a figure of over 47 million was arrived at. When now to this is added the acreage representing special crops (like raisins, prunes, and apples), which also were produced in a volume which could not be consumed within the country and could not be sold abroad on free and

[1] Cf. L. H. Bean, "Planning Our 1935 Farm Program," *The Annals of the American Academy of Political and Social Science,* November 1934, Vol. 176, pp. 111-20.

open markets without subsidy, except at very low prices, it is fair to raise the figure to 50 million. The Secretary of Agriculture remarked further:

> ". . . Forty million, if we take out good land; 100 million if we take out the worst." (*America Must Choose*, pp. 10-11.)

This range corresponds to the amount of acreage adjustment to be sought within the dimensions of the several acreages given above in the table of distribution of land in farms.

Of course, the table for 1929 in the Fifteenth Census of 1930 does not closely forecast the facts for 1935. Farms have been abandoned, both by individuals and corporations; abandoned in the sense of having fallen into disuse, even deserted. Lands have reverted to counties, to states, and to reclamation, irrigation, and drainage districts, in some states to quite large extents. Such lands may be leased out, but probably lie fallow. Lands have been foreclosed for non-payment of debt; some of these are continued in operation, but others lie unused. Therefore, the land in (active) farms from which the 25, 50, or 100 million acres are to be subtracted is to an indeterminate extent less than 987 million acres.

Also the segregation within the "land in farms" has changed from the prosperous years to the unprosperous years. The Department of Agriculture makes no annual estimate of farm land corresponding with that in the decennial census. There is probably now less land devoted to crops and more land classified as pasture. Also there is probably more land lying under the classification "other land" (that is, neither crop land nor pasture land) than there was five years ago. Low prices for cash crops and relatively high prices for the goods and services purchased by farmers, and the special relatively high prices for machinery and fertilizer, have already led to some internal contraction within many farms, leading to less land in crops, more land in pasture, and more land under the residual group of "other land," with the least productive use. Beginning with 1933-34 occurred a corresponding contraction in the farm plant of animal husbandry for which, however, other explanations are in hand. All in all, whatever scope of contraction of operations might be adopted, it would apply to a smaller figure for all land in crops than that of the last decennial census. But the difference can hardly be of significance generally, though perhaps important locally.

With contraction by only 25 million acres, as under the "planned middle course," the several considerations adduced above would apply to lesser extent. But it is doubtful whether the problem would be greatly eased. Many farmers would resist small contraction less than larger contraction; but they would still resist. A small contraction would hold a lesser obvious incentive than a larger one. If our embarrassing surpluses are so small as to be remedied by a small contraction of crop-land acreage, then the surplus problem loses its emergency character. Farmers might tolerate large measures for a large surplus better than small measures for a small surplus. There is poor political expediency in emergency measures when there is no emergency, in huge undertakings for a minor project. If our export market would take the surplus with only a small acreage contraction, then why not leave the acreage alone and try to support the exports in some direct or indirect way, for example, with an export debenture? In our view the lower acreage contraction of the "planned middle course" could well turn out to be about as hard as the larger contraction, with the results less promising to farmers.

SUMMARY

The classification of farm land in the decennial census is described and reproduced, together with a short discussion of the categories. Then follows a discussion of the nature of so-called submarginal farming. On the basis of the census classification, three progressive degrees of retirement of acreage in crop land are presented—namely, subtraction of 25, 50 and 100 million acres—with reclassification of the subtracted crop acreage into idle and fallow land, plowable pasture, and wood land. Then follows a discussion of the technique of retirement of crop land, whether by application to the individual farmer or to the particular crop. Emphasis is laid on the circumstance that land taken out of crop use must be set aside in such fashion that it cannot be indirectly cultivated to defeat the object of the retirement. Fallowing, with and without cover crop, is described as probably the best form of use of the acreage withdrawn from crop land. Particular emphasis is laid on the necessity of preventing the retired crop land from being used for cash-crop animal husbandry. The possibility of retirement in bulk is explored, with negative result. The particular problems involved in a program of retirement of acreage by states are presented, with special reference to wheat, corn, and hogs. The direct and indirect effects of acreage retirement on farm management, especially in relation of overhead to contracted tillage, are discussed. It is pointed out that if we had many more cattle and many less hogs, more acreage would be required; also, if animals were raised less on concentrates and more on grass, larger acreage would be used. An especial point is made of the possibility of avoiding any contraction of crop land through regimentation of the national diet—reducing the use of high-calorie foodstuffs, such as cereals, dried legumes, sugar, fats and oils, and increasing the use of low-calorie foodstuffs such as fresh and canned fruits and vegetables. Finally, the application of the program of contraction now under way is briefly considered, and the suggestion advanced that it would be possibly almost as difficult to contract crop land acreage by 25 million as by 50 million acres.

It is to be kept in mind as the outcome of a broad historical survey of modern agriculture that we have many illustrations of governmental and competitive expansions of agriculture; but we have few illustrations of competitive contraction of agriculture outside of those determined by migrations of population. In particular we have practically no illustrations of governmental contraction of agriculture under conditions at all comparable with those existing today. Therefore, in a governmental undertaking to contract agriculture in a formal manner we embark on the making of new history.

CHAPTER V

POPULATION INFLUENCES

IT seems rather curious in the statement of Secretary Wallace that so little consideration is given to the subject of size of farm population. There is comment on unemployment of farmers; but the larger aspects of the implications of a reduced rural class are not explored:

". . . Furthermore, if we continue year after year with only 25 or 30 million acres of cotton in the South instead of 40 or 45 million acres, it may be necessary after a time to shift part of the southern population, and there is a question as to just what kind of activity these southern farm laborers should engage in. We will find exactly the same dilemma, although not on quite such a great scale, in the corn and wheat belts." (*America Must Choose,* p. 11.)

In the census of 1930, the rural population was given as 53,820,223, and the urban population as 68,954,823, or respectively, 43.8 and 56.2 per cent. The classification of urban includes all cities and incorporated places having 2,500 inhabitants or more. This, of course, indicates that the rural population is much larger than the farm population. While it is true that a few farmers live in incorporated places of over 2,500 and are there classified as urban, a large number of non-farming persons in town with fewer than 2,500 inhabitants are classified as rural. The rural population contains two groups, those living on farms and those living in towns of less than 2,500 inhabitants, whose occupations are directly or indirectly related to the trade into and out of farms. The farm population (rural-farm plus urban-farm), without regard to occupation, was given as 30,445,350. The gainful workers in agriculture were reported as 10,471,998. The number of farm operators in this gross figure was reported as 6,288,648. Of the rural population of 53,820,223, no more than 30,157,513 were classified as rural farmers, while the large number of 23,662,710 were classified as rural non-farmers. The total so-called farm population (30,445,350), which included 287,937 urban-farmers living in towns over 2,500 was 24.8 per cent of the total population. But not all of these were farmers by occupation.[1]

A vital question for the future concerns the social and technical utility of this farm population. The slowing-down of rate of growth of the total population is not the same as that of the farm population: indeed, the total population will grow slowly for several decades while the farm population will presumably decline again after the depression is over. In the present state of American agriculture, is it technically wasteful, i.e., redundant, to have 30,445,350 persons living on farms, of whom 6,012,012 are owners and tenants, 67,222 are farm managers and workmen, with a total of 10,471,998 total gainful workers employed in agriculture? Could not 5 million efficient farmers on that number of farms conduct our agriculture? Or perhaps even as few as 4 million?

In consideration of the particular circumstance that our agriculture is based on outturn per man and not per unit of area; having regard to the character, quality, and diversity of our soils; taking account of the present state of the art of husbandry; and in particular giving adequate consideration to the present development of machinery on the farm

[1] According to the census of 1935 the farm population has risen to 32,779,000. That figure represents the all-time high record for farm population. This increase has been due to the depression. Despite apparent reduction of the acreage in harvested crops, the number of farms probably has been increased. Beyond that, the existing farms have directly absorbed a larger population, a true drift back to the land.

(whether hand-driven, animal-driven, or power-driven), is the outturn of crops secured in the United States, year after year, to be regarded as adequately efficient? If we regard the gross outturn of agricultural products as an efficient expression of the activities of the farm population, then the size of such farm population is justified on that score alone. If, however, the gross outturn of farm products is not large enough to be regarded as the expression of an efficient national operation, then the size of the farm population is to be justified, if at all, on grounds other than employment. Is the actual outturn per man rising as fast as the potential outturn per man? Is extensive farming becoming intensive farming as rapidly as the art and science would permit?

It is everywhere a trite remark, past and present, in sociology as well as in politics, that the rural population is the "backbone of a country." As the urban population, decade after decade, grew disproportionately to the rural population, following every census we read lamentations on the decline of the rural population. It seems nowhere to be accepted that the size of the rural population ought not to exceed the size of the rural function. With continuing improvement in agricultural operations, there is a widespread resistance against having the farm population adjusted downward to its employment. In short, the farm population is widely regarded as possessing certain peculiar and cardinal virtues. The topic is not peculiar to the United States nor to this period of history. Indeed, in the new states of the Europe of today, the prestige of the peasant class is perhaps higher than ever before in modern history; nor does this derive directly from military considerations.

Three separate considerations have been advanced in support of the view that the farm population possesses a peculiar value for society. (a) The first consideration is that the rural population tends to be more conservative than the urban population, in the sense of capitalism and the established order. It occupies the middle of the road on new policies, between extreme right and extreme left. It is true that urban workers with revolutionary tendencies have in many countries endeavored to make political alliances with farm workers. But the outcome, as in Russia, is usually one which sooner or later illustrates the essential divergence of the pecuniary interests of the two classes. (b) The second consideration, of which one hears less recently is to the effect that life on the farm is more healthful than in cities; that the migration of the country children to the cities provides fresh and invigorating human material to the urban population. This may have been true, for example, one hundred years ago in England; but it does not hold in the United States. This view is not now supported by scientific surveys and health reports; in general, conditions of sanitation tend to be worse in the country than in the town. The war records of soldiers from town and country, like the physical reports on enlistment, do not support the view that country boys are stronger and healthier than city boys. (c) The third consideration is that the birth-rate in the country is higher than in the city; therefore, a fecund rural class is to be conserved, in order to maintain the rate of growth of population of the nation. It is true that the birth-rate in the country is usually higher than in the city; but since the war (with cessation of immigration) the rural birth-rate in the United States has fallen significantly. Certainly, the older argument that the countryside was the "spawning ground of the nation" is in the first place ceasing to be true, in fact; in the second place, it is not a good argument, even if it were true. Back of this consideration abroad was once the accepted notion that the country provided more "cannon-fodder" than the town; this was true in Europe, but again proves nothing for this country. It is perhaps not out of place to remark that the one outstanding country in the world with an accomplished stationary population, France, is a country where the influence of the peasant class upon national characteristics and policies is very strong—showing that a high rural birth-rate is not needed to make rural influence predominant.

The exact grounds on which a farm population in excess of the technical (occupational) requirements of farm work may be supposed to hold a peculiar utility to a country, are obviously difficult to indicate; there is really very little more than intangible sentiment. If the farm population is larger than the work requirements of agriculture, this means part-time employment of a kind; it implies that gross farm income must be large enough to support a somewhat redundant population. At a time when land values were doubling every decade (as was roughly the case for thirty years before the war) a redundant farm population did not represent an economic burden of consequence; but after the war, when farm values and the gross income of agriculture fell to a low level in dollars, and especially in purchasing power, the situation became entirely different.

There are other occupations which may be cited in com parison. In coal mining, for example, more or less over the world, we have the situation of a class too large for the work; there is either widespread part-time employment, staggering of work, or total unemployment in practically every coal field in the world. It is very difficult to move the miners out of coal mining into other occupations; little has been accomplished in this direction, despite particular efforts made, for example, in Great Britain. But one does not read that it is important for a country to maintain a certain size of the class of coal-miners in order to safeguard the fuel supplies of the country in the future. There are more seamen than jobs on ships, but we do not hear that extra men ought to be carried along in order to maintain a larger class of seamen for future emergencies. In every large industry it is coming to be accepted as inevitable policy, that the size of the working group shall be apportioned (as costs) to the work of the industry—just as the size of the financial structure shall be apportioned to the work of the industry.

Accepting this general view for agriculture, despite its unpopularity in political circles, what is to be said of the present farm population in this country? Without question, it is too large. The farm population must be contracted to fit the occupation, or, more slowly, a migration maintained from country to town at a rate in excess of expected urban birth-rate. The average farm is now too small to make effective use of the boys of the family. For illustration, the average size of the farm in Iowa today is practically what it was thirty years ago, despite enormous improvement in agricultural technique. It is not to be questioned that 5 million farmers could readily carry the agriculture (for domestic requirements) of the United States at present. Possibly with the best methods and the use of the best land, the best 4 million farmers could carry on the national agriculture, for domestic requirements. The farm population in excess of requirements of the home market is far too large for the present or prospective foreign outlet for our farm products. It strikes us that it is an inherent weakness in the statement of Secretary Wallace that a continuation of the present size of the agricultural class seems apparently to be accepted as inevitable (apart from drastic official acreage contraction), instead of having an inevitable gradual reduction of farm population incorporated into the plan for adjustment of agricultural supply to demand. Otherwise, we face the problem of maintaining a farm population redundant for domestic requirements and dependent directly and solely on the foreign outlet for farm products. Thus export trade becomes the work-dole of the redundant farm workers.

It seems to be accepted in agrarian circles that agriculture ought to have close to 20 per cent (at least 15 per cent) of the national income. In recent years, the share of the national income contributed by agriculture has been below 10 per cent. In other words, one-fourth of the population on the land would be content with let us say one-sixth of the national income. In such an estimate of "balance" are four variables: total population, farm population, total national income and income contributed by agriculture.

The Secretary of Agriculture makes, further, no adequate reference to the rate of growth of our population, as affecting the home market. It now seems clear, from careful studies, that the rising rate of growth of the American population is slackening. The rate of increase from 1930 to 1940 will be less than that from 1920 to 1930; and a further retarded rate of growth will appear between 1940 and 1950. It is possible that around 1950-60 we shall have a practically stable population, provided that we continue our rigid exclusion of immigrants.

This means that with each decade the added new domestic market for agricultural products declines. In the past we have raised foods to sustain a domestic population increasing annually at a relatively rapid rate of growth; each year there was an added new market for the added new population. This change in our rate of population growth implies that unless the plant of agriculture is relatively contracted, we shall need to seek a continuously larger outlet abroad. If the rate of growth of population from 1920 to 1950 were to be the same as it was from 1890 to 1920, the present problem of our supply of agricultural products would not have arisen.

At the same time, the per capita need for food is declining. The exposed occupations are being gradually reduced or eliminated. There is not only lessened exposure to cold in outdoor occupations, there is lessened exposure indoors, on account of improved heating of buildings. The heavy occupations are being reduced; more and more, machines are supplanting human hands. There is also an influence in the age distribution with increasing expectation of life; the proportion of the population living in the later period of low activity is enlarged, which lowers the per capita need of foodstuffs. With a population at customary body weights, the demands for foodstuffs is very inelastic; but with our wide range of selection, substitutability is enhanced and the per capita requirement of staples lowered. These developments imply a significant reduction in the per capita need of food in terms of calories, which means, of course, a reduction of the home market.

Finally, we have a better disposition and utilization of farm products. There is less waste in the harvesting of foods; less waste in transportation; better grading and less waste in retail marketing; less waste in the home. All of this means that the utilization of the gross crop is improved, which implies an indirect lessening of the total demand, a contraction of the home market.

Over the period of the last thirty or forty years, these several reductions have amounted to 200 or 300, or even more, calories per person per day. This means that demand for food has declined relatively by over 5 per cent since the close of the last century. At the same time, more efficient methods of caring for and feeding domesticated animals have effectuated a corresponding contraction of the home market for feeding stuffs. Farmers turn out more per man and per area, consumers use less through numerous savings in disposal of crops.

If 50 million acres of harvested crop land are taken out of cultivation, that means a reduction of 14 per cent; if 25 million acres of crop land are taken out, that means a reduction of 7 per cent. Contraction of area of tillage by withdrawal of 25 million acres of crop land raises at once a direct population inquiry: shall fourteen-fourteenths of the farm population cultivate thirteen-fourteenths of the crop land, or shall one-fourteenth of the farm population leave the countryside when one-fourteenth of the crop land is closed down? Of course the redundancy of farm population will not be horizontal but will be concentrated in certain regions; this, however, will make the solution rather more than less difficult.

Some of the broader aspects of population have an indirect bearing on the international market for farm products. As has been mentioned above, our rate of growth of population is tapering off, which means a slower rate of growth of the domestic market. The population of Europe west of Russia also shows for the continent a declining rate of growth, which implies either a lessened reliance on domestic agriculture, or a reduced demand for imported farm products. In Russia, on the other hand, the rate of growth of population is rising, according to the official reports, which with the increasing industrialization of the country probably implies a declining exportable surplus of grain. Finally, we have to take account of the small population of the countries which are our principal competitors in the export trade in farm products, outside of cotton. The combined populations of Argentina, Australia, Canada, Denmark, and New Zealand approximate 35 million. For these countries the export market is the major outlet; for the United States the export market is a minor outlet. These five countries, when they come to negotiations with importing countries, have a much smaller inlet for manufactures to offer to European countries than has the United States, which gives us an advantage; but they must pay debt obligations with farm products, which may compel them to cut export prices.

Finally, when it is recalled that the net-creditor countries of the world have a population of less than 250 million, or one-eighth of the population of the world, it is obvious that the competition between the net-debtor countries to supply these 250 million people with their requirements of industrial raw materials and farm products is bound to continue to be intensive. If we had in the world a pressure of population on food supply, this would be a circumstance favoring American export of farm products. But since we have instead a pressure of food supply on population, the relatively small proportion of the world's population living in net-creditor countries seems certain to work to the disadvantage of our country, which desires simultaneously to be a heavy exporter of industrial raw materials, of farm products, and of manufactures of various kinds and especially those proceeding from rationalized industry with the highest technique of mass production. In a sense, one might from these circumstances infer that our foreign investors stand a poor chance of repayment. In the case of Canada, however, the somewhat paradoxical outcome will be further export of American capital. Despite the extreme disparity in populations on the two sides of our northern international border, our active balance of merchandise trade with Canada precludes payment by her of service charges due us, except as they may be paid in new gold. This leads to annual fresh lending to balance the account, which both sides regard as an agreeable transaction on account of identity of language, similarity of populations, and contiguity of location. But in the case of our debtors in Europe, their large populations enforce imports from this country, which preclude, or make difficult, payments by them of service charges due us, creating a situation not to be relieved, as in the case of Canada. by fresh American lending.

SUMMARY

Despite pre-depression decline in farm population relative to total population, it is evident that our farm population is larger than the occupation of the class. The present farm population is the largest in our history in absolute numbers, but this is the expression of urban unemployment and not an evidence of rural occupation. The number of farm operators was reported in 1930 as 6,288,648. In the present state of the art, 5 million, possibly 4 million, would suffice to cover domestic requirements of farm products. The number of farmers in excess of those needed to cover domestic requirements is much in excess of the size of the export market. The rate of growth of population of the United States is declining, and the reduced per capita food requirement will decline still further. The rate of growth of population in western Europe is declining, which implies presumably a lessened demand of import of farm products. The populations of the countries mainly competitive with ours in export trade in farm products (outside of cotton) are relatively small; for them the export market is the major market, for us it is the minor market. These considerations, and others, all tend towards a lowering of foreign demand for American farm products. The proposed contraction of 25 million acres of crop land represents a reduction of 7 per cent in the active agricultural plant. Such a contraction merely intensifies the existing redundancy of farm population.

Three considerations are commonly adduced in favor of maintenance of size of farm population in excess of occupational requirements: the farm population is conservative in a capitalistic sense, life on the farm is supposed to be more healthful, and the higher birth-rate in the country is needed to maintain rate of growth of population in cities. Qualifications are advanced tending to show that these arguments are special pleading and not well founded. Sooner or later, farm population will need to approximate occupation on farms. Our agricultural problem is intensified by our failure concretely to realize that pressure of population on food supply has been replaced by pressure of food supply on population.

A general observation may not be out of place in a summary. Our biological instincts are rebellious to the idea of a stationary population, our pecuniary ambitions revolt at the idea of a stationary or stabilized economy and our traditions bind us to definitions of classes even within a democracy. Nevertheless, all social stabilizations are relative. The changes that have occurred in the relations of town and country in Russia, Germany, and Italy should impose caution on prophecy of the future status of agriculture and industry in the United States. It is precisely in countries possessing the broadest categories of resources that changes in social classes are most approachable in the technical sense. Resources and techniques eventually control populations.

CHAPTER VI

FOREIGN NEED OF AMERICAN FARM PRODUCTS VERSUS AMERICAN NEED OF AGRICULTURAL EXPORTS

WE have here to explore important implications of the planned foreign trade. Secretary Wallace seeks to promote:

". . . an effective foreign purchasing power for our customary exportable surplus of cotton, wheat, lard and tobacco at prices high enough to assure social stability in the United States." (*America Must Choose*, p. 6.)

In another place he refers to the

". . . foreign purchasing power enough to sell abroad our normal surpluses of cotton, wheat and tobacco at a decent price, . . ." (p. 18)

It is presumably taken for granted that when we export farm products we do not deplete natural resources but only export products of labor, which is continually renewable and if unemployed would be a public charge.

We have first to arrive at an estimate of the additional export of farm products desired in order to improve the "balance" within our agricultural operations and also the "balance" between town and country. Once such an estimate of desired level of export of farm products is arrived at, it will be appropriate to consider the food requirements of the countries which we expect to take these exports; also the state of agriculture, in both surplus and deficiency countries, to both of which our added exports of farm products will be competitive.

DESIRED LEVEL OF EXPORT OF AMERICAN FARM PRODUCTS

Secretary Wallace refers to our "customary exportable surpluses," or to our "normal surpluses." One gathers the impression that an increase of at least a half a billion dollars' value over the exports of recent years would be necessary, even with a contraction of 25 million acres of land in harvested crops. It is possible to prepare a rough statistical estimate to confirm this.

TABLE II.—UNITED STATES FOREIGN TRADE IN AGRICULTURAL PRODUCTS, 1909-14 AND 1924-34 *

(Million dollars)

July-June	Exports in Current Dollars	Imports in Current Dollars	Balance	All-commodity Wholesale Price Index Number (1926=100)	Exports in 1926 Dollars	Imports in 1926 Dollars	Balance
	(1)	(2)	(3)	(4)	(5)	(6)	(7)
1909-10..	871	794	+ 77	70.8	1,230	1,121	+109
1910-11..	1,031	773	+258	66.4	1,553	1,164	+389
1911-12..	1,051	888	+163	66.8	1,573	1,329	+244
1912-13..	1,124	917	+207	69.8	1,610	1,314	+296
1913-14..	1,114	1,000	+114	68.9	1,617	1,451	+166
Average..	1,038	874	+164		1,517	1,276	+241
1924-25..	2,280	2,057	+223	100.5	2,269	2,047	+222
1925-26..	1,892	2,530	−638	102.5	1,846	2,468	−622
1926-27..	1,908	2,281	−373	97.0	1,967	2,352	−385
1927-28..	1,815	2,194	−379	96.1	1,889	2,283	−394
1928-29..	1,847	2,179	−332	96.2	1,920	2,265	−345
1929-30..	1,496	1,891	−395	92.5	1,617	2,044	−427
1930-31..	1,038	1,163	−125	79.0	1,314	1,472	−158
1931-32..	752	834	− 82	68.2	1,103	1,223	−120
1932-33..	590	612	− 22	62.9	938	973	− 35
1933-34..	787	862†	− 75	72.0	1,093	1,197†	−104
Average..	1,440	1,660	−220		1,595	1,832	−237

* Data for exports and imports in current dollars from *Yearbook of Agriculture,* 1934, p. 660, and from U. S. Bureau of Agricultural Economics. Index numbers from Bureau of Labor Statistics of U. S. Department of Labor.

† Imports for consumption.

The above table contains the reported exports and imports of agricultural products of the United States during the past ten years and during the five pre-war years. Columns 1 and 2 are taken from Table 440 on page 660 of the 1934 *Yearbook of Agriculture,* and column 3 presents the balance between imports and exports in columns 1 and 2—these all in currently reported dollars. Columns 5 and 6 show the same figures reduced to the 1926 dollar; column 7 gives the balance of such trade on that basis.

The table is unsatisfactory on account of the system of classification. In the case of cereals, fruits, and vegetables, both unmanufactured and manufactured products are included; but in the case of the fibers, tobacco, and rubber only unmanufactured products are included. This passive balance of trade in agricultural products, however, is not of much significance, since imports of rubber, silk, coffee, tea, cocoa, and chocolate are noncompetitive, though the imports of sugar, tobacco, vegetable oils and wool are competitive to varying extents.

The data in the table indicate that before the war we had an active balance of trade in agricultural exports, to the average extent of some 240 million (1926) dollars. The balance became passive after the war; it is to be noted that such imports exceeded exports, except in 1924-25. Imports and exports of agricultural products started to decline in 1929-30, and the recessions have continued. These declines express both reduction in amount and lowering in price, but the figures give no indication of the relative extents of these two kinds of decline. We surmise, however, that declines in price have been more conspicuous than declines in quantity.[1] Using either the estimates in current dollars or in 1926 dollars, it is apparent, judged by values, that both exports and imports have declined by something more than one-half. In gross figures, the exports may fairly be said to have declined in value to the extent of more than a billion dollars per year. Accepting the average of the first five years (1924-29) as base line, the exports that might be called "normal" or "cus-

[1] Expressed as index number of volume, the export of farm products from the United States in March 1935 stood at 45 per cent of the pre-war level of 100.

tomary" would approximate 1,800 or 1,900 million dollars per year: the average of the last three years was 710 million dollars. Restoration of these exports in terms of 1926 dollars would be very difficult; restoration in terms of current dollars would seem entirely out of the question. When we speak of increasing all imports to the extent of a billion dollars' value, this to cover service charges on our foreign investments and the desired increase in export of farm products, it seems natural to suggest that about half of this would apply to the export of farm products. Adding a half-billion dollars to the reported exports of the three years 1931-34 would still leave the exports considerably below the average of the years 1924-29. But since we take it that the objective can hardly be the amount of the average of the five high years 1924-29, the estimate of a half-billion-dollar gain sounds reasonable. At the same time, it is to be recognized that many farmers will regard this estimate as too low; if farmers have a "right" to exports, why limit the right?

Since some figure of illustration must be used, let us employ that of a half-billion dollars, to represent the value of added export of farm products over the otherwise level, this to be paid for by added imports over the otherwise level. How the half-billion dollars of added exports would be divided between cotton, tobacco, wheat and hog products, in the order named, need not detain us,[1] though some indication of the partition is presumably revealed in the program of acreage contraction. It is perhaps not inconceivable that the foreign purchasing power for the added export of a half-billion dollars' value of farm products might be secured through the added import of a corresponding value of agricultural imports, rather than of manufactures. We shall

[1] It is not impossible in the corn belt that corn may be replaced with soya beans and these prove exportable when corn is not exportable. That is, rather surprisingly, Manchuria would be easier to compete against in the export market than Argentina.

return to this later when considering noncompetitive imports. We have now to consider the food needs of the importing countries and thereafter the agricultures of the competing importing and exporting countries.

FOOD REQUIREMENTS IN THE COUNTRIES ENGAGED IN INTERNATIONAL TRADE

One reads a great deal about "unsatisfied" food needs in many countries, and, indeed, to some extent in all countries. Hunger and want have been exaggerated by the depression; but hunger and want exist in the most prosperous times in the richest countries. Famines appear here and there, relief is always in operation in one place or another. Rarely is general or scattered want due to actual shortage of foodstuffs in the country concerned; hunger (even in India and China) is most often due to unemployment, lack of purchasing power, lack of relief organization, lack of revenue or limitation of taxing power by the state. Whatever differences exist now in nutrition in the United States, in contrast with the 'twenties, are due to unemployment and lack of purchasing power and not to shortage of foodstuffs.

Subnutrition may be general, due to shortage of calories; or special (best called malnutrition), due to shortage of indispensable elements such as vitamins. Malnutrition is much more common than subnutrition, even in deficiency countries dependent on imports. The food requirements of a people depend on the birth-rate, the age distribution in the population, the average size of the body, the extent of exposure to cold, and the character of manual occupations. If there is a shortage of calories in the gross food supply of a people, this will not be evenly distributed but will fall mostly on lower-income classes; the result will be reduction of body weight if the shortage is moderate and emaciation if the shortage is extreme. A shortage in the special constituents of the diet, such as vitamins, will be revealed in various deficiency diseases, affecting children predominantly. Europe, during and after the war, had all forms of undernourishment; but malnutrition was more prominent than subnutrition.

Now, in a depression, with general reduction of national income, subnutrition does not appear for some time, because of various adaptations and adjustments. Indeed, public health and nutrition may seem to improve for a time, just as the first two years of the war "cured" the Germans of gout, diabetes, and obesity. Up to the end of 1933, possibly, it was reasonable to claim in this country that reduction in weight among the adult population had affected mostly the obese, that children had been well provided with indispensable nutrients. Inevitably, however, the relief operations tended to fail to cover the ground, and there is no question that since 1933 it has been possible in some classes in our cities to show definitive subnutrition in adults and malnutrition in children. This occurs at a time when our politicians are struggling with the problem of surplus of foodstuffs. Whenever unemployment is very extensive and has persisted for a long time, the task of relief tends to exceed administrative and financial capacity, particularly where private charity breaks down and public charity is not promptly and efficiently brought into the field.

The same situation occurs of course more easily in countries which are net food importers. Such countries have different administrative problems in public relief, since foods for distribution must be secured from outside countries; any existing shortage of foreign exchange directly intensifies the difficulties. But the internal problems of distribution and of raising the revenue are the same in both cases. If it be true, as has been claimed, that during this depression the nutrition of the unemployed has been better maintained relatively in the United Kingdom than in the United States, this must indicate that in the United Kingdom the administration of relief with imported foodstuffs is more efficiently carried out than in the United States with domestic foodstuffs. In countries with unstable governments, depreciated currencies, and low taxing powers, relief is ineffectively administered, whether the country be a food-surplus country or a food-deficiency country, with of course a natural advantage in favor of the food-surplus country.

Under these circumstances, the natural indignation of the public over "hunger in the midst of plenty" ("the tragic nonsense of misery and want in the midst of tremendous world stocks of essential goods," in the words of Secretary Wallace), in the international sense at least is to little practical effect. If a net-food-importing country has low internal tax-raising power, faulty internal administration, and little external purchasing power, it makes no difference how many outside countries have a surplus of foodstuffs; unless the country with a surplus of food can offer that food without return in trade, the surplus avails nothing. If the net-food-importing country had adequate external purchasing power, this would insure securing the needed supplies even if no considerable outside surplus existed. The problem is really not at all one of agricultural surplus here or want there; it is a problem of disequilibrium. And if the disequilibrium persists, it makes little difference whether the world as a whole contains a heavy surplus of foodstuffs.

The physiological food need of the world is lower in a depression with heavy unemployment than in normal times with full employment. Nevertheless, in many food-deficiency countries subnutrition and malnutrition exist widespread, simply because the peoples of the deficiency countries cannot exchange even the products of their lowered labor for the surplus foodstuffs of other countries. It is therefore a futile lament for the people of the United States to feel that because we have surplus foodstuffs and the needy countries cannot buy them, this is a peculiarly outrageous misfortune for the needy countries, and perhaps a still more outrageous misfortune for us. Our indignation is due partly to the fact that because we cannot sell our surplus we suffer from low prices; if we happened to have no surplus in this country, our indignation over foreign hunger in the midst of international plenty would be less acute than it is. The situation is quite similar to that of the city people who blame farmers for seeking to adjust relative overproduction to effective demand so long as unemployed urban classes suffer from undernourishment. In the final analysis, the problem resolves itself into economic, not nutritional, terms.

THE STATE OF AGRICULTURE IN THE FOOD-SURPLUS AND FOOD-DEFICIENCY COUNTRIES

Secretary Wallace recognizes that for the time being our surplus problem in this country is a part of a world surplus problem.

"It should be recognized that our surplus problems here in the United States, and the resulting necessity of keeping parts of our factories idle and withdrawing acreage, or of widening foreign markets, or of doing these things in combination, is really part of a world surplus problem. This country has more industrial as well as more agricultural capacity than it needs for home consumption. Surplus capacity in industry shows up mainly in unemployment, rather than in a persistent accumulation of commodities; but in all branches of our economic life there is an identical tendency for production to outrun consumption. Other nations have just the same trouble, as we know from the prevalence of unemployment and dole systems throughout the world." (*America Must Choose*, p. 30.)

One observes in the United States, and in other countries lying overseas from Europe, a curious attitude towards European agriculture. It is rather incoherently felt that the changes in European agriculture during and since the war were essentially transitory and reversible. Europe seems to be regarded as perverse and provocative because she has not reversed her agricultural practices back to the pre-war position. In fact, however, Europe is in no better position to reverse the changes of the past twenty years than are the other countries of the world. The exigencies of war taught Europe, combatants and neutrals alike, intensification of agriculture, altered incentives, and new objectives. The war gave Europe a measure of the sense of security in the food supply which the present generation cannot forget. The desirability of raising bread-grains instead of feed-grains, the advantages of using colonial oil-seeds instead of foreign grains, the utility of importing feeding stuffs instead of animal products, the expediency of raising domestic beet sugar over importation of cane sugar—these and other lessons were learned to different degrees by the several countries of Europe west of Russia. New developments of the agricultural art have arisen, based to some extent on the circumstance that Europe is now relatively independent of imported chemical fertilizers.

There is considerable agriculture in Europe that may fairly be called artificial and "exotic." In Belgium and Holland are literally miles of cultivation under glass. This would be "exotic" in our country; but is it so over there? And on what grounds would we ask these countries to give up their hothouses and import the produce from Florida and California? Is the new growing of tobacco in China "exotic"? Why should China continue to import tobacco from the United States if on her soil her coolies can raise suitable tobacco on their accustomed plane of subsistence?

An outstanding result of modern researches in agronomy is the poleward migration of wheat growing. New varieties of spring wheat are more resistant to cold and mature within a shorter time, whereby it becomes feasible to raise wheat on appropriate ground in higher latitudes. The meaning of this advance for Canada, northern Europe, northern Russia, Siberia, Mongolia, and Manchuria is certain to be considerable. The southward migration is to be observed in Argentina. A particular implication of this advance lies in the circumstance that these regions tend to be mostly adapted to one-crop agriculture, namely wheat. These newly developed areas cannot be expected to relinquish wheat growing in favor of older regions nearer the tropics.

Is Europe to be expected to relinquish the use of new devices and improvements, while other continents continue them? Is Italy to give up the "battle of the grains" and are northern Europe and Russia to make no use of new rugged wheat varieties, while the wheat belt expands northward in Canada and southward in Argentina, and towards higher and drier regions on the eastern slopes of the Rocky Mountains? Are new chemical advances in the manufacture of foods from tropical oil-seeds and marine fats to be disregarded, in order to maintain a world market for butter and lard of pre-war type? Are the countries of western Europe not to make the best technical use of their colonies? Why should we object to Japan having wheat raised in Manchuria to supplant wheat previously imported from Canada and Australia? (Incidentally remarked, the history of the American steel industry, contrasted with that of the steel industries of northwestern Europe, illustrates the progress of self-sufficiency in essential commodities.) Such questions indicate that it is to no purpose for the *estanciero* of Argentina, the hog raiser of Iowa, or the wheat grower of Saskatchewan to get peeved over the agricultural policies of foreign countries. The expediency of contraction of agriculture in each European country is a special problem for each people.

Political, technological, and monetary elements are involved, and it is quite as futile for us to offer advice to other countries as it would be for them to give advice to us. A recent survey of agriculture in Germany by E. von Borsig [1] makes clear at once the difficulties of further self-sufficiency and of return to greater industrialization.[2] The problem of relation of town to country in Germany is not new. Indeed, it is a half-century old and was a live public question when Adolf Wagner first issued his *Agrar- und Industriestaat* in 1901.

Self-sufficiency has been a policy forced on most countries by economic disequilibrium. The net-food-surplus countries endeavor to cover their requirements of the particular foods they were accustomed to import. The net-food-deficiency countries endeavor by stimulation of intensive and enlargement of extensive agriculture to reduce their dependence on imported supplies. So long as the importing countries, of Europe especially, simultaneously stimulate agricultural production and restrict or modify consumption, the restoration of international trade in foodstuffs will not be accomplished. And with this failure of restoration will continue a failure in reciprocal movement of industrial goods. Secretary Wallace pictures, as an eventual contingency, the total loss of our export trade in farm products if we persist in intense "nationalism," decline to accept merchandise in return for merchandise, and in addition insist on payment of international debts. It remains equally true, though less insisted on, that the same result of loss of export trade in our

[1] *Reagrarisierung Deutschlands?* (Jena, Fisher, 1934).

[2] It is becoming painfully evident to certain interests in the agriculture of Europe, especially landlords of large holdings, that the stimulation has been overdone. There is an old peasant proverb in Europe which one finds in the rural dialects of their languages: "Prayer won't help, use more manure." Without being sacrilegious, some of the wiser heads are beginning to feel that too much emphasis has been placed on manure (and subsidy) and too little on prayer.

farm products may follow from intense nationalism in the importing countries of Europe. To dispute whose "nationalism" came first is waste of words.

The policy of self-sufficiency in foodstuffs has usually two major bases: the augmented importance of agriculture and the defense of the national currency. With increasing autarchy, the international movement of agricultural products tends to decline. Autarchy has been developing, on special grounds, since the close of the World War; but when the depression intervened, the lack of international purchasing power in terms of money lent an added force to the decline of international movements of agricultural products. At the same time, the tendency of decline in trade does not hold for all farm products: for example, during recent years foreign trade in wheat has declined, but not in corn, a very low price acting to sustain the movement in quantity. Secretary Wallace seems to feel that we have lost our foreign outlet for comparably priced wheat and hog products largely on account of foreign tariffs. But our wheat and lard have not been comparably priced, our prices have been too high. There are added reasons, beyond mere lack of purchasing power abroad, why our exports have declined so heavily. In *New Frontiers* Secretary Wallace seems more keenly alive to the circumstance that the huge European borrowings from the United States will tend to check their activity as customers for our farm products. Rather paradoxically, it may be remarked that France represses imports because she has so much gold, while Germany and Italy take the same action because they have so little gold.

Not only does the increase in autarchy among the countries which are net importers of foods and feeding stuffs tend to reduce their imports, it also brings about shifts in the sources from which they are derived. With heavy carryovers in several surplus countries, the importing countries can pick and choose.[1] The importing countries stipulate qualities and they purchase in the cheapest markets. This is clearly shown in the case of wheat and hog products; our prices are high, our products are not of the choicest grade, and are often distinctly lower. During the past decade we have exported practically no Dark Northern Spring wheat, very little No. 1 Soft Red Winter wheat, and little No. 1 Hard Winter wheat except in occasional years when large crops in Oklahoma and Texas have permitted such exports through the Gulf. The wheat exports through Puget Sound and the Columbia River have been partly second-grade. The domestic mills naturally select the best of the representative wheats, those of highest protein content in the case of the bread wheats; what remains for export is below the average of the crop. On the other hand, in the case of Canada, Argentina, and Australia (countries with small populations and large wheat crops) the best of the wheats go to export. The same thing holds for hog products from the outstanding countries of export. The lard, bacon, and ham shipped from this country to Europe are for the most part of lower quality than the best grades consumed at home. These products are distinctly inferior to the best products they meet in competition in Europe. Of this fact the quotations on the several bacons on sale in London afford ample confirmation. Our export lard, usually shipped in tierces, is called "prime steam lard"; it is inferior to the special brands marketed by the same packers in this country and ranks below the best domestic lards in Europe. These considerations of quality have an influence in markets which are crowded with surplus stocks from all over the world.

Finally, with respect to prices, the prices of American

[1] In direct furtherance of an old project, the agrarian bloc of central European states is urging acceptance of a working principle that the service charges due from these states to western European states shall be paid for in farm products.

farm products, unsatisfactory as they have been to American farmers, tend to rank relatively or even absolutely above the prices in the other surplus-producing countries of Europe, except when grossly inflated by governmental devices. This circumstance is due at least partly to the influence of trading in futures on established commodity exchanges. A striking illustration is afforded by wheat. More or less during the past three years, the future price of wheat in Chicago has been close to or above that in Liverpool, sometimes above it to a preposterous extent. Most of the time the wheat price in Chicago has stood relatively, and even absolutely, far above the prices in Canada, Argentina, and Australia. Since the autumn of 1934 we stand on the verge of importing duty-paid bread-wheat from Canada.[1] Of course, under such conditions, practically no export of wheat is possible. The same fact tends to hold to a lesser degree in the case of all other farm products which are bought and sold in futures contracts on commodity exchanges. The combination of high price and unrepresentative quality forms an insuperable bar to exports in volume, in a world filled with temporary excessive carry-overs, with importing countries striving for agricultural self-sufficiency. Tariff changes abroad would in themselves make little difference. When our farmers seek abroad an outlet for a half-billion dollars' worth of added export of farm products, the position of our prices and the quality of our offerings must both be considered.

In short, the state of agriculture in the food-surplus and food-deficiency countries is now such as to give to international trade the complexion of a buyers' market. There is an excess of carry-overs, there is the tendency towards self-sufficiency in the importing countries, there is demonstrable underconsumption below the otherwise level, due to restric-

[1] Small importations of duty-paid durum wheat and bread wheat have in fact occurred.

tions of various kinds in the importing countries. The Secretary of Agriculture speaks truly when he refers to the embarrassments of all the surplus countries. Beyond this, however, it is significant to point out that for a number of reasons the embarrassment of American agriculture exceeds that of the agricultures of other surplus-producing countries. When, finally, one adds the major circumstance that our chief competitors in the export of agricultural staples are debtor countries with a natural active balance of merchandise trade, the almost insuperable obstacles to (unsubsidized) export of agricultural staples from the United States arise as a matter of course.[1]

Finally it is here appropriate briefly to advert to the contradiction of effects in two of the departments of the government. The AAA is engaged in driving up prices of the farm products which the Secretary is trying to get exported in larger volume. The more successful is the AAA in driving up prices, the less successful will Secretary Wallace be in expanding exports except under subsidy. We can hardly hope to get foreign countries to pay us higher prices for farm products by offering them higher prices for their exports to us, because our consumers have been told that by lowering our tariffs the prices of imported articles will be brought down. This contradiction between the two policies of the Department of Agriculture is so patent that there seems to be no purpose in elaborating further on the discrepancy.

SUMMARY

As basis of discussion, it is expedient to possess an estimate of the desired additional export of farm products re-

[1] We have made no reference to cotton. Here lies the most obvious future point of weakness in our agriculture. If we contract cotton acreage substantially and raise our price of export cotton, the effect will be stimulation of raising of cotton abroad and substitution of other cotton for American cotton, for which the adaptations of machinery are already available. Once the low-grade populations of the hot countries are engaged in raising cotton, the development will tend to be irreversible.

garded as necessary to achieve a balance in our country. Such an estimate may reasonably be based on statistical grounds. Before the war we had an active balance of trade in agricultural products, annually approximating 240 million (1926) dollars. During nine of the last ten years we have had a passive balance of foreign trade in agricultural products, to the average extent of over 200 million dollars. During the five years 1924-29 the annual value of our export of agricultural products approached or exceeded two billion dollars. Decline set in during 1929-30, and since 1930-31 the value of annual export of agricultural products has approached or fallen below a billion dollars. This heavy decline has been partly in quantities but still more in prices. It would be going too far to aim at a restoration of the export level during 1924-29; but if anything worth while is to be attempted, an additional export to the extent of the value of 500 million dollars is a reasonable objective. This figure we shall use as the minimum added export of farm products sought per annum, to be paid for by a corresponding addition of imports of merchandise.

A survey of requirements, surpluses, and deficiencies in foodstuffs throughout the world makes it clear that the problem is not one of physical units. The explanation of nutritional suffering in the midst of plenty rests on decline of purchasing power, depreciation of currency, loss of export outlets, and disequilibrium between the trading countries of the world. Our concern over the food needs of various unfortunate countries is almost like shedding crocodile tears; that is, we are truly concerned over nutritional suffering of others in the midst of plenty, but we are still more truly concerned over our economic suffering in the midst of plenty.

Finally, the state of agriculture in foreign countries, especially in net-food-importing countries, is casually surveyed. The impulse towards self-sufficiency, especially in Europe, is not a perversion, but a natural reaction resting on solid ground. European countries seek security. Europe has lost foreign purchasing power and export markets and feels forced to apply the newer knowledge of agriculture. It is out of place to expect importing countries to forego improved agriculture while exporting countries continue to practice it. Our country is peculiarly vulnerable in such an argument, because we expect Europe to pay premium prices for discount farm products (outside of cotton), especially in wheat and hog products. Subsidy of export of farm products is usually based on desire to maintain standard of living on farms. Autarchy is not a state of mind, it is partly a stage of emergency and partly a stage of progress. In any event, the autarchy of the deficiency countries and the congestion of the surplus countries are not to be solved with adjectives. The balance of merchandise trade between countries has become in part an expression of the relations of debtors to creditors, just as the balance of trade of a farm is partly the expression of the debtor status of the farmer. With advances in agriculture, dispersion of urban industries and enlargement of the invisible items of trade, the needs of foreign countries for our farm products are not to be predicted.

Chapter VII

BALANCE OF MERCHANDISE TRADE BEFORE AND SINCE THE WAR

In order to provide American agriculture with what Secretary Wallace regards as an indispensable foreign outlet, it is necessary to have our imports of goods enlarged to take account of this, as well as to cover service charges on our foreign loans and investments. The "planned middle course" hinges on shifting a (predicated) active (positive, miscalled favorable) balance of merchandise trade into a moderate, or fairly heavy, passive (negative, miscalled unfavorable) balance of merchandise trade. But just what is the demonstrable extent of the predicated present active balance of merchandise trade? And just what is the extent of the shift in merchandise trade contemplated, or implied? As will be shown, the position of our merchandise trade is not so unfavorable to agriculture as Secretary Wallace interprets it to be; the balance is not really active, but instead is passive.[1]

[1] Since the early descriptions of the balance of trade in the seventeenth century (of which perhaps the most notable was that of Mun, *England's Treasure by Forraign Trade*) different usages have prevailed in different languages. What is sought in one respect is the separation of visible from invisible items; in another respect, the separation of goods from services; and in still another respect, the separation of commodity movements from capital movements. For our purpose we need an expression to indicate the preponderance of export or import of merchandise, including the correlated services, but excluding the movements of investments and loans. We have the choice of the following, on the credit and debit sides:

favorable balance of merchandise trade	unfavorable balance of merchandise trade
active balance of merchandise trade	passive balance of merchandise trade

For a dependable understanding of the movements of goods in international commerce, the balance of international payments in the account of the country must be studied. The subject of foreign trade becomes more intelligible if we picture it as a sort of bank; just as the business of a bank consists of creation, transfer and cancellation of credits, so foreign commerce consists of order, transfer, and delivery of goods, with appropriate instruments of payment. Foreign trade, in the ordinary sense, is primarily exchange of outbound for inbound goods. It was once bare barter, then it became a money barter, then a money exchange; last of all, it has become a transaction through bills of exchange, through bankers' acceptances. These gradual developments have had the effects of improving comparability of prices and lowering of risks. The incoming and outgoing transactions cannot simultaneously cancel in international commerce; time is used in transactions and the lapses of time become variable lags. There is also seasonal variation in movement of goods and of prices in international trade. Risks, changes of prices, lags, seasonal fluctuations, changes in volumes due to crop variations and other causes—these and other factors would continue to complicate trade if commerce consisted only of directly reciprocal exchanges of goods for goods. But associated services enter the picture

---

positive balance of merchandise trade	negative balance of merchandise trade
credit commodity balance	debit commodity balance
credit balance on commodity account	debit balance on commodity account

Each of these terms has undesirable connotations in one direction or another. The terms "active" and "passive" enjoy perhaps the widest usage today, and are the terms to be used in these pages. Under "active balance of merchandise trade" is understood a preponderance of sales of goods and associated services over purchases abroad; under "passive balance of merchandise trade" is understood a preponderance of purchases of goods and associated services over sales abroad. One must always bear in mind that the balance of trade of a country is a different thing from the balance of payments.

also; those of shipping, insurance, commissions and interest and others, all magnified by distances between countries and the circumstance that different countries have different currencies. Thus including all the factors that are variable in relation to the sales of goods and to the services attending the contracts, dispatches and arrivals, our international trade would still be complex to a degree if it consisted only of goods and the services attending sale, transportation, and delivery. But the growing invisible items have come to disturb the clarity of the visible items.

The export of capital. The picture becomes confused when currency, gold, and capital movements enter. Before the war there was very little movement of gold to balance the merchandise accounts. Gold was shipped as a metal from countries of origin to countries seeking it for metallic base in their currency systems, and for use in the arts, sciences, and industries. Under the so-called gold standard of the decades before the war (it was really a sterling standard with a gold handle), very little gold was used in settlement of international accounts. These accounts were mostly equated at a central point used as clearing house, which was London. The small sums out of equilibrium were covered mostly with forward balances or short-term credits, occasionally with transfers of gold. Silver had no part worth mentioning, outside of Asia.

Following the Napoleonic Wars, long-term foreign investment proceeded steadily. The heaviest foreign lending was after 1865. There were only six net-creditor countries—United Kingdom, France, Germany, Holland, Belgium, and Switzerland. There were few inter-governmental debts. The debts between countries were mostly the lendings of nationals in creditor countries to nationals and to governments in the borrowing countries; these transactions were therefore private enterprises. Most of the lendings were direct investments in enterprises and properties; bond-loans to governments were less conspicuous, except in a few instances. Most of these foreign investments were designed for developmental and productive projects. Perhaps the gross total in 1914 was equivalent to some forty billion dollars. The group of creditor countries lying along the English Channel and the North Sea had been the leaders in the industrial revolution. Their peoples had saved; these savings they were willing to place abroad to aid in the development of backward countries, to bring potential resources into active being, to supply the countries of western Europe with raw industrial materials, foods, and feeding stuffs, and to bring pecuniary rewards to the lending persons and companies. The achievements of science in transportation and communications were thus brought to the outlying parts of the world. Both sides profited; the lending countries secured primary materials to support their growing populations, the borrowing countries secured active capital before they could otherwise acquire it by internal savings.

The capital thus exported went abroad mostly as goods, partly as services. The repayment of capital was arranged through sinking fund and amortization or on term maturity. These payments, called "loan service charges," came back to the lending countries in the form of goods and services, only occasionally and under exceptional circumstances in gold. While a foreign investment was being paid off, over the period there was an excess of goods into the lending country; goods for interest went back as well as goods for principal, whereas in the act of lending, only goods for principal went out.

This natural excess of goods bound for the mature creditor countries was in many cases unwanted. Then the service charges were left in the borrowing country; that is, in effect were reinvested. The gross capital sum due on paper to the six creditor countries at the outbreak of the war consisted in good part of unpaid interest that thus had been added to principal. Sometimes the interest was defaulted; but often the excess of goods was simply not needed and the sum therein represented was added to loaned capital. To some extent it was recognized that foreign investments were not expected to be paid off—they were like "perpetual bonds." Heavy losses were not infrequently encountered, and extensive refundings were necessary; but the stream of foreign investments grew steadily, if irregularly, from 1815 to 1914.

Visible trade grew with each decade, disregarding fluctuations; invisible trade also grew alongside. The two-sided progress worked well so long as foreign loans were mostly for developments, currencies were fairly stable, and there was a central point and an effective machinery for settlement of the accounts as they became due. During this long period, short-term balances were small and mostly associated with merchandise trade; the long-term balances were settled usually by refunding, in ways that little disturbed the flow of goods. Before the war the tariffs of the world were tending to decline, certainly they were low in contrast with the position today; and this may be ascribed in part to the smooth working of the transfer system in relation to movement of goods.

Before the World War operated a massive, and at the same time most delicate, mechanism of equilibrium in the trade relations of the world. This equilibrium, commonly ascribed to the gold standard, was in reality due rather to an effective credit system centralized in the clearing center of London. The equilibrium was not a rigid relation at a point, but a flexible relation over a range. It was an equilibrium in the sense of an ebb and flow—between supply and demand, imports and exports of merchandise, production and consumption of goods and services, internal and external prices, gold and credit, prices and costs, interest rates and investment returns—these all between countries, but reflecting prior equilibria within countries. This flexible equilibrium was the outcome of a long hand-in-hand development of foreign investment with production and trade, with a rising standard of living in the advanced countries and a proportionate or even more rapid relative rise in the standard of living in the backward regions. It is important to re-emphasize the relatively easy working of the old system. The gold standard, under British leadership, worked out its principal effects by raising and lowering prices, with corresponding adjustments in costs and production, and thereafter in volumes of goods moved.[1]

Our pre-war debt to foreigners was between 4 and 5 billion dollars; but our nationals had invested in Canada, Cuba, and Mexico (disregarding other small investments) between 2 and 3 billion dollars. Therefore, our net position just before the war was net-debtor to the extent of between 2 and 3 billion dollars. In payment of loan service charges (interest, dividend, and principal) we annually sent abroad goods to the value of some 200 million dollars. This statement of our pre-war position cannot be derived directly from reports and public records, but is made on the basis of fairly trustworthy inferences brought out during and since the war.

The interrelated price, cost, and income structures of different financial areas, that is, in different countries, evinced a relationship that was seldom seriously out of equilibrium. Transfers of payments between countries were practically as easy and riskless as transfers of payments within the distant parts of a large country. According to a calculation of Sir Josiah Stamp, the per capita level of real income in Great Britain, just before the World War, was four times as high

[1] For an exact and lucid description of the working of the gold standard before the war, see T. E. Gregory, *The Gold Standard and Its Future* (London, Methuen, 1934).

as a century earlier; in the United States the multiple must have been still larger; and certainly all countries profited materially over the period. Considered in the light of the present breakdown, the statement is not to be questioned that during the century elapsing between the close of the Napoleonic Wars and the outbreak of the World War, the economic system of the international world at no time, not even in a trade cycle, showed serious signs of breakdown of the kind now experienced. Now in consequence of the World War, the framework of international trade has suffered an earthquake, with shifting of foundation and twisting of the superstructure.[1]

The post-war export of American capital. The war effected a convulsive reversal of the trade positions of the United States and Germany. Before the war, Germany was a net-creditor country to the extent of some seven billion dollars; now Germany (reparations disregarded) is a net-debtor country almost to the same extent. We were a net-debtor to the extent of perhaps three billion dollars. Prior to the entrance of the United States as a belligerent, our nationals sold to Europe huge amounts of civilian and military supplies which were paid for, in large part, by sale in the United States of American securities previously held abroad. Following our entrance into the war, our country delivered to the Allies huge amounts of civilian and military supplies, against credits extended by the American Treasury. Following the Armistice, finally, we delivered to the ex-Allies, to the ex-enemies, and to new European states huge amounts of civilian supplies and reconstruction equipment, again on loans from the American Treasury. These advances

[1] The latest summary of balances of trade of many important countries is to be found in the League of Nations, *Balances of Payments, 1933* (Series of League of Nations Publications, II. Economic and Financial, 1934, II, A. 19), Geneva, 1934. See also Bertil Ohlin, *Interregional and International Trade,* Harvard Economic Studies, Vol. XXXIX (Cambridge, Harvard University Press, 1933).

all became inter-governmental loans. These loans, with accumulated interest prior to refunding agreements, approximated 12 billion dollars.

Secretary Wallace has made the following remark:

> "We went into the World War owing other nations 200 million dollars annually on interest account, and came out with other nations owing us 500 million dollars annually." (*America Must Choose*, p. 5.)

The expression is inexact and tends to be inadvertently misleading. On entering the World War "we" did not owe other "nations"; it was our nationals who owed the nationals of other countries. Coming out of the war, however, other governments owed our government "war debts," equivalent to annual payments of some 500 million dollars. The "war debts" (13,438 million dollars) are now in default and repudiation, which, in fact if not on diplomatic paper, should erase the 500 million dollars in the quotation above. The item of war debts should be dropped from the bookkeeping of our international account. Since the war, in transactions of totally different nature, American nationals have loaned to foreign nationals or governments, or invested in foreign countries, a sum which at the peak a few years ago probably approximated 17 billion dollars, but which has latterly, through losses, liquidations, and repatriations, been reduced to the equivalent of perhaps 13 billion dollars. The service charges annually due on the portfolio securities may be estimated between 350 and 400 million dollars; if the direct investments are expected to show comparable earnings, this adds another 400 million dollars, which, however, does not need to be transferred into dollars. Therefore, the 500 million dollars due from governments in the quotation above should be replaced by a range of 400-800 million dollars, due in the debtor countries from nationals and governments to private American investors. The sum of 200 million stated above, previously due to foreigners from our borrowing nationals, is presumably to be reduced; we know less about foreign investments in this country than about American investments abroad. (See p. 126.)

Beginning soon after the Armistice and reaching a peak in 1929, American nationals loaned to, or invested in, foreign countries a sum which at the peak, as stated, approached the equivalent of 17 billion dollars. This "export of capital" was mostly of three kinds, broadly considered: (a) New issues of dollar-bonds of foreign governments, floated by American bankers in the United States and sold here to individual investors under a system of high-pressure salesmanship exceeded only by the system developed during the war for the sale of Liberty Bonds. (b) Purchase by American nationals of pre-existing foreign securities, partly of governments and partly of private enterprises. (c) Direct investments abroad, including the purchase of enterprises and properties and the erection of subsidiary plants.[1] We have a fairly exact record of new issues of foreign securities floated in the United States. We have no exact figure of the purchase by Americans of pre-existing securities of foreign governments and of private foreign enterprises. We have a fairly exact estimate of the direct investments abroad. We have not even an approximate estimate of the present holdings of American securities by foreigners: the figure was probably as low as a billion dollars directly after the war, rose to over three, perhaps four, billion dollars in 1929 as foreigners were tempted to "share in our prosperity," then declined as foreigners came to distrust us in our depression, but has since risen.

It is a common statement that the export of capital from

[1] Of direct investments abroad, probably a fourth are in branch factories. It is not generally appreciated that direct foreign investments have a longer and larger significance than dollar-bond foreign loans.

the United States since the war was done for the purpose of "aiding" export of surplus farm products and manufactures. This statement confuses economic effect with investors' incentive. Many individual American investors placed their capital abroad in the expectation of securing higher returns than were to be had at home.[1] Many Americans invested abroad with the sheer objective of diversification; others have lately invested abroad as a form of flight of capital. The direct investments abroad were mostly for the purpose of retaining foreign markets for American manufactures, which, for one reason or another (often tariffs), could no longer be remuneratively supplied from the United States. To say that the American Radiator Company or General Motors established their numerous subsidiaries in Europe, and that our various investing companies have established public utilities in South America, for the purpose of facilitating the export of wheat, cotton, and lard from the United States, is absurd. But, of course, the export of capital had the effect of facilitating movement of outbound goods and services.[2] The huge exports from 1921 to 1930 depended, in the mechanism of foreign trade, upon dollar-exchange placed in the hands of foreigners by export of American capital. With the depression, the export of American capital has declined to next to nothing. The exports of wheat, cotton, and lard have declined heavily, partly because export of capital no longer furnishes abundant dollar-exchange to foreigners.

The character of our lending to foreign countries since the war has been in black contrast to that of other creditor countries before the war. The rate of our foreign lending in the 'twenties far exceeded the rate of growth of produc-

[1] Never in the modern history of rates of interest have such wide differences of rates in return on capital been known as since the World War.

[2] It is not amiss to regard foreign lending in support of exports as comparable with installment selling in the domestic market.

tion and trade in the borrowing countries, which acquired thereby more of foreign debt than of domestic productive investment. An abnormally large proportion was placed in dollar-bonds of weak governments, for purpose of more or less unwise expenditures. Certainly at no time since the Napoleonic Wars was so large a sum so unwisely loaned abroad. As a German writer has remarked: "Americans looked at interest rate, not at 'rentability.'"

American investments of all kinds are now contracting through default, liquidation, refunding, and repatriation. According to the United States Department of Commerce as of December 31, 1933, the portfolio investments were given as 6,032 million dollars and the direct investments as 7,767 million dollars. A later private estimate as of July 1, 1934, gave the foreign dollar debt (disregarding amounts just previously repatriated) as 8,675 million dollars, of which about 23 per cent was in complete temporary default. Many of the portfolio investments are in default on interest payments, some quite as much through lack of facility of transfer as through lack of earning. Many of the direct investments are insolvent, others are being taxed out of profits or even out of existence; the prosperous ones are compelled, for the most part, to impound their earnings in the foreign countries, where they are located. Obstructions to international trade have, of course, the effect of enhancing the difficulties of transferring debt payments; but they have also reduced the earning capacities of the borrowers. Defaulted interest is being added to principal, either as a bookkeeping entry or by actual lending for that purpose. Considerable gold has been transferred as payment.[1] It is obvious from the history of foreign investments that fresh

[1] It was not strange or unprecedented that, when depression set in, our country tended to receive interest on foreign debt in the form of gold rather than in the form of goods; this has been observed in earlier, smaller trade cycles.

lending will be required to salvage some of the old investments; foreign bondholders' associations were never so busy —and perhaps never less effectual.[1]

A boomerang effect of foreign lending, now coming to be appreciated, lies in injury to particular producer groups in the creditor country. During the period of active lending, exports of certain goods are inordinately stimulated. When active lending abroad for fresh investments ceases, or is reduced to a small amount, some producer groups encounter inordinate contraction of their foreign markets. The producer groups favored in the stage of active lending may be, but need not be, the same groups injured in the subsequent stages. The experiences of trade between creditor and debtor countries since 1920 clearly reveal this boomerang effect. It is not strange that this effect has struck the United States with particular severity.

The world is now gravely advised by historians and

[1] In a very recent reappraisal of our foreign relations by George N. Peek, former Adviser to the President on Foreign Trade, as of December 31, 1934, significantly different estimates are advanced on the basis of statistical investigations not disclosed in the report. According to Peek, the foreign bonds now held in the United States have a face value of 5,270 million dollars and a market value of 4,016 million dollars. The book value of American direct investments in foreign countries is given as 7,823 million dollars. The value of American stocks and bonds held abroad (market value for shares, face value for bonds) is given as 6,000 million dollars. The book value of direct investments of foreigners in this country is given as 1,000 million dollars. According to these estimates, the net value of our foreign loans and direct investments on private account is only 6,093 million dollars.

Peek suggests that we need realistic reappraisal of the present value of our loans and investments abroad and of the loans and investments of foreigners in our country. It is intimated that such a reappraisal would indicate a greater shrinkage in our loans and investments abroad than in the loans and investments of foreigners in our country. A reappraisal, however, introduces such intangibles as face value, book value, market value, original cost, reproduction cost, and deviations due to changes in currencies, including under- and overvaluation. Proceeding from the agreeable assumption that the United States is solvent and the rest of the world insolvent, one might indeed declare that our country has reverted to the position of a net debtor country! It is in order to make the comment that international bankers regard the above estimate of foreign investments in this country as too high and the estimate of our loans and investments abroad as too low.

economists that further lending is required of Americans, and of others, not merely to save existing foreign investments but also to "re-establish export trade." We are told that the annual "need" of the world for fresh foreign capital is at least one, and maybe two, billion dollars. Up to the present, it has been accepted that the export industries of net-creditor countries depend for their export markets upon a continuing simultaneous export of capital. We are told that, having for a decade sold goods abroad on credit, in effect, through the device of export of capital, we can hope to recover the foreign outlets for our surplus goods, and raise the price level, only by lending further fresh capital abroad.[1] But such a suggestion makes little impression now on the ears of investors made deaf by the din-din of default of existing foreign investments. Therefore, we are told that (to secure customers and raise the price level) the government should step in and make loans, not alone to foreign governments but also to nationals in foreign countries. Cessation of foreign investment had obviously an inevitably deflationary effect in both net-creditor and net-debtor countries.[2] It is one of the grave faults of inflation of credit, through excessive foreign lending, that it generates collective errors by producers of capital goods which, however, become apparent only at a considerably later date. Then confidence collapses. That was the status of American foreign investment at the close of 1934.[3]

[1] Compare A. Feiler, "International Movements of Capital," *American Economic Review,* March 1935, Supplement, XXV, 63-73.

[2] During 1934 there was a large inward flow of capital, both long-term (by transfer of securities) and short-term, accompanied by really huge inflow of gold, into the United States.

[3] In the open letters to the President issued by George N. Peek (appointed Special Adviser to the President on Foreign Trade), are to be found summations of loans and foreign investments of the United States government and American nationals over the period 1896-1933. It is a misfortune that the war debts of the United States government are lumped with the loans and investments of American nationals. As influences on future foreign trade of the country and finding expression in the inter-

Short-term capital movements. Far worse, in the early effects at least, than our hasty and ill-judged long-term investments was the extraordinary expansion in what are commonly called short-term balances (also termed floating balances), which are really short-term loans. Before the war, short-term balances were nearly all of the nature and purpose of trade acceptances. Following 1924, however, they took on huge expansion, strange distribution, and untoward uses. The figure for gross, total short-term balances in all countries at the peak in 1929 has been estimated equivalent to ten billion dollars. These balances had no relation to movements of goods. They were used for speculation, for flight of capital, as implements of monetary policy, to protect gold reserves, to supplant gold reserves, to cover long-term interest, and to settle trade differences which arose through abnormal price differences and inability to transfer gold. To some extent, a bank in one country would borrow short-term from another country and relend short-term, or even long-term, into a third country. Great Britain, France, Germany, and the United States were the glaring illustrations, on one or the other side, of these balances. In 1929, for illustration, when the United States was a heavy long-term net-creditor, we were a heavy short-term net-debtor. Banks all over the United States carried these accounts, to enjoy the high interest rate secured. When, in country after country, these short-term balances became frozen (of which Germany remains the glaring illustration), then the world was forced into a defensive system of currency protection and budget defense through exchange regulation, which exerted profound and widespread injury to foreign merchan-

---

national account, the war debts ought to be ruled out. It is commonly stated by otherwise well-informed observers that the United States is the heaviest net-creditor country. This is incorrect. Great Britain is a heavier creditor, also a heavier net-creditor. The point is of little importance, but there is no purpose in perpetuating a statistical misstatement.

dise trade. In estimating the implications of the abnormal short-term balances, it must not be overlooked that these proceeded in part from misplaced and really abnormal long-term foreign lending. These short-term balances are now mostly liquidated (except in the case of Germany), with greater or lesser losses; but the injury to national currencies and foreign exchange rates, and to trade in commodities, remains.

Export of American goods. Since the war our exports of goods have been larger than our imports of goods, judged by reported values. If American investors are to receive full payments due on service charges on foreign investments, other things equal (war debts disregarded), we must have instead a passive (negative, miscalled "unfavorable") balance of merchandise trade. If, thereafter, we are to export an added half a billion dollars' worth of farm products, we must import a further half-billion dollars' worth of foreign goods of some kind. This is the dilemma indicated by Secretary Wallace in the following remark:

". . . If we are going to increase foreign purchasing power enough to sell abroad our normal surpluses of cotton, wheat and tobacco at a decent price, we shall have to accept nearly a billion dollars more goods from abroad than we did in 1929. We shall have to get that much more in order to service the debts that are coming to us from abroad and have enough left over to pay us a fair price for what we send abroad." (*America Must Choose,* p. 18.)

There are implied, according to this formulation, three categories of increased imports: (a) those necessary to balance the present so-called excess of exports, (b) those representing the payments on foreign debt, and (c) those covering the added export of farm products at the "decent," "fair" price. In order to appraise the exact position of our visible trade and our hypothetical place in the picture at the low level of imports under "nationalism," at the high level of imports under "internationalism," and at the middle level of imports under the "planned middle course" of the Secretary of Agriculture, it is necessary to examine our foreign commerce in somewhat greater detail.

In attempting to determine the value of merchandise, annual acceptance of which (other things equal on exact balance) would be required to cover the payments of interest and principal annually due us on private loans and investments abroad, we must not fall into the error of oversimplification. Qualifications must be applied to the data both of visible and invisible items; by this we mean special qualifications quite apart from gaps in our information. The preliminary qualifications are as follows:

(1) The reported dollar valuations of merchandise sent out and brought in are not strictly comparable for purposes of accounting in the balance of trade. Quite generally, in countries which have import tariff duties, declared valuations of imported goods are likely to be more accurate than declared valuations of exported goods; the customs officials give particular attention to declared values of imports to prevent undervaluation and consequent loss of revenue.

(2) Practices vary in respect of treatment of costs of packing, value of packing materials and charges of transportation, insurance, and other commissions. There is no standardized practice generally enforced in the accounting of these items throughout the commercial world.[1]

(3) In recent years, depreciations and fluctuations of foreign currencies make estimates of valuation highly uncertain.

[1] In the *Balances of Payments,* issued by the League of Nations, the attempt is made to "adjust" the reported values in order to arrive at commercial value f.o.b. and c.i.f. Such procedures illustrate the difficulties of the accounting.

BALANCE OF BARE MERCHANDISE TRADE

We have the traditional statement, uncritically reiterated, that the United States, a net-debtor, had before the war an active (positive, miscalled "favorable") balance of merchandise trade; and that since the war, despite our net-creditor position, this has continued. This traditional statement must be subjected to a far-reaching correction. It is true that before the war our country had an active balance of merchandise trade, correctly defined. But it is incorrect to state that this has continued since the war. On the contrary, the data contained in the successive annual publications of the United States Department of Commerce on *The Balance of International Payments of the United States* indicate that when the term "merchandise trade" is fully amplified and correctly construed, our country has in recent years had a small passive balance of merchandise trade, in conformity with our net-creditor position.

Let us first consider what may be called bare merchandise movements, of which the successive annual reports are not identical but improved from year to year. We have here the reports of valuations of goods going out and coming in, including silver but not gold, including parcel post and contraband liquor items (very incomplete), also outgoing bunkers of coal and oil. Gold has been excluded because it is a monetary metal, despite the fact that some of the gold imported was a commodity to be used in the arts and sciences. As is evident at first sight, outbound and inbound merchandise movements thus defined tend to exaggerate exports over imports. The following table presents the data for the past ten years in current dollars as reported, and also reduced to a common 1926 dollar by dividing the figures for each year by the all-commodity wholesale price index number of that year, with highs, lows, and averages.

TABLE III.—BALANCE OF UNITED STATES IMPORTS AND EXPORTS OF MERCHANDISE (WITH MERCHANDISE ADJUSTMENTS), IN CURRENT DOLLARS AND IN 1926 DOLLARS, 1925-34 *

(Million dollars)

Year	*Receipts from foreigners for "exports" (credits)*	*Payments to foreigners for "imports" (debits)*	*Net credit (+) or debit (—)*	*All-commodity wholesale price index number (1926=100)*	*Receipts from foreigners for "exports" (credits) in 1926 dollars*	*Payments to foreigners for "imports" (debits) in 1926 dollars*	*Net credit (+) or debit (—) in 1926 dollars*
1925....	4,934	4,268	+666	103.5	4,767	4,124	+643
1926....	5,010	4,744	+266	100.0	5,010	4,744	+266
1927....	5,037	4,489	+548	95.4	5,280	4,706	+574
1928....	5,334	4,497	+837	96.7	5,516	4,650	+866
1929....	5,490	4,756	+734	95.3	5,761	4,991	+770
1930....	4,097	3,339	+758	86.4	4,742	3,865	+877
1931....	2,481	2,197	+284	73.0	3,399	3,010	+389
1932....	1,717	1,470	+247	64.8	2,650	2,269	+381
1933....	1,760	1,612	+148	65.9	2,671	2,446	+225
1934....	2,133	1,655	+478	74.9	2,848	2,210	+638
High ...	5,490	4,756	+837		5,761	4,991	+877
Low ...	1,717	1,470	+148		2,650	2,210	+225
Average.	3,799	3,303	+496		4,264	3,701	+563

* Based on data from U. S. Department of Commerce, Bureau of Foreign and Domestic Commerce, annual reports on *The Balance of International Payments of the United States.*

The all-commodity wholesale price index number is from the U. S. Department of Labor, Bureau of Labor Statistics.

According to this table, we had a pronounced excess of exports over imports of merchandise; the highest excess was 837 million dollars in 1928, the lowest was 148 million dollars in 1933, and the average was 496 million dollars. In terms of 1926 dollars the net credits are raised over the net credits in current dollars, except in two years; the highest net credit was 877 million dollars, the lowest was 225 million dollars, and the average no less than 563 million dollars. Without question, if these reports told the entire story, it would follow that our net-creditor country has continued to display an active balance of merchandise trade.

Now, the United States has further rather extensive imports and exports of goods not so classified, but instead hidden under tourist expenditures. American tourists abroad use goods and services; food is ingested, clothes are worn out, dutiable articles are smuggled back into the country, dutiable articles as well as those on the free list are openly brought back, since there is an allowance for duty-free importation by the individual traveller. In fact, every item of outlay on the returning travellers' lists tends to be underestimated in dollars. The foreign traveller in the United States also uses American goods and services, food is ingested, clothes are worn out, and there is no record of the carrying out of articles by the departing traveller. The (frequent) expenditures of American tourists on goods bought and used abroad and on those brought in are obviously equivalent to imports; the corresponding (infrequent) transactions of foreign tourists in this country are equivalent to exports.

Of course, one may separate goods and services. The American abroad who wears a British suit while on travel abroad, might as well have imported the same suit into the United States; but when he pays for a railway ticket the transaction is different. It becomes a matter of some interest, therefore, to estimate in the total expenditures of tourists in foreign countries how much is spent for goods whose valuations strictly belong as debits in the international merchandise account, and what proportion on the contrary represent transfer of money abroad which cannot be directly accounted as debit items in merchandise trade. Let us assume that on each side of the credits and debits of tourist expenditures, half would be regarded as expended for goods, equivalent to imports of goods, and the other half regarded as transfer of money, equivalent to immigrant remittances, let us say. Let such a reformulation of the balance of merchandise trade now be attempted.

Table IV presents the valuations of exports and imports of goods over the ten-year period, adjusted to take account of the suggested division of tourist expenditures. That is, half of the reported expenditures of American tourists in each year are added to imports, and half of the reported expenditures of foreign tourists in this country are added to exports.

The influence of the correction is immediately obvious. Since expenditures of American tourists abroad so greatly exceed those of foreign tourists here, the effect of the correction is to raise the valuations of imports, relative to exports, to a significant extent. In terms of current dollars, the highest excess of exports was equivalent to 574 million dollars, the lowest excess was 38 million dollars. In one year imports exceeded exports by 18 million dollars. The average of excess of exports was 259 million dollars, practically one-half of the corresponding figure for excess of exports of bare merchandise revealed in Table III. When these valuations are reduced to the 1926 dollar, the highest excess of exports is raised slightly to 594 million dollars, the lowest excess of exports is 58 million dollars, and the average is 289 million dollars. Therefore, this quasi-correction has the effect of re-

TABLE IV.—BALANCE OF UNITED STATES IMPORTS AND EXPORTS OF MERCHANDISE (WITH ADJUSTMENTS FOR HALF OF TOURISTS' OUTLAYS), IN CURRENT DOLLARS AND IN 1926 DOLLARS, 1925-34 *

(Million dollars)

Year	*Receipts from foreigners for "exports" (credits)*	*Payments to foreigners for "imports" (debits)*	*Net credit (+) or debit (—)*	*All-commodity wholesale price index number (1926=100)*	*Receipts from foreigners for "exports" (credits) in 1926 dollars*	*Payments to foreigners for "imports" (debits) in 1926 dollars*	*Net credit (+) or debit (—) in 1926 dollars*
1925....	4,984	4,598	+386	103.5	4,816	4,443	+373
1926....	5,081	5,099	— 18	100.0	5,081	5,099	— 18
1927....	5,114	4,874	+240	95.4	5,361	5,109	+252
1928....	5,418	4,844	+574	96.7	5,603	5,009	+594
1929....	5,580	5,129	+451	95.3	5,855	5,382	+473
1930....	4,183	3,745	+438	86.4	4,841	4,334	+507
1931....	2,537	2,482	+ 55	73.0	3,475	3,400	+ 75
1932....	1,753	1,693	+ 60	64.8	2,705	2,613	+ 92
1933....	1,796	1,758	+ 38	65.9	2,725	2,667	+ 58
1934....	2,180	1,816	+364	74.9	2,911	2,425	+486
High ...	5,580	5,129	+574		5,855	5,382	+594
Low ...	1,753	1,693	— 18		2,705	2,425	— 18
Average.	3,863	3,604	+259		4,337	4,048	+289

* See Table III for source.

ducing heavily the supposed active balance of merchandise trade.

ADEQUATE REVISION OF MERCHANDISE TRADE POSITION

The requisite correction, however, must go much further. In order to clarify the situation and specify the items, it is necessary to analyze and classify the various services rendered by us to foreigners and by foreigners to us in furtherance of our international commerce. These services may be classified, on the basis of their internal significance, into three groups:

(a) Government expenditures. Our government maintains abroad embassies, legations, consulates, and various special representations; other governments maintain these institutions in the United States. The payment of expenses requires transfers of funds, which transfers may occur in gold, silver, bills of exchange or paper money, according to circumstances. The records of our expenditures abroad are readily obtained; the records of the expenditures of foreign governments in this country are not so readily obtained. In our view, these inward and outward transfers do not belong to movements of goods, nor yet to loans and investments; they are neither visible nor invisible, attached to neither movement of goods nor movement of capital, though possibly affecting both. Thus we omit them in the table of balance of merchandise trade to be given below, though in fact without significant influence since the figures are not large.

(b) Services attached to imports and exports of goods. A long list of services rendered by us to foreigners or to us by foreigners are directly connected with movements of physical goods, are incidental thereto, represent special transactions of sale, or have an influence on movement of goods, and are not classifiable as loan or investment, as long-term or short-term balance. Such are freight charges on the Great Lakes and the oceans and canal tolls; insurance, commission, and interest on shipments; royalties on patents and moving pictures; advertising expenses; cable charges; payments on export of electrical power, and other smaller items. These stated services are related to inbound and outbound movements of merchandise, they are the accessory and ancillary parts of visible trade. We term these *commercial services.*

(c) Service charges on foreign debts and investments. Here we have interest and dividend on short-term and long-term foreign debt and investment, including amortization, sinking fund and payments on maturity. These are part of import and export of capital, to be separated as strictly as possible in an annual account from imports and exports of goods and their attending services as stipulated above in (b). We term these *loan and investment services.*

Now to prepare a true balance of merchandise trade, an accounting that shall be dynamically correct, one must attach the credit and debit figures for the items under (b) to the figures for valuations of outbound and inbound goods. One must further attach the figures for tourist expenditures at home and abroad, for immigrant remittances and so-called charitable remittances. These return no interest or dividend, they are not repaid; they correspond with a movement of goods in one direction but not a later movement of goods in the opposite direction, as is the case with foreign loans and investments. Inherently and essentially these several items belong with the items of outbound and inbound movements of physical goods. Such a corrected balance of merchandise trade is given in Table V.[1]

Here is revealed a totally different state of affairs from

[1] Compare statement of A. H. Hansen in *International Economic Relations,* pp. 135-38.

that currently accepted. In only two of the ten years did export credits exceed import debits, and the amounts were small; in eight of the ten years import debits exceeded export credits, and in each of these years the amount was greater than in the two years, 1928 and 1934, in which credits exceeded debits. That is, over the decade we had a passive balance of merchandise trade in conformity with our net-creditor position.

The highest figure for excess of imports in current dollars was 552 million dollars in 1926, the lowest excess of imports over exports was 137 million dollars; and the highest excess of exports in the two exceptional years was 116 million and the average excess of imports over exports was 192 million dollars. When these figures are adjusted to the 1926 dollar, the significant change is the elevation of the average to 229 million dollars.

In summary, it appears that, correctly stipulated and construed, our country has had over the past decade a true passive balance of merchandise trade. This passive balance has, however, not been so large as it ought to be in view of the extent of our foreign loans and investments. It is, however, in striking contrast with the trade of the previous five years (1919-24), which we may say (without minute proof) did show an active balance of merchandise trade. The transition from the calendar years 1919-24 to 1925-34 illustrates clearly that despite all mercantilist doctrine and tariff legislation, the United States has moved into the position appropriate to our net-creditor status, namely, we have a passive balance of merchandise trade. This circumstance makes a difference of perhaps a half-billion dollars in the computation of the objective of the trade development proposed by Secretary Wallace. To pay service charges on foreign debt and investment and to export a stated added amount of farm products, we do not need to reverse an active balance

TABLE V.—BALANCE OF UNITED STATES IMPORTS AND EXPORTS OF MERCHANDISE (FULLY ADJUSTED TO TAKE ACCOUNT OF ASSOCIATED SERVICES), IN CURRENT DOLLARS AND IN 1926 DOLLARS, 1925-34 *

(Million dollars)

Year	*Receipts from foreigners for "exports" (credits)*	*Payments to foreigners for "imports" (debits)*	*Net credit (+) or debit (—)*	*All-commodity wholesale price index number (1926=100)*	*Receipts from foreigners for "exports" (credits) in 1926 dollars*	*Payments to foreigners for "imports" (debits) in 1926 dollars*	*Net credit (+) or debit (—) in 1926 dollars*
1925....	5,184	5,371	—187	103.5	5,009	5,189	—180
1926....	5,518	6,070	—552	100.0	5,518	6,070	—552
1927....	5,653	5,845	—192	95.4	5,926	6,127	—201
1928....	5,869	5,815	+ 54	96.7	6,069	6,013	+ 56
1929....	6,040	6,233	—193	95.3	6,338	6,540	—202
1930....	4,670	4,807	—137	86.4	5,405	5,564	—159
1931....	2,793	3,182	—389	73.0	3,826	4,359	—533
1932....	1,945	2,236	—291	64.8	3,002	3,451	—449
1933....	1,978	2,124	—146	65.9	3,001	3,223	—222
1934....	2,491	2,375	+116	74.9	3,326	3,171	+155
High ...	6,040	6,233	—552		6,338	6,540	—552
Low ...	1,945	2,124	+116		3,001	3,171	+155
Average.	4,214	4,406	—192		4,742	4,971	—229

* See Table III for source.

of, let us say, a quarter of a billion dollars; we have only to expand an existing passive balance of, let us say, a quarter of a billion dollars into a larger passive balance of, again, a billion and a quarter dollars at the outside.

Import and export of gold. Our country is not now an extensive source of new gold, the average outturn of which in recent years has been about 90 million dollars. We have a fairly heavy use of gold in the arts and sciences. Our law provides for a relatively heavy gold reserve. In consequence of our inability otherwise to balance our annual account of international trade, gold has been accumulating in the possession of our government. There was a heavy net import of gold during 1934. In terms of our present formal revaluation of gold, the gold bullion reserve of the federal government stands in the neighborhood of 9 billion dollars. With continuation of present trends, it is possible that within a short time our gold bullion reserve might approach the equivalent of 10 billion dollars. This is an utterly unheard-of quantity of gold and without direct usefulness as currency reserve under the law, or in relation to the outstanding importance of bank credit in the money supply of the country. Without entering into any digression, it may here be stated as accepted by competent students of the subject that the commerce of the United States would gain if some of our gold were in the possession of other countries for the stabilization of their currencies. In any event, it is not in the interest of the higher price level desired in this country for producers of industrial raw materials and of farm products to acquire further imports of gold to balance the international account. Nor would it be in the interest of our internal economy to have the new gold of South Africa indirectly diverted to this country in payment of service charges on our foreign loans and investments.[1] A healthy foreign trade

[1] The new gold production of the world is now over 27 million ounces annually.

ought to be equated with goods and services and not annually balanced with gold to a significant extent.[1]

The current position of export of capital. The current annual estimates of new investments by Americans abroad and by foreigners in this country may be taken as approximately accurate. But the net change in position at the end of each year is by no means so well known. Every year foreign investors buy from and sell to American investors securities belonging to old issues on both sides of the international account. Repatriation of foreign securities and flight of capital into foreign securities go on almost side by side, or follow each other. This "backwash" in the annual movement of domestic and foreign securities, considered merely in long-term paper, becomes more important as time passes and has become particularly important during the past five years. Before the World War the United States was a net-debtor nation to the extent of perhaps 3 billion dollars; but there is still no adequate account of the extent of persistence to 1934 of old foreign investments in the United States. (The writer has friends in Europe whose sole remaining foreign securities still yielding dividends are American railway and public utility bonds.) The tendency is now towards reduction in the net figure for long-term foreign investment, due to sale to Americans of American securities held abroad. The figure of long-term American investments abroad was given at the end of 1930 at 15,134 million dollars, probably too low; the estimate for the end of 1933 was given as 13,799 million dollars. From this we deduct, let us say, two to four billion dollars representing long-term foreign investments in this country, in order to obtain a rough estimate of our net position as creditor, which is probably now less than 10 billion dollars. Rather paradoxically in one sense, but inevitably in another, as foreigners default on their borrowings

[1] The recently reported statement of the Secretary of the Treasury, in a radio address, on the acceptability of gold in return for exported goods is a striking recrudescence of old mercantilism.

from Americans, the gross sum owed to Americans declines.

Short-term movements of capital (almost satirically called "floating" balances), which especially since the war have become in large part the substitute for movement of gold, introduce uncomputable confusion into the international account. Some of the current short-term movements are true trade acceptances, to cover past accounts or provide for new ones. Some are true short-term investments, some represent flight of capital, some reveal movement of "equalization funds," some are acts of monetary policy, some take the place of gold reserves, some are loans to cover unpayable or defaulted service charges, some are speculative deposits, others are political deposits. Short-term balances have a valuable, if sometimes hazardous, function, but they are not well enough reported to clarify the international accounts.

Service charges currently due. It is historically and technically incorrect to assume that all so-called foreign loans and investments must annually offer to the countries of the lenders the equivalents of their service charges in goods. This is true only, by definition, of portfolio securities. Borrowers abroad whose obligations are in dollar-bonds must, if they are to escape default, in the absence of gold offer goods or convertible foreign exchange secured in other countries through goods. According to the latest estimate of the Department of Commerce, American investments in foreign countries, as represented in portfolio securities, are only 6,032 million dollars (as of December 31, 1933), from which must be subtracted the unestimated holdings by foreigners of portfolio securities in the United States, perhaps a half of that figure. At 6 per cent, the service charges due us would represent only 362 million dollars a year, to which must be added a figure for amortization or sinking fund payments, which might bring the sum to over 500 million dollars.[1] From this must be subtracted the sum due foreigners on American portfolio securities owned abroad. The net figure of payments due on portfolio securities is the only obligation which must be offered in gold or goods during the current year.[2]

This follows from the simple fact that direct foreign investments as a class are under no formal obligation to transfer their earnings in dollars, or even to transfer them in goods at all for the time being. The earnings merely accumulate, in terms of foreign currencies, in the foreign countries in which the direct investments are located. In prosperous times, with easy exchange rates, the earnings on the direct investments are returnable to the lending country; in other times such earnings accumulate abroad (or are formally impounded), and added to the gross sum of direct investments. The history of Great Britain as a foreign lender illustrates that investments are, in effect, by choice often perpetuated, are not returned as principal; owners do not transfer their earnings, but allow them to accumulate abroad as accretion of capital in the foreign investments. In fact, the rising foreign debt of some countries (for illustration Australia and Argentina) represents essentially the accumulation of unpaid interest added to principal. Keynes has made the amusing computation that the share of Queen Elizabeth in the loot of one expedition of Drake would equal, at compound interest over the long interval, the present foreign investment of Great Britain.

IMPORTS OF GOODS TO BE EXPECTED

These several considerations, with others of lesser impor-

[1] The relation between payments due on principal and on interest varies, but in total the latter exceed the former.

[2] If one accepts the low estimate of American net-creditor position offered by Peek and quoted above, the sum due annually on service charges to this country would be less than a half-billion dollars, including both direct and portfolio investments.

tance, prevent one directly from using the annual amount of interest and dividends paid by foreigners (or due) to American investors (a credit item), contrasted with interest and dividends paid to foreign investors (or due) by American borrowers (a debit item), in reaching a figure to be used to express the value of imports of goods over exports regarded as necessary to equate the international account. The annual figures for bare merchandise are in themselves, as stated above, misleading. Some of the reported payments of interest and dividends represent money borrowed in the creditor country, short-term and long-term. In each year the payments of interest and dividends due the United States are relatively less complete than the payments due from the United States; the payments of interest and dividends due the United States are shortened by defaults, which have been conspicuous in recent years. The list of our foreign investments contains portfolio securities (in unknown but exaggerated volume) which have become worthless, and from them no future payments are to be expected; the list contains direct foreign investments which have gone bankrupt and passed through liquidation. One cannot use an average rate of interest applied to the gross paper figure for American long-term investments abroad, to arrive at a figure to be used to suggest the value of goods we ought to receive in annual payment. Nor can one take the figures for actual payments and assume that such figures represent a known proportion of what ought to be expected in the future.[1] A glance at the reported annual balance of trade of Great Britain since the war will show that the figure for passive balance of merchandise trade tends to stand lower than the

[1] It is to be kept in mind that many foreign loans now termed in default are in that situation through failure of transfer rather than through failure of earnings; when transfer again becomes practicable, the accumulated earnings (as well as transfers due on refunding operations) will raise considerably the sum of the payments to be expected during the next few years.

figure for payments due on foreign investments. One may use the sum due us as a basis, level of tariff permitting, for suggesting the passive balance of merchandise trade to an approximate extent; but we do not know what proportion of the payments may not be transferred but left abroad.[1]

Assuming no lending for payment of interest due from abroad, if imports of goods during 1933, based on Table V, had been sufficient to pay interest on foreign debt and investment, and provide purchasing power for an added export of a half-billion dollars' worth of farm products, the passive merchandise account of the year would have stood somewhat as follows, in million dollars:

Receipts from foreigners for "exports" (credits)	2,478
Payments to foreigners for "imports" (debits)	3,124

This, of course, is merely an arbitrary illustration, but it indicates that according to an accurate interpretation of the real balance of merchandise trade, the estimate of Secretary Wallace that we shall have to import practically a billion dollars' worth more goods in order (a) to secure payment of service charges on foreign loans and debts, and (b) simultaneously sell abroad an added half-billion dollars' worth of farm products, is broadly correct.

As a rule, in the history of other net-creditor countries, well illustrated in the balance of trade of the United Kingdom, the full sum due (on paper) from foreign debtors in normal times at least has not been accepted in goods and services; a variable part has almost routinely remained abroad to swell the figure for foreign investments. Indeed, one of the methods employed in London to make an estimate, in an indirect manner, of new foreign investment for the year

[1] According to Hansen (*International Economic Relations,* p. 162), an increase in exports up to 500 million dollars would be required to service our foreign investments and an increase up to 800 million dollars would be needed to facilitate foreign purchase of any substantial additional volume of farm products.

to be compared with the sum of new issues, is to secure that estimate as the difference between the sum presumably due on the account of foreign investments and the sum of receipts on passive balance of merchandise trade and services. Such a method has large present difficulties. If we were not lending new sums for any purpose, short-term or long-term; if debtors were not receiving advances to cover service charges; if our net-creditor position were not being changed by buying or selling, at home and abroad, short-term or long-term paper; if we were not sending out or receiving gold; if short-term capital movements were being employed solely in facilitation of trade acceptances; then, with appropriate allowances for tourist expenditures and remittances for charity and governmental expenses abroad, one would rather expect to see the account "balance" for the year (additional exports of farm products disregarded), with shipping services a stand-off, by the acceptance of 400-600 million dollars' worth of goods. But it might be more or less. Further assumptions are made, of course, of continuation of current relations in the price levels at home and abroad, together with still other assumptions on the high or low level of imports and exports in the world in general. The figure would depend in part upon the extent of foreign long-term investments remaining in this country and on the degree to which owners of direct investments abroad were able to transfer their earnings into the United States. Much depends on the willingness of unseasoned foreign investors to leave their earnings abroad.

Though it is to be regarded as oversimplification to state that relative to 1929, under a system of "internationalism," the United States would need to accept nearly a billion dollars more of goods from abroad, the figure sounds rather low. It seems likely to be that much under the "planned middle course." Of course, the Secretary has hedged his position with the use of the term "decent price"; the Secretary has reserved "decent" prices only for cotton, wheat, and tobacco, and has not stipulated them for any exportable manufactured products. Nor have "decent" prices been implied for the imported goods. No other net-creditor country has the peculiar problem of a heavy natural export both of farm products and factory products. When one deals *ad misericordum* with "emergencies," "decent" prices and "social stability" as predicated terms in an argument, one is reminded of the Pope who said he cared not who conducted the arguments so long as he framed the definitions.

The estimate of the desired shift in merchandise trade may be checked by the paper record of our long-term foreign investments. We have for 1930 a tabulation of income and debt-service receipts of the United States from long-term foreign investments and loans.[1] In this tabulation receipts in payment of war debts, principal and interest were reported, but for our purpose ought to be excluded from the grand total, which amounted to the apprehensive sum of 1,380 million dollars. The figure given for war-debt payments was a little over 241 million dollars. In respect of portfolio securities, the sum including interest, bond redemption payments, and sinking-fund payments aggregated 740 million dollars, of which interest was 437 million dollars. As return for direct investments was given the sum of 398 million dollars. The combined sum (740 + 398) is therefore 1,138 million dollars. From this must be subtracted the sum due from us on long-term investments held by foreigners in the United States. This was reported in 1929 as equivalent to 4.5 billion dollars; the service charges may be estimated at 300 million dollars a year. Subtracting this sum from 1,138 million dollars leaves a net figure due us annually of 838 mil-

[1] U. S. Department of Commerce, Bureau of Foreign and Domestic Commerce, *The Balance of International Payments of the United States in 1930* (Trade Information Bulletin No. 761).

lion dollars. If, now, we estimate our present real passive balance of merchandise trade as equivalent to 229 million dollars per year, and subtract this from the 838 million dollars, and then add 500 [1] million dollars of further imports to cover the added export of farm products, we arrive at the sum of 1,109 million dollars, representing the value of imports necessary to cover estimated service charges on foreign investments and loans and the added export of agricultural products desired by the Secretary of Agriculture. It will be noted that this sum is in excess of the estimate of "nearly a billion dollars more goods" under "internationalism" suggested by the Secretary. Such an enlarged estimate would make the problem of adjustment of American industries to increased imports more difficult. However, the rejoinder would be made that full payment of service charges on foreign investments and loans is not to be expected. Much would depend on the temper of the American investors; they might be willing to let payments on principal be suspended if interest were paid; some might prefer to reinvest interest abroad; dividends on direct investments might be transferred or reinvested abroad.

When, now, we come to the change in imports envisaged by Secretary Wallace in "the planned middle course," his estimate seems far below the requirements. The Secretary suggests that

> ". . . we would lower tariffs enough to bring in another half-billion dollars worth of goods annually, and permanently retract of our good agricultural land some 25 million acres." (*America Must Choose*, p. 27.)

An added import of a half-billion dollars' worth of goods annually would do little more than cover the interest charges on foreign investments alone (as of 1930), or it would merely pay for the added export of a half a billion dollars' worth of

[1] In contrast with our export of farm products in 1929, an added 500 million dollars of such exports above recent levels is not excessive.

farm products annually. If the estimate of contraction of 25 million acres is directly contingent on the estimate of import of only a half a billion dollars' worth of goods annually, then the estimate of contraction cannot be correct. If Secretary Wallace aims at an added export of a half a billion dollars' worth of farm products, not an excessive ambition, then the passive balance of merchandise trade will need to be possibly more than the equivalent of a billion dollars. The estimate of "another half-billion dollars' worth of goods annually" will not fill the bill at all if service charges on foreign investments and loans are to be paid in goods. In a word, the Secretary has stopped short in a correct argument.

The Secretary draws an interesting contrast (by implication more than direct exposition) between pre-war Great Britain and Germany, to point a moral for the United States. This was the acceptance by Great Britain of a passive balance of merchandise trade, as appropriate to her net-creditor position, with the disinclination of Germany to do the same. In our view, the comparison is not directly appropriate for the two decades before the war, because it fails to take account of the outstanding and indeed controlling circumstance that during this time the Germans were making technical advances at an extraordinary rate while Britain was slowing down. The Secretary further suggests a comparison between Germany before the war and the United States since the war, as illustrations of net-creditor countries disinclined to accept passive balances of merchandise trade. Again, in our view, the comparison is inadvertently misleading, because Germany was a net-food-importing country, whereas the United States is a net-food-exporting country; and Germany's export problem was largely in manufactures, whereas our export problem, as the Secretary points out, is especially in agriculture.

It strikes us as unexpected to find that the Secretary of

Agriculture lays undue stress upon the visible items of trade and accords to the invisible items a much lesser rôle. It would be perhaps unfair to judge the Secretary by the respective attentions accorded to the visible and invisible items in *America Must Choose.* Yet it seems clear that it is in part this lesser attention to the invisible side of commerce which leads the Secretary to exaggerate the rôle of tariff rates in the international movement of commodities. Annually over the past three years the League of Nations has issued a *World Economic Survey.* This is the period in which has developed in the mind of Henry A. Wallace the policy he now enunciates as Secretary of Agriculture. It is possible that the Economic Intelligence Service of the League of Nations exaggerates the importance of the invisible items in commerce, the difficulties of transfers of payment, and the immediate and residual effects of short-term and long-term investments and debts. But certainly if the scope of the problem, as conceived by the League of Nations and revealed in the successive issues of the *World Economic Survey,* represents an equitable weighting of the forces under consideration, then we have an all-too-simplified presentation in *America Must Choose.*[1] Secretary Wallace insists on the importance of the shift of the United States from the net-debtor to the net-creditor position; but this is only one figure in the large painting of the invisible items in international trade.

In a broad sense, a review of the visible and invisible commerce does not throw a genial light on the prospect of a large extension of our passive balance of merchandise trade. If we regard American foreign investors, American farmers, and American industrialists as alike entitled to a "balanced foreign trade," with the emphasis on farm products upheld

[1] The *World Economic Review 1933,* issued by the Department of Commerce and prepared under Willard L. Thorp, contains much well-selected information and judicious comment.

by Secretary Wallace, our annual passive balance of merchandise trade will need to exceed a billion dollars.[1]

SUMMARY

The several visible and invisible items in the foreign commerce of the United States are briefly discussed. For the purpose of a dynamic analysis of the balance of merchandise trade, this part of our commerce is subjected to a more detailed scrutiny. A balance of what might be called "bare merchandise" is first presented, which shows, in accordance with the usual statement, an excess of reported values of exported goods over reported values of imported goods. This is next supplemented by a suggestive division of tourist expenditures into goods and services. This partial correction still gives an excess of reported values of exported goods over reported values of imported goods, though to a much smaller extent. Finally, what is believed to be a full and adequate correction is undertaken. The large group of services is divided into two sets, (a) those associated with movements of goods directly and indirectly and really a part thereof, and (b) those associated with payment of interest, dividend, and principal on foreign loans and investments. When the credit and debit items of the first group of services, those directly and indirectly associated with movements of goods, are added to the credit and debit items of bare merchandise, with appropriate consideration of tourist expenditures and immigrant remittances, there emerges a passive (negative, miscalled "unfavorable") balance of merchandise trade,

[1] Apparently an immediate influence on the trade of the country by the advice of Secretary Wallace is not in evidence. During the calendar year of 1934, the first full year of the New Deal, the positive balance of bare merchandise trade (excess of goods exported over goods imported) was reported as 478 million dollars. This was more than the combined positive balances of 1932 and 1933. Incidentally remarked, Secretary Wallace and Secretary Morgenthau do not seem to hold the same view on the acceptability of export of goods for gold.

which we believe is the true position in our commerce and which is appropriate to our situation as net-creditor country. This corrected formulation and appraisal of the true balance of merchandise trade is not new, but has been elsewhere derived and expounded. The average passive balance of merchandise trade during the past ten years was thus computed as 192 million dollars in terms of current dollars, and 229 million dollars in terms of 1926 dollars.

The importance of this correct formulation of our balance of merchandise trade lies in the fact that our country is thereby shown to occupy the position theoretically and practically demanded of us as a net-creditor country. The extent of the passive balance of trade is, however, not sufficient to correspond with the extent of our net-creditor long-term position. If we are to receive a sufficient excess of imports of goods and associated services to permit of the payment of service charges on foreign loans and investments, and to cover an additional export of a half-billion dollars' value of farm products, our passive balance of merchandise trade must be enlarged to the extent of a figure exceeding a billion dollars.

Chapter VIII

RAISING THE PASSIVE BALANCE OF MERCHANDISE TRADE

In an expanding export of farm products, according to the so-called "planned middle course" of Secretary Wallace, it is implied that the gross value of imports of merchandise shall be raised or, alternatively and perhaps simultaneously, the gross value of merchandise exports must be lowered. The dollar credits (receipts from foreigners for exports of merchandise) must fall and/or the dollar debits (payments to foreigners for imports of merchandise) must rise. The equation of merchandise values may be shifted from either side; but the sum of debits is annually to outweigh the sum of credits. Since gross foreign trade is sought to be expanded, this implies that exports are to be somewhat enlarged but imports much more enlarged. When, now, one undertakes at a certain price level to formulate a schedule of imports and exports which shall give a stated passive balance of merchandise trade—a shift from a small passive balance of merchandise trade of 100-300 million dollars into a heavy passive balance of merchandise trade up to 900-1,200 million dollars—one must leave generalities and deal with concrete items, with amounts and prices. Such an appraisal is tentatively approached in this chapter.

"A neighborhood of trade—with actual goods exchanged, not goods for promises to be collected on later at any cost—here, admittedly is a situation far from present realities; but it is worth considering." (*America Must Choose*, p. 21.)

By this quotation, the historically-minded may be led to inquire how commerce would have developed in the half-century before the war on the limited basis of "actual goods exchanged, not goods for promises to be collected on later."

We must receive (a) more imports and/or (b) higher-priced imports; or deliver (c) less exports and/or (d) lower-priced exports. Or we may buy more, or sell less, of commercial services (see pp. 136-7). These demand separate consideration. Dealing first with imports, the end may be approached either by increasing the quantities introduced, c.i.f. duty-unpaid prices considered equal, or by increasing the import prices, quantities considered equal.

INCREASING QUANTITY OF IMPORTS

To increase the quantities of goods accepted in a planned program of international commerce may be left either to natural competitive forces—to the arbitrage of costs and prices—or to treaty arrangements. Secretary Wallace leans strongly to trade agreements; the cumulative effect of bilateral trade agreements would be to reduce merchandise credits and/or enlarge merchandise debits.

". . . international planning must include a complete survey, item by item, of all the products that enter into our annual output, and a conscious decision as to which kind of products we might receive in large quantities from abroad, . . ." (*America Must Choose*, p. 18.)

". . . If we are going to lower tariffs radically, there may have to be some definite planning whereby certain industries or businesses will have to be retired." (p. 18)

"A truly practical readjustment of our own tariff policy would involve the careful examination of every product produced in the United States or imported, and the determination of just which of our monopolistic or inefficient industries we are willing to expose to real foreign competition." (p. 28)

A large number of goods now enter duty-free,[1] and under a progressive policy of decline in tariff rates (towards such a low level as might be termed historically a low tariff or a tariff-for-revenue), the free list would be enlarged. It is not generally realized how long is the list of primary raw materials which are subject to no duty. Using a conventional tariff argument we may take it for granted that whenever import duties are applied on ores, or to the early stages of processing, production costs abroad are supposed to be lower than in the United States. If, now, such tariffs were reduced or repealed, the effect would be to encourage imports, and presumably so much more as to enlarge the debit figure in the merchandise account of our foreign trade. Of course, the local consequences would be unpleasant, injurious, or destructive, as the case might be. To draw duty-free copper from the cheapest foreign sources in Africa would mean closing many of the copper mines in the United States, in which high production costs, due to low concentration of copper in the ore and extreme depth in the operations, are not to be avoided; further, it would imply pitting our fairly low-cost copper mines against the lower-cost mines of South America and the supposedly lowest-cost mines in Africa. A similar situation exists, or could develop, in lead, zinc, and bauxite. In the case of certain of these metals our production may fairly be called "exotic," [2] i.e., the development of the native deposits is almost artificial; illustrations are magnesite and tungsten ore. If all the metals were duty-free, and our more or less higher-cost deposits reserved for future use, while lower-cost foreign deposits are drawn on in the immediate future, the debit figure for merchandise trade would presumably be increased. Copper represents the most

[1] These are included in the 40 per cent of our peak imports that represented goods not produced in this country.

[2] The word "exotic" has acquired a wider use than that found in the high school dictionaries; perfume is no longer the classical example.

outstanding case for the future, but the considerations involved apply to all the metals of which the deposits in the United States are under protection in the interests of the owners and workers. That the copper mines are not monopolized would hardly help their cause.

In the case of fibers we have important items. Short-staple cotton (under 1⅛ inch) is on the free list; but the fiber from 1⅛ to 1⅜ inch is dutiable, and long-staple cotton is dutiable. The purpose of the duty on the longer lengths is to compel the American manufacturer to use the short American fiber in place of longer imported fiber. Cotton waste is free; but the cotton yarns and warps, thread, and the cloths (unbleached, bleached, colored) are dutiable. Here we have an illustration of a domestic raw material, the export disposition of which, in the current excess of the crop, constitutes an important political problem. We have import duties on the raw material of certain qualities and on the material in the earliest stages of processing. Presumably, if the dutiable raw cottons were free, imports would be larger in value; but the exportable surplus of our cotton would also be larger.

Wool has been nailed to many mileposts in the history of the American tariff. Carpet wool, in the grease or on the skin, is free or dutiable according to a minute classification which laymen do not understand, but which was worked out partly in the star chamber of legislative committees and partly in the open forum of political controversy. Clothing wool and combing wool are all dutiable, according to a scale which again the laymen cannot understand, nor yet the politicians, but which wool growers understand partly and wool importers and manufacturers appreciate thoroughly. All yarns and fabrics are dutiable. In the case of the tariff on wool, we have not merely the agricultural backing of wool growers, but the far-flung support of woolen mills. If wools were duty-free, or had lower duties, imports would be larger in value, since we are a heavy net-importer of wool.

Raw silk, cocoons and silk waste are free; spun silk and yarn, singles or plied, are dutiable. Silk could readily be raised in the United States, but will not be raised because our women and children do not lend themselves to such farm work. Silken fabrics are dutiable except silk bolting cloth, used not for habiliments but in flour mills and other factories. If silk cloth were duty-free, the debit item of silk imports might be larger. It is not out of place to remark that the older attitude which regarded silk merely as a semi-luxury has within the last decade come to regard foreign silk as a competitor of domestic rayon, whereas in Japan domestic rayon has become the competitor of domestic silk.

Incidentally remarked, in the case of textiles, we must have regard for an extraordinary range of substitution and replacement. This holds not merely for clothing, but also for household and industrial fabrics. In the case of clothing and household furnishings, the range of substitution is largely between the different fibers; but in the case of industrial uses, processed forest products, paper, and processed agricultural by-products enter the list. In the case of clothing, there is a quite clear, if moderate, inelasticity of demand; with all consideration of perishability of style of wearing apparel, it still holds that to wear more of one fabric means to wear less of another. In the international sense, we must recognize that when we endeavor to induce foreigners to use more cotton, directly or indirectly, we are likely to find in effect that we take it on ourselves to use more silk, linen, wool, and jute. The wide range of substitution, and the adaptations induced or imposed thereby, are the outstanding variables in the international disposition of fibers. This remains true whether the fibers are considered in the raw states as competitive primary materials or in finished goods.

Sugar furnishes a pertinent illustration. It is a moot question, politically and agriculturally, to what extent the United States ought to endeavor to become independent of foreign sugar, including as domestic of course the sugar of Porto Rico and of the Hawaiian Islands, with the sugar of the Philippines regarded as domestic until their independence occurs. As a statement of agricultural potential, it is not to be questioned that the continental United States is capable of raising, let us say, 4 million tons of beet sugar. Of course we cannot raise 4 million tons of beet sugar so cheaply as Cuba can raise 4 million tons of cane sugar. At the same time, to intimate that beet sugar is an "exotic" product is far-fetched, in the light of experiences in northern Europe. If there be an "exotic" sugar-raising in the United States, this is to be found in old cane sugar in Louisiana and new cane sugar in Florida, and not in beet sugar in the scattered regions that extend from Michigan to California. There is an unsolved labor problem in connection with the raising of beet sugar, the labor of thinning the plants and the first weeding; this is done abroad largely by women and children and is in any event a form of minute, "bending-over" work which is repulsive to the mechanistic spirit of American agriculture. To a large extent such work is done in this country by (usually colonized) aliens. Perhaps it will soon become practicable to raise sugar beets in hills instead of in rows; sooner or later the entire culture will be mechanized, including the chopping of the leaves from the roots.

There are unsolved problems of depredations by parasites. But when all is said and done, price permitting, we have the soil naturally adapted to the sugar beet in such large tracts in different regions as to enable us to turn out 4 million tons of sugar. In fact, in certain areas an intensive type of agriculture with the most advantageous crop rotation will not be developed except with the inclusion of the sugar beet, as is the case in some parts of northern Europe. We may be sure that if the world did not face a profusion of cane sugar —in Cuba, Java, and India as outstanding examples—in short, if the agriculture of the United States faced a domestic sugar shortage with limitation of foreign supplies, we would reproduce in beet sugar culture in this country the success it has attained in northern Europe and Russia. And when it becomes officially incumbent upon the Secretary of Agriculture, as has occurred in the allocation of sugar imports, to set an upper limit to what inferentially may be termed "normal" beet sugar production and beyond which production is to be called "exotic," this is to expose that official to the risk of a blunder, which may turn out to be as devious technically as it may be disastrous politically. The tendency in the application of the Jones-Costigan Act is to enlarge the imports of raw sugar, from Cuba at least, which would raise the debit side of the international trade account.

Let us now leave the raw materials selected for illustration and consider semi-finished and finished goods. The hypothesis of the new plan implies that with lowered import duties larger amounts would be imported, and presumably amounts sufficiently larger to make the gross figure of debits higher under the lower duties. The exact effect of a lowering of the import duty upon volume of importation and duty-paid price of a particular article cannot be reliably predicted. The domestic manufacturer will endeavor to cut costs and meet the lowered price of the imported competitive article. Much depends on the extent of the reduction of the import duty; but if forced to lower costs in order to stay in business, American manufacturers could accomplish a great deal in that direction. The outcome would, of course, vary from one commodity to another. On the whole, however, it seems clear that the operation of the plan of the Secretary of Agriculture could not rest on the effectiveness of mere competition between foreign and domestic goods. In the case of bilateral treaties, foreign goods would presumably need to be accorded a stipulated admission, permissive or even definitively set in quotas. The general viewpoint of Secretary Wallace would be to "plan" the imports, which must include planned quantities and prices as well as planned selections. If the outcome on the basis of competition were to be one of commercial trial and error (since reliable precedents for this country are not contained in the operations of the Underwood Tariff), certainly the outcome of planned importations would still be quite as much a question of trial and error. A great deal would depend upon the extent to which controlling technical circumstances were given consideration in the planning of imports. Broadly considered, we take it that the objective of the plan would be to raise the sum of valuation in the debit column of the international account of the country and at the same time secure as large a volume of goods as possible.

It is a familiar experience that returning American tourists are subject to exacting restrictions designed to prevent them from smuggling in dutiable articles. If we are planning to increase the debit side of the international account, this could be aided by granting a larger exemption than the present small sum of one hundred dollars—for example, five hundred dollars. Or, in the direction of still greater liberality, selected classes and grades of goods might be exempted in any amount. A liberalization of the custom-house treatment of returning tourists, on declared but exempted goods, might possibly have the effect of bringing in an added hundred million dollars' worth of imports of goods.

INCREASING PRICE OF IMPORTS

We approach here the rather novel possibility of influencing the international account of the country, enlarging the passive balance of merchandise trade, by importing goods in a higher state and at a higher price—just the opposite of the so-called improvement trade in exports. The possibility of such a procedure—just in line with the objective of the new plan—may be illustrated with several important commodities.

If the consistent policy were adopted of permitting the smelting or other first primary processing, or concentration, of ores and raw metals to be done abroad, and these products admitted duty-free, the debit figure in the merchandise account would be somewhat increased, assuming volume of imports unchanged. Of course, this would raise a tremendous protest in the states where the mines are located, and still more at the seaboard, where imported ores, or first concentrates, are now smelted or otherwise processed.

The import duties on the yarns, threads and cloths are now imposed not merely to keep out articles made from foreign raw cotton, but to prevent American raw cotton being shipped out and returned in processed form. A policy of permitting yarn, warp, sewing thread, and unbleached cotton cloth, made abroad from American raw cotton, to enter the United States duty-free, would bring about a notable increase in the debit figure of the international merchandise account; but to suggest such a thing would be regarded by textile mills as preposterous.[1]

In the case of jute, the raw material and waste are duty-free; jute yarn, cordage, bagging for baled cotton, jute burlap, woven fabrics, and bags are dutiable. We raise no jute; the objectives of the duty on manufacturers is to favor the processing in American mills. India could of course favor her jute mills by levying an export tax on raw jute, sufficient to overcome our import duty on jute manufactures. We

[1] Just to give expression to an exaggeration—what would have been the position of our foreign trade balance over the past decade if we had exported no raw cotton but only cotton manufactures?

could retaliate by raising our duties and India could again raise the export duty on raw jute; fortunately such a tariff war has thus far been avoided. Unmanufactured flax, hemp, and ramie are dutiable, the yarns, threads, and fabrics are dutiable. Sisal, manila, kapok, and istle are free, some manufactures are free; binding twine is free, but cordage is dutiable—presumably because farmers use a great deal of binding twine and only a little rope. In these cases, import prices would be raised by bringing in the products in the early stages of processing, not the raw fibers.

In the case of processed wool, the tariff on carpets and rugs represents an endeavor not merely to secure protection against directly competitive articles, but also to favor American substitutes for so-called Oriental rugs, which latter are not made in the United States at all. Weavings of wool definable as "art" are indeed admitted free to some extent; but this extends only to old tapestries used as wall hangings and to antique rugs and carpets.

In view of the large amount of wool imported, and of the significant difference in c.i.f. price between raw wool and the cleaned and scoured wool, the gross sum representing the value of a stated amount of imported wool would be appreciably increased if no wool were imported in the grease. Further, if wool were imported combed and carded, or as tops, the gross value of the import would be still further augmented. Of course, we would lose the wastes and by-products, and capital and labor now employed in these early stages of processing would be disemployed. But since the objective would be to increase the gross debit figure in the balance of merchandise trade, this could be done to a significant extent by having a higher tariff on raw wool than on processed wool.

Rayon is a manufactured article made from cellulose, usually from the cotton fiber or wood pulp, according to one of several methods of manufacture. The primary material involved is the filament, from which the yarns are spun. Rayon and other synthetic textiles are dutiable in all stages and forms. We take it this is not done to protect the lumber baron or the one-mule cotton grower, but is purely a protective tariff safeguarding a domestic infant industry against the corresponding European and Japanese infant industries. But was it perhaps "exotic" to set up rayon mills here when the Europeans were prepared to furnish us with the filament?

The paper group presents an interesting illustration. Pulp wood (whether rough, peeled, or rossed) is free. Wood pulp, whether mechanically ground or chemically treated, is free, bleached or unbleached, whether sulphite, sulphate, or soda pulp. American timber interests producing pulp wood and wood pulp have been able to secure no protection in the face of the opposition of paper users, aided by the general recognition of the menace in the decline of our forest resources. Newsprint and other printing papers are of course free, under the influence of the press. But wrapping papers, writing papers, tissue papers, paper boards, cigarette papers, wall papers, in fact most paper for special uses, are dutiable, as protection for mills. That newsprint should be free and most other manufactured papers dutiable is of course a violation of the theory of protection. Canada could of course impose export taxes on pulp wood and wood pulp, hoping thus to compel us to accept manufactures. In fact, we already accept these for the most part; and from the other countries of origin (Finland, Norway, Sweden, Germany, Newfoundland, and Labrador) we import practically no pulp wood or wood pulp but only newsprint. Conceivably Russia could supply us with pulp wood and wood pulp if appropriate efforts were made in this direction. Covering the paper industry, we find it fair and important to point out that American newspapers have in this case accomplished what a consistent tariff reformer would suggest for many commodities—namely, the importation not of the raw material nor of the material in the early stages of processing, but of more advanced or even finished manufactures. If the users of producers' goods throughout the United States had been in position to impress their interests to the extent accomplished by the newspapers, the American tariff schedules on articles made from imported raw materials would read very differently from what they do.

One of the most active fields of technical development in recent years, conducted largely under governmental supervision and support, is in the utilization of timber residues. In the broad sense the objective sought is to utilize in manufactures diverse varieties of trees which previously had only a fuel value. When the wood of a particular tree is unadapted to this or that use, this is usually not on account of the lack of positive traits, but on account of the presence of undesired characteristics; when these are removed, the wood becomes adaptable to various commercial uses. Newsprint, for example, may now be made out of varieties of timber which a few years ago were regarded as unadapted to the making of newsprint. The aim of the forest-product researches is to have the trees which grow well in each locality made available to varied commercial uses. As these developments are perfected, the tendency will be to import less and less timber products. Shall, now, these developments be halted, in furtherance of a larger gross figure for value of imported merchandise? The words "exotic" and "inefficient" are but the limitations of the present day, the state of the art but not a bar of nature. If it becomes practicable to make newsprint, cellophane, and rayon from yellow southern pine and western digger pine, shall these methods be repressed because it was earlier found out how to make such products cheaply from other pines, let us say in northern Europe? Is making newsprint an exotic industry?

In the history of the importation of sugar into the United States, the practice was developed of introducing it in the state of raw crystallized sugar, of about 94 per cent pure sugar content, to be then refined into the customary white granulated sugar. Large refineries were constructed at the seaboard to accomplish this refining. Only within recent years has it come about (through what was apparently a blunder in differential tariff rates) that refined sugar has been imported from Cuba as well as raw sugar. Cuba and Java of course have always wished to refine their sugars, but the importing countries wished also to refine them and naturally had their way.

If, now, we wish to increase the debit figure of imports of sugar, we can do so by importing it refined instead of raw. The difference between the c.i.f. duty-unpaid price of Cuban raw and Cuban refined sugar in New York is now around 9 mills per pound. Two million tons of sugar imported refined instead of raw would therefore represent an increment on the debit side of the international account of some 36 million dollars, other things equal. (Whether Cuba would be able to retain this is another question.) Of course, this would close our refineries; also, it would deprive us of certain by-products; further, we would not get refined sugar in so many forms as it is now offered to the trade for various purposes. But it would have the effect of increasing the gross figure of debits, which represents in the ultimate sense the Cuban purchasing power for American farm exports.

It is unnecessary to give further illustrations of the thesis than in the metals, the fibers, and sugar adduced above.[1] We face here the possibility of the reversion of the age-old

[1] Sometimes the objectives become incompatible. This crop year we shall certainly be a net-importer of wheat. This will enlarge the debit side of the international account, which fits in with the official plan, and also tend to raise the price of wheat. But the high price of wheat will reduce export of wheat, and thus operate against the added export of farm products desired in the official plan.

trend incorporated in the so-called "improvement trade." Importing countries desire for internal consumption to secure raw materials in the earliest practicable stages, thereafter to be refined, processed, elaborated, and finished into processors' goods, producers' goods, and consumers' goods for final consumption. Countries with technical equipment strive also to import raw materials in order later to re-export the refined, processed, and finished commodities. Each country wishes for its capital and labor to secure the "added value of manufacture," both on the fraction consumed at home and that shipped abroad. The basis of such policy is to secure the raw material at the lowest possible cost, other things equal; disposing of the various products at the highest practicable price, domestic capital and labor are employed in the elaborations.

There is a world-wide contest between the countries still in the extractive stage of development and the more advanced countries which possess older manufacturing equipment. The countries producing raw materials wish to carry on the elaborations; they are doing so in some cases with success, in others without success. India has built up a significant iron industry to enable her to export iron instead of iron ore. Finland exports newsprint instead of pulp. Germany exports purified salts of potash instead of crude concentrates. We export petroleum products instead of crude oil. The United Kingdom and Germany export the products of the fractional distillation of coal instead of exporting coal for that purpose. But there are numerous illustrations on the other side. Australasia, Argentina, and South Africa export raw wool instead of processed wool. The world trade in wheat greatly exceeds that in wheat flour. Most of the sugar of commerce is raw rather than refined. Most of the Japanese export of silk is raw rather than in thread or tissue. Whether a country must export its materials raw or processed depends upon many circumstances—historical and technical, related to the state of financial development and to the dispersion of industries. Whenever possible, exporting countries have tried to enlarge the credit item in the international account by exporting materials in the most finished state possible; importing countries have tried to reduce the debit item in the international account by importing materials in the rawest possible state.

Now, as part of a planned economy for our country it is hypothetically possible, however heretical and impracticable it may seem, to reverse this tendency on both sides; that is, to endeavor to obtain our imports of materials not in their earliest stages but more or less refined and processed; and on the other hand, to endeavor not to send our exports in the most finished state, but processed to a lesser degree. This would imply, on the one hand, importing refined sugar instead of raw, and, on the other, exporting wheat instead of wheat flour. It would mean importing refined vegetable oils instead of oil seeds, and exporting crude cottonseed oil and unrefined lard instead of highly processed products. It would mean importing newsprint instead of wood pulp (which is the fact already), and exporting raw cotton in preference to cotton cloth. It would mean importing silk tissues instead of raw silk, and exporting crude petroleum instead of gasoline and the other refined fractions. This all looks so extraordinarily hypothetical, even in a planned economy, that one is tempted to reject it as absurd. But if one will enter carefully into the analysis, one will find that adaptations in this direction are really not more complicated than changes "planned" in the tariff (to be considered later) in order to admit the added amounts of selected imports in substitution of materials and articles now produced at home.

Such a motivated shifting in the credits and debits of our international account is of course abhorrent to the spirit of mercantilism as well as to protectionism. But it accords with the dispersion of industries, discussed below, and it may yet turn out to be a policy acceptable to the New Deal. And it would be a new and pretty thing for professors to play with.

DECREASING QUANTITY OF EXPORTS

Since an international trade account may be influenced either on the credit or the debit side, the predicated balance of merchandise trade may be secured either by reduction in credits or by increase in debits. Reduction of credits may be sought either through lowering of quantity or lowering of value, and these we shall briefly consider separately.

A lowering of the quantity of exports of merchandise is of course a somewhat novel but by no means unprecedented or indeed infrequent procedure. If gold be considered as a metallic commodity, restraint of export has often happened. We have the impression that importers of saltpeter from Chile were once pledged not to extract the iodine and thus the export of isolated iodine was restricted. At times, the export of diamonds has been restrained. The valorization plan of Brazil involves restraint in the export of coffee. The Stevenson Plan for rubber control contained a similar provision. The export of sugar from Cuba is now restricted by the island. The International Wheat Conference of 1933-35 has had before it a quota restriction on export of wheat. In the far-flung trade agreements of the United Kingdom, several extractive countries are pledged to restriction of exports of agricultural products to the United Kingdom; thus the bacon shipments of Denmark to the United Kingdom are limited. The blockades of war ruthlessly apply restrictions on export of materials regarded as essential, directly or indirectly, to continuation of the conflict. Novel and abhorrent as restriction of quantity of exports must appear to a mercantilistic world, nevertheless it is becoming clear that in bilateral trade negotiations such proposals must frequently arise as practical questions.

How, now, in a world of reviving trade, is export of goods from the United States to be restrained?[1] An export tax would be effective, but is expressly prohibited in the Constitution. Repeal of course would take too long to be considered; perhaps, however, it might be possible to regard a reduction of the credit side of the international trade account as an "emergency," and to suspend in the "public welfare," as in the state of war, the operation of the constitutional prohibition against export tax. Otherwise, the only method of restraining flow of exports in quantities would be to stipulate with the foreign buying countries that only stated limited amounts could be accepted by them. That is, we would employ restriction through export quotas in the commercial treaties to be negotiated.[2] In this manner the largest part of the export outlet could be controlled, and there is apparently no other known method by which a control of exports can be effectuated. A planned export policy, the predicated balanced economy, obviously includes planned restriction of certain goods as well as planned expansion of others. Such a general policy is certainly implied in the following words of Secretary Wallace:

". . . If we are going to lower tariffs radically, there may have to be some definite planning whereby certain industries or businesses will have to be retired. The government might have to help furnish means for the orderly retirement of such businesses, and even select those which are thus to be retired." (*America Must Choose*, p. 18.)

[1] It is misleading to adjudge export trade by the proportion of our total production going to export. One has only to recall the proportion of cotton going to export. Each commodity must have its export trade judged on individual merit.

[2] How this fits in with "most-favored-nation treatment" is becoming a superciliously superfluous question.

"... We may have to have government control of all surpluses, ..." (p. 11)

Inevitably, by implication such a policy would need to be applied to competing surpluses abroad as well as to competing surpluses at home; and if we exact from foreign countries a lowering of export of agricultural products to us, we must be prepared to impose a lowering of our export of industrial products to them. It is clearly not practicable to have all of the restrictions apply on the importing side; in the "idealistic cooperation" that is implied as well as invoked in the plan of Secretary Wallace, it may become necessary to have restraints on certain exports on both sides, as well as enlarged acceptance of certain imports on both sides.

DECREASING PRICE OF EXPORTS

Under the previous heading we considered the lowering of quantities of exports, with prices considered equal; we have here to consider the lowering of prices of exports, with quantities considered equal. Both have occurred in the decline of trade during the last five years of the depression; usually prices have declined more than quantities. But the price declines have not been motivated. Low export prices have been the particular cause of agrarian dissatisfaction in all surplus-producing countries. Is it now possible to contemplate influencing the international balance of merchandise trade by lowering the credit items through reduction of export prices? Certainly the administration is not considering it; it seeks higher prices on the wheat, lard, cotton, and tobacco to be exported. We might agree to lower export prices for manufactures; but certainly not for farm products, for which we seek "decent" prices. If processing taxes apply to our exports, then our foreign competitors are favored in importing countries; if processing taxes are not applied to our exports, then the importing countries obtain the goods at prices below ours. And yet high export prices will actually tend to nullify the stated objective, that is, the enlargement of the passive balance of merchandise trade.

It is, of course, proclaimed that "rationalized industries" should lower their costs to such an extent as to supply foreign markets with goods at lower prices. But, in fact, when the rationalized industries face this problem many seem to prefer to establish subsidiary plants in foreign countries. In theory, everyone supports the doctrine of enlarging consumer demand by lowering prices, so as to bring in new increments of demand at successively lower income levels— of which movement Henry Ford was the conspicuous leader. But in practice, producers try to eat their cake as well as keep it, by falling back on high-pressure salesmanship, rather than on low price, to dispose of enlarged outturn. We may be sure that even the New Dealers, trying to lower the credit balance of our international merchandise account, will not have a sufficiently strong motive to adopt a policy of lowering the prices of exports of American goods in order to contribute to this result.

A concluding observation may not be out of place. From the beginning of our history, irrespective of the political party in power, we have followed the more or less masked mercantilist policy, to have the value of exported merchandise exceed the value of imported merchandise, if not in return for gold, then for other valued considerations. Now we contemplate putting into operation a plan to have the value of imported merchandise greatly exceed the value of exported merchandise. To acquire, or enlarge, a passive balance of merchandise trade, one may reduce amount or values, or both, on the export side; and/or one may increase amounts or values, or both, on the import side. The lower the price level, the more difficult to plan any change in the balance of merchandise trade; the higher the price level, the easier. The theory of the passive balance of merchandise trade appropriate to a net-creditor country is self-evident; the practice will be found anything but self-evident. To influence prices, as well as quantities, of exports, as well as imports, in order to modify the balance and terms of trade, will sound hypothetical and far-fetched in this country; but we may be sure that among the astute delegates of other countries engaged with us in negotiation of bilateral trade treaties will be found experts who will find these devices on our exports applicable to the advantage of their countries.

The entire subject of relations of prices of exports and prices of imports is for the time being historical rather than factual. Now, with all manner of obstacles to inbound goods operative in importing countries, with open or concealed subsidies to outbound goods in exporting countries, and with regulation of issue, and even price control, of foreign exchange, the prices of import and export merchandise do not have the meanings or implications naturally attached to them. With free markets, quantities influence prices and prices influence quantities; but under the conditions forecastable for the next few years, prices are likely to be little more than arbitrary figures.[1]

IMPORTS OF GOLD

In the past decade an abnormal balancing of our foreign trade account has occurred through imports of gold. At the

[1] The war debts cast a shadow on revival of world trade, and for this reason alone a settlement should be sought, if not on the ground of equity. The only propitious settlement would be by lump sum. The European debtors could issue fresh securities, sell them to American nationals, and turn in the cash to our government. Or they could buy up American securities held abroad, sell them in the United States, and turn in the cash. Or our government could "board it out," so to speak, by having the debtor governments pay the current expenses of the American government in their countries; this would not be a large sum, unless extended over a long time. It is imperative that Americans realize two points: the lump sums will be small and the debts must cease to be inter-governmental, and if not liquidated in cash must be commercialized.

present formal valuation of gold, with the trend revealed by the imports during 1934, the total monetary gold of the country will soon approach the value of ten billion dollars. This accumulation of gold may be regarded in part as the expression of an ineradicable faith in mercantilism. It seems quite clear that such accumulations of gold as lie in the hands of the governments of the United States and France confer no benefits on the foreign trade of those countries. Whatever the shade of opinion one may hold on the future use of gold as monetary standard, it seems to be generally accepted that movements of merchandise between countries would be stabilized and facilitated if imports and exports of gold (outside of new gold) could be limited to the true balancing of merchandise trade accounts. Secretary Wallace does not specifically (and consistently) urge increased imports of goods in order to avoid imports of gold.[1] It is, however, obvious that when once again the price of gold is fixed and free export of gold and sale of foreign exchange are restored, tariff reduction may be the only method of preventing the resumption of import of gold into this country.

INCREASING PAYMENTS FOR FOREIGNERS' SERVICES

There are many services which are associated with the collection, movement, and distribution of goods, and thus really are an essential part of import and export of merchandise. These "commercial services" were briefly discussed on pages 136-7. The items here under consideration have nothing to do with, and expressly exclude, payments of interest, dividend, and principal on foreign debts and investments. The receipts from foreigners for services we render are credits in the international account, ranking as exports; pay-

[1] There is an undeniable element of humor in the fact that in 1934, in the first year of the advocacy by Secretary Wallace of an enlarged passive balance of merchandise trade, the country had, largely through gold imports, a substantially enlarged active balance of trade.

ments to foreigners for services they render to us are debits in the international account, ranking as imports. These debits considerably exceed the credits, i.e., we buy more services than we sell. In 1933 we paid out for such services (including government expenditures but excluding war debt items) about 512 million dollars and took in about 218 million dollars; therefore we had a passive balance of about 294 million dollars. (All figures are minimal estimates.)

Now, unorthodox as it may appear in history and politics, it is orthodox in economic theory to enlarge the passive balance of merchandise trade by buying more services from foreigners and selling less, like importing more goods and exporting less. We can discourage the American merchant marine and have foreign ships carry goods to and from our shores.[1] We can employ foreign bankers, brokers, commission merchants, and insurance agents instead of our own, on incoming and outgoing goods. We can use foreign insurance companies for life and fire insurance,[2] employ international instead of domestic advertising, use foreign instead of American cables and radios, buy rights to moving pictures instead of selling them, take as much electrical power from Canada as possible. We can encourage churches, schools, philanthropic bodies, reformers, and medical institutions to do as much work abroad as possible, with American money. We can encourage the second generation of immigrants to keep up the remittances established by the first generation. We can urge the building of elaborate embassies, legations, and consulates abroad, and the maintenance of expensive staffs. Finally, we can encourage Americans to travel abroad and induce them to go over and return in foreign ships, while discouraging the travel of foreigners in this country. These

[1] The difference arising from payment or acceptance of shipping charges becomes the difference between f.o.b. and c.i.f. prices.

[2] Few realize that premiums paid by Americans to foreign insurance companies annually exceed 100 million dollars.

various devices are politically heretical, socially more or less inexpedient, offend the canons of commercial taste, and sometimes provoke risibility. But it is merely a question of what we are accustomed to. To stimulate such services of foreigners to American nationals is inherently no more absurd than to assume with the mercantilist that it is good to export goods in order to bring in gold and silver. If it is advantageous to import raw silk from Japan, it may be correspondingly advantageous to have it brought here in a Japanese vessel. Secretary Wallace has made a guarded reference [1] to the circumstances that stimulation of the American merchant marine makes it more difficult for foreigners to buy goods here and pay debts due to us; but he has not entered into consideration of these foreigners' services as a group. If one will scan the individual items in the list over a period of years, one will readily make the inference that a national policy applied to this group might easily enlarge our passive balance of merchandise trade to the extent of 50 or even 100 million dollars a year. But when it is pointed out that Great Britain, the premier net-creditor country, is also the country most prominent in selling the services we are considering, nothing will come of a project to enlarge our passive balance of merchandise trade by buying instead of selling these commercial services. Indeed, none of the net-creditor countries which are willing to take goods are in the same manner willing to accept services. So we shall merely follow their example.

SUMMARY

To enlarge the passive balance of merchandise trade of the United States, changes might be introduced in movements of goods and/or of gold and/or in execution of services associated with imports and exports of goods. Imports

[1] *New Frontiers,* pp. 71 and 86.

of goods might be expanded in quantity, prices considered equal; or higher-priced imports might be brought in, quantities considered equal. It is pointed out that if fewer materials were imported in the raw state, and more in various stages of processing, the value of the debit item would be thereby increased. The export of goods might be reduced in quantity, prices considered equal; or lower-priced exports might be sent out, quantities considered equal. It is pointed out that if we exported more in the raw state and less in processed form, the figure for the credit item in the account would be reduced. Comment is made on the circumstance that while these several devices are equally sound in theory, they would not appeal as equally feasible, or even reasonable, to the affected classes in this country.

Brief comment is made on the experience that much gold has been imported to balance export of goods, and therefore in effect import of gold tends to reduce import of goods. Under these circumstances, with restoration of free markets for goods, gold, and foreign exchange, tariff reduction may become the most effective method of checking importation of monetary gold.

Finally, emphasis is laid on the experience that we have a strongly passive balance of the services associated with movements of goods, excluding services representing payment of interest, dividend, and principal on foreign debt and investment. The passive balance of the merchandise account might be further enlarged by buying more of such services—for illustration, ocean shipping—and selling less. These services have always occupied a favored position in public esteem, which has however no justification in economic theory. Whether the passive balance of merchandise trade is enlarged by increasing the debits and/or decreasing the credits of such services, or by increasing the debits and/or decreasing the credits of merchandise movements, is a question of expediency and in no wise one of doctrine. In the negotiation of each bilateral trade agreement, each of these above-stated possible methods will need to be appraised for practicability. We shall know more of international double-entry bookkeeping before we are through with these devices.

We are told that we cannot sell unless we buy. This observation is true and old. But it also appears that we must accept today in goods the payment for goods sold by us decades ago. There is the rub: the lag in the payment, which provokes a conflict between generations. Raising the passive balance of merchandise trade is essentially the completion by the son of the bargain of his father. But the son has the same feeling toward the bargain of his father that he has toward the social, economic, and political traditions of the earlier generation. The attitude of the younger generation is unlogical. But, as Pareto has exhaustively demonstrated, much of human conduct is unlogical.

Chapter IX

BILATERAL TRADE TREATIES

After preparatory discussions, we now come to the pièce de résistance in the menu of the New Deal foreign policy, as prepared by Secretary Wallace. The policy sounds simple, possibly because it is so extraordinarily complex. There are five planks in the Wallace foreign trade platform:

(1) We are to secure the export of an additional half-billion dollars in value of American farm products.

(2) We are to accept an additional billion dollars in value of imports, presumably mostly manufactures, in order to pay for the aforementioned added export of farm products and to cover service charges due from abroad on American loans and investments.[1]

(3) The planned outgoing and incoming movements of goods are to be stipulated through bilateral trade agreements, each such treaty to bind two countries, to be contracted separately between the United States and some thirty-six[2] foreign countries (our estimate), and to channelize the trade between the United States and these thirty-six foreign countries according to a planned bilateral development of commerce.

(4) In order to facilitate the execution of our treaties with other countries, it will be necessary for many of these

[1] The order of priority between planks (1) and (2) may depend upon whether the program is being enunciated by the Secretary of Agriculture or the Secretary of Commerce.

[2] The exact number (not a question of importance) is considered below.

countries also to contract bilateral trade agreements with one another. Otherwise, the other countries would be in conflict with one another over the fulfillment of their treaties with us; and harmony, not conflict, is essential in the new economic international "balance" envisaged in the New Deal.

(5) Our bilateral treaties are to be so designed, constructed, and executed as to facilitate in the foreign countries with which these agreements are contracted the developments in the direction of the same planned "balance" in their internal affairs which is envisaged in the internal policy of the New Deal in the United States.[1]

From the simple to the sublime is sometimes but a short distance. In this program we cover the span from profits at home to ideals abroad. Without cynicism, it may be remarked that before the series of bilateral trade agreements is completed, plank (4) will be honored in the breach more than in the observance and plank (5) will be moss-grown.

GENERAL CONSIDERATIONS

Just as every play has back-stage and front-stage, so in every international situation we have background and foreground. The background of the problem of revival of international trade lies in the history of the development of multangular commerce; the foreground is the field of "balanced" internal economy. Direct trade between countries was the rule, for good reasons, up to modern times; exchanges (outside of barters and sales for gold or silver) depended largely on direct contracts, based on integrities

[1] Let credit be given where credit is due. The views of Werner Sombart have led him in his study of the future of capitalism to forecast many of the developments now being tried by the New Dealers of all countries. Sombart made the forecast long ago that the forms in which the future international economic relations will be conceived and developed will not be in free trade nor yet in the most-favored-nation treatment clause, but rather in commercial treaties, customs unions, preferences, import quotas, etc. One wonders to what extent our Secretary of Agriculture has dipped his bucket into the Sombart well of wisdom.

of individuals. Multangular trade as we know it arose out of the exigencies of the industrial revolution, since the manufacturing countries of western Europe could not distribute their wares abroad and bring back the diverse raw materials within the narrow confines of direct trade between two countries. With growing export of capital, direct trade became still more inexpedient. Multilateral trade expanded in consequence of growth of arbitrage, under a system of clearing of transactions at a central point, which became London. The gold standard and the credit system which centered around the pound sterling, the delicate equilibrium described in Chapter VII, the establishment of futures markets in many countries, the perfection of transportation and especially of communications, and finally the gradual adoption of most-favored-nation treatment between trading countries —these were the supports on which rested the highly efficient multangular commerce of the world which broke down under the Great Depression. Multangular trade, clearance at a central point, balancing of merchandise accounts eventually by gold, and most-favored-nation treatment constitute the outstanding points in what may be called the classical story of foreign trade.

This has broken down. Despairing of early restoration of multangular trade, we find a widespread movement now emerging to organize instead direct trade, channelized trade between two countries. Howsoever this now may be regarded as new, essentially it is but a reversion to the trade practices of the centuries before the industrial revolution.[1] If in contradistinction to the "classical doctrine" of foreign

[1] It is fitting to know, not imagine, what is new and what is old. The officials in governments all over the world to whom are entrusted the devising of trade restrictions were apparently drawn from the ranks of archæologists. All the recent obstructions to trade are relics of medieval regulations, used over and over again before the Middle Ages and even before the Christian Era. They are not the products of new human ingenuity, any more than any other form of modern devilment.

trade, venturesome spirits might be tempted to call this the "romantic doctrine," it suffices to make the rejoinder that it is merely pre-classical—though in another sense of the word it may well turn out to be "romantic."

For central clearing of accounts is now to be substituted a direct clearing of balances. Instead of most-favored-nation treatment fairly available to all, we are to seek preferential treatment, barters and quotas, channelized trade. Since multangular trade rests on uncontrolled competition, channelized trade is assumed to require controlled competition. Controlled competition, with preferences, barters, and quotas, is readily reformulated to mean balanced trade in external commercial relations second to balance in internal economies. Planned foreign trade thus emerges as a logical development of the New Deal. At the same time, the New Deal has reverted to mercantilism.

At the outset it is necessary to avoid a misconstruction. At the height of foreign commerce in 1928-29 it was probably correct to say that on the record multangular trade constituted one-third of the total and direct trade as much as two-thirds. Some such ratios would be obtained by summation from the reports of foreign commerce of the trading countries. But it is misleading to assume that the previous one-third could drop out and the previous two-thirds remain. Nothing of the sort. To a large extent, direct trades were made possible because of the existence of multilateral trades. Viewed from the inside of the adjustment of balances, appraising both invisible and visible items, a good case could be made out for the statement that at the peak of world trade the larger proportion was essentially multangular and the lesser proportion inherently direct.[1]

Any scheme for enlarging foreign trade, whether through

[1] Cf. statement of A. H. Hansen in *International Economic Relations*, pp. 146-57.

multangular or direct channels, must take account of certain basic differences between the trading countries.

(1) We first divide the countries into net-creditor and net-debtor nations, an important segregation, since the vested interests in the invisible items will have influence in the determination of policy. It is well to bear in mind that some of the countries are close to the border line, and therefore scarcely reveal the traits of net-debtor countries. Such for example are Sweden and Italy.

(2) We divide the countries into those having respectively an active and a passive balance of merchandise trade. This grouping rests on insecure statistical grounds for many countries. In the long run and under so-called normal conditions, separation according to active or passive balance of merchandise trade would bear a relationship to separation of net-debtor from net-creditor countries, but this does not hold at present.

(3) Countries are divided into (a) tropical lands that are primarily exporters of raw materials, (b) non-tropical lands predominatingly exporters of raw materials, and (c) countries that are predominatingly exporters of manufactures, none of which happen to be tropical. *The United States is the only country which is at the same time a heavy actual and potential exporter of raw materials, of raw foodstuffs and feedstuffs, and of manufactures in all stages.*

(4) Each country will separate the foreign countries with which it trades into two groups: those with which exports of goods exceed imports and those with which imports of goods exceed exports. This segregation, the recognition of the existence and extent of a natural surplus or deficit of foreign exchange, is much more important in direct trade than in multangular trade. In the case of the United States, we have an active balance of individual merchandise trade with sixty-six countries and a passive balance with forty-five, the total

trade with the sixty-six, however, being larger than with the forty-five.

(5) Finally, it is important to segregate trade into regions or continents. While it is clear for our commerce as a whole that we have a true passive balance of trade (see Chapter VII), this is not now large enough to correspond with the service charges due us as a creditor nation. But a different statement holds for most regions. Goods received from Canada have a lesser value than goods sent to Canada, and obviously Canada pays no service charges with merchandise; it is a striking circumstance that we sell more goods to Canada than we buy from her, despite the extreme disparity in populations. From Central America and the West Indies the goods we receive are so greatly in excess of those we send that the difference in value is more than enough to cover debt payments due from them to our nationals. If we regard South America as a unit, we receive from that continent so much more goods than we send there that the difference is more than enough to cover debt payments due from there to our nationals, and this despite the circumstance that several countries, like Argentina, sell to us less than they buy from us. In the case of Asia (excluding the Philippines), we buy of goods so much more than we sell that the difference is much more than the amount necessary to cover debt charges due from that region to our nationals. It is Europe that disturbs the equilibrium of our foreign trade, or rather it is the debts of Europe. Our imports of goods from Europe are so far below our exports of goods to Europe that the difference strikingly exaggerates the figure due our nationals on debt payments from Europe. If we arbitrarily construe trade directly by regions, it is only by an immense increase of imports of merchandise from Europe that we can be paid for our exports of merchandise to Europe and at the same time receive service charges on our

foreign loans to and investments in Europe. It was this fundamental and inherent discrepancy which led far-seeing men like Somary and Bonn to denounce our loans to European countries as abnormal. If we had no foreign investments in Europe, portfolio or direct (disregarding war debts), our excesses of imports of goods from other parts of the world in multangular trade would cover the debt payments due our nationals from all borrowing regions. Or, if our loans and investments in Europe were scattered over the other regions of the world, it is possible that we would naturally accept from them large enough excesses of imports of goods over exports to cover service charges on foreign loans and investments of 10 million dollars. The trouble lies, in this sense, less in the total volume of our foreign investments than in the abnormal localization of part of them in Europe. The divergent case of Canada does not weaken this argument. Canada is a neighbor, with a long frontier and a naturally extensive border trade. Canada looks more to us than to Great Britain for capital imports. We can avoid a future passive balance of merchandise trade (specifically the imports of raw materials, foodstuffs, and feedstuffs) with Canada only by annually increasing our investment in that country, unless the new gold of the expanding mines of Canada comes to this country. In any event, in view of the contiguity, our relation to Canada is no urgent problem.

A broad survey of the background of our foreign trade thus makes it clear that whatever may be the desirability of direct trade agreements on other grounds, the lay of the land of commerce, so to speak, is more naturally in favor of multangular rather than of direct trade. The natural presumption in favor of multangular trade has, however, been (for the time being) discounted in this country in favor of direct trade.

It seems to be the view of the State Department, entirely

orthodox in this regard, that world trade in a restored prosperity ought to recover rapidly, of which the United States ought to reacquire 20 per cent by making a "supreme effort to restore the normal processes and methods and the normal volume of international finance and commerce," to use the words of Secretary Hull in an address to the American Farm Bureau Federation. The relation between growing volume of domestic production and trade and growing volume of export trade involves a circuitous interaction. When exports expand, this increases the volume of production so that the fraction domestically used can be sold at a lower price, which will stimulate demand. When domestic absorption expands, the increase in volume will lower costs and lead to expansion of exports. As total outturn expands, the proportions going to domestic and foreign markets do not remain constant, but both grow with lower prices based on lower costs with larger outlet. To influence foreign trade directly, three prerequisites are needed. These are, in the order of their importance in our view: (a) restoration of monetary relations and exchange processes; (b) removal of various obstacles outside of tariff duties; and (c) lowering of tariff rates, with maintenance of most-favored-nation treatment. We shall return to these prerequisites below.

It is important that Americans appreciate just how we have changed routes at the crossroads. Politicians the world over just now favor bilateral trade agreements on external grounds; economists the world over disapprove of bilateral trade agreements on internal grounds. The politicians do not favor bilateral trade agreements because they favor direct trade against indirect trade; most of them have no ideas on international trade. They favor bilateral trade agreements because at the moment they seem expedient; they are tangible, plausible, and negotiable. Economists disapprove of bilateral trade agreements because they believe in multangular trade and do not believe in direct and channelized trade. Many economists concede that in an emergency, in a period of trade disorganization, it may be expedient to set up artificially direct trade movements; but they regard bilateral trade agreements as a secondary reflection of economic nationalism. In particular, economists feel that if the processes of trade were again set free from artificial controls, the pressing alternative between bilateral trade and multilateral trade would largely and quickly disappear.

Why, now, did the Administration make the decision, quite out of harmony with the traditions of the Democratic party, to establish a policy for promotion of foreign trade mainly through the instrument of bilateral agreements? Without reference to the priority of tariff stabilization over monetary stabilization, why was federal legislation enacted which placed in the hands of the Executive, under stated conditions, the authority to contract trade treaties? Some twenty years ago a Democratic administration under Woodrow Wilson made a comprehensive revision of the tariff in the Underwood Act, which effectuated a sharp reduction in import duties. Now with an overwhelming majority in both houses of Congress, competent bureaus devoted to economics in the Departments of Commerce and Agriculture and a well-organized Tariff Commission, why did not a Democratic administration proceed to enlarge imports of goods to the extent envisaged by Secretary Wallace through a comprehensive lowering of duties by Congressional action, with retention of most-favored-nation treatment? Such lowering of duties could not have been horizontally applied either to specific or to *ad valorem* rates; but they would have been chosen reductions, varying from article to article, selected with reference to internal conditions, but retaining externally the principle of most-favored-nation treatment. The future historian through a study of documents will surely find more adequate explanations than are at present available on the record. But the student of trade will find the explanation of the change of policy largely in the following considerations.

(1) A general revision of the tariff ranks as a plague. The history of the enactment of the Hawley-Smoot, the Fordney, and the Underwood Tariffs was enough to throw dismay into the ranks of industrialists. Such a revision implied a long session of Congress. The Congress contained many novices, who were unqualified to study the tariff and disinclined to break bread, or break lances, with their constituents on the subject. The administration had specific projects of legislation, and a general revision of the tariff looked too much like "old stuff."

(2) The extensive unemployment prevalent in the country made a general overhauling of tariff rates hazardous. Even free traders, at home and abroad, had counselled against radical reduction of tariff duties during a trade cycle; tariff duties might be lowered during a boom, but adjustments ought not to be enforced during a depression. Neutral commentators have in general supported this position. Horizontal lowering of tariff rates is unwise because the effects are unequal, old injustice is not corrected but new injustice is committed, and discrimination is inevitable, which cannot be foreseen but is revealed only by trial and error.

(3) The abnormal and for the most part depreciated currencies of the world made computation of tariff rates insecure or even irrelevant. At the time of the entrance of the new administration most of the countries of the world were struggling with actual or potential undervaluation or overvaluation of the currency. When a currency is overvalued, it is priced on international exchanges at a higher

level than that corresponding to purchasing power within the country itself. This tends to stimulate imports into that country and depresses exports from it. This was the case with Great Britain after return to the gold standard at par in 1925. When a currency is undervalued, it is priced on international exchanges at a lower level than that corresponding to purchasing power in the country itself; this tends to stimulate exports from that country and depress imports into the country. This was the case in France after revaluation of the franc in 1927. These variable over- and undervaluations contribute to disequilibrium between countries, prevent costs from influencing prices and prices from influencing volumes of movement and vice versa, in the normal manner, thus making settlement of balances unforeseeable and difficult. In order to meet such situations, foreign countries had found tariff rates ineffective and had taken recourse to various arbitrary regulations. Under these circumstances, it was obviously not a propitious time to lower protection and expand free trade, on the classical doctrine that free trade means not only free movement of goods, of services, of capital, and of monetary gold, but also of labor, i.e., of immigration.

(4) The commerce of the world was rampant with dumping and subsidies, direct and indirect. With domestic interests almost daily protesting the admission of dumped and subsidized imports of one kind or another, there was obviously no basis of assessment of lower duties as expression of demonstrable (?) differences in production costs. Russia has taught the modern world that a production cost does not, or need not, apply to the individual article but to the system of industry. Our traditional policy on monopoly could not be enforced with coexistence of governmental monopolies abroad.

(5) The practice as well as the principle of most-favored-

nation treatment had gone into eclipse. Already at the time of the meeting of the International Economic Conference in 1927, it was evident that most-favored-nation treatment was being evaded covertly and grotesquely by subterfuge and indirection. This deterioration of international morality has continued, and when the new Secretary of State first officially viewed the horizon of foreign trade he saw violation not only of the spirit but also of the letter of most-favored-nation treatment agreements. Of the several devices for beating this devil about the bush, the use of quotas and barters is perhaps the most ingenious. In a manner at once illogical and perversive, it is covertly held that so long as formal duties and other conditions of importation apply to all outsiders, it is not a violation of most-favored-nation treatment to carry out a barter or to contract for stipulated deliveries of goods between one country and another. By means of numerous devices the evasion of (conditional or unconditional) most-favored-nation treatment is transforming international trade into a form of "racket." Since our tariff policies have always contemplated equal treatment for all, under these circumstances a revision of the tariff, downward or upward, presented few attractions.

(6) Finally, too many bilateral treaties had been contracted abroad for the movement to be disregarded. There were literally hundreds of petty agreements. It was clear that such trade agreements as the Runciman-Roca treaty, the scheme of Imperial preference within the British Empire, and the barter contracts between Danubian and western European countries represented the cue of the play. Our only recourse was to follow the same rules, if possible. It required no argument to make it clear that the Congress could not create bilateral trade agreements by legislation; in the very nature of the transactions, these could be carried out only by the executive branch of the government. In

order to do this, the idea of a general revision of the tariff was scrapped and legislation enacted (the Reciprocal Tariff Act) granting to the Executive under stated conditions the power to contract bilateral trade treaties with individual countries.

But, it will be interjected, if a general revision of the tariff is impossible, why was it not possible through international conferences to secure a lowering of trade barriers? The answer is that this had been tried without results. At the meeting of the World Economic Conference in Geneva in 1927—when the world was still in the New Era and most of the present New Dealers were marching in that procession—a serious attempt was made to secure comprehensive international action (a) towards lowering of tariff rates; (b) towards removal of the various extra-tariff obstacles to trade, ranging all the way from import licenses, blending regulations, and exchange penalties to embargoes; and (c) to a strengthening and general acceptance in spirit and letter of most-favored-nation treatment. This conference was a success in resolutions but a failure in results. The International Wheat Conference of 1931 followed the same course, with the same outcome. It was here that the quota was informally christened as a (bastard) child of most-favored-nation treatment. Numerous small trade conferences, like the "truce-to-tariffs" and the more political than economic attempts to create a "United States of Europe," had the same result. When the World Economic Conference of 1933 met in London, among the principal items on the agenda were reduction of tariff rates, elimination of extra-tariff obstructions, and reaffirmation of most-favored-nation treatment. The conference broke down when a declaration of the President of the United States on domestic monetary policy made it clear to the delegates of all countries that tariff revision could not be approached without preliminary stabilization of money and exchange.

". . . Three courses are then open to a nation that desires to negotiate reciprocal trade agreements. It may refrain from making reciprocal trade agreements in order not to be compelled to extend the benefit of such agreements to high fixed tariff nations with which it has most-favored-nation treaties. It may cancel its most-favored-nation treaties and then proceed to negotiate reciprocal trade agreements. It may by one device or another circumvent its most-favored-nation obligations." (*International Economic Relations,* p. 39.)

Some nations have followed the first course, a few have followed the second, many have followed the third. Widespread disregard for existing most-favored-nation agreements, both devious and open, exists today, especially in Europe.

In summary, unless we, in absolute isolation, are to occupy the position that foreign trade is governed only by tariff rates and most-favored-nation treatment, no other course seems possible than the policy of bilateral trade agreements, so long as the invisible trade relations remain in almost inscrutable disequilibrium. For good or for ill, for the time being the world has deserted the classical doctrine of trade for that of movement of goods and services by negotiation.[1] In Great Britain and in the United States are Victorians who feel that if the British Empire and the United States would stand together, we could "lick the world." This rather complacent reflection, reminiscent of the London clubs, assumes, however, that India and Egypt would go with Britain; also, it disregards the circumstance that however divergent the views of Russia, Japan, and the countries of continental Europe may be in respect to their independent trades, they would join for offense and defense against a policy specifically defined as Anglo-American. And finally, Britain and America have not convinced other countries that

[1] A disillusioned journalist remarked during the negotiation of the Treaty of Versailles that one difference between the United States and the countries of Europe was that Europeans did not believe in their own lies while we believed in ours. Something comparable to this distinction may be expected to develop in the negotiations of the bilateral trade treaties.

they would prefer to "lick the world" in trade rather than "lick" each other. Blood is indeed thicker than water. But history does not show that policy of trade follows the lines of blood; and this is yet to be proved within the British Empire by a successful outcome of Imperial preference.

METHOD OF TARIFF REDUCTION

Within the projected scope of bilateral trade agreements, we still face the important questions of (a) methods of reduction of tariff taxes,[1] (b) retention, modification, or suspension of most-favored-nation treatment, and (c) efforts to secure contractual abolition by others of extra-tariff devices or eventually acceptance by us of such devices in bilateral agreements. Let us consider these in succession.

Proponents of expansion of international trade have an extraordinary belief in the meaning and implication of varying rates of tariff duties on direct imports of goods. As the rate rises, less tends to be imported: with decline in rate, more goods come in. Some appear to view the relation of tariff rate to import volume as corresponding with a straight line; others apparently would picture instead either a concave curve or a convex curve. There are practically no worth-while analytical studies of the question—not because of lack of interest, but because of uncontrollability of the numerous variables which must be measured or ruled out if correlation between tariff rate and import volume is to be established. No topic is more filled with assumption, postulation, predilection, and prejudice than the tariff; to this may be added political misinformation and perversion by inter-

[1] Particularly interested readers are referred to the following: F. A. Southard, *American Industry in Europe* (New York, Houghton, Mifflin & Company, 1931); J. M. Jones, *Tariff Retaliation* (Philadelphia, University of Pennsylvania Press, 1934); J. G. Smith, *Economic Planning and the Tariff* (Princeton, Princeton University Press, 1934); George Pavlovsky, "Planned Economy and Agriculture," *International Review of Agriculture,* January 1934, XXV, 1-48.

ested parties. Nor are these distortions confined to the protectionist side; they are as prevalent on the free trade side.[1] Of factual analysis, there is little which is devoid of special pleading.

Even the determination of comparative production costs of a specified article in two countries, which sounds simple enough, is so complex as to be answerable only over a range and not at a point. Indeed, it may fairly be asserted that the political hypothesis of basing a protective tariff on demonstrated differences in production costs is factually fallacious. No tabulation of production costs takes account of the standard of living; correct and comparable cost accounting is not applicable. It is important to emphasize that the fallacy of "protectionism" based on differences of production costs holds equally for those who, like the Secretary of Agriculture, desire to reduce tariffs in order to stimulate imports, and for those who, like ex-Senator Smoot, have tried by raising the tariff to restrict imports. The hypothesis of tariff duty based on differences of production costs is now almost universally rejected, since it is based on "a principle untenable on general grounds of reasoning and impossible of precise application in practice." [2] It would probably be more difficult to predict what would happen when tariff rates go down than it would be to predict what would happen if tariffs were raised.

Secretary Wallace, it may be remarked, pleads for more extended foreign trade throughout the world, without reference to the question of the respective advantage of a stable internal price level versus a stable foreign exchange rate; this, however, must be settled domestically before any policy

[1] In Geneva is a three-dimensional map, which shows around each country the height of the tariff wall. The implication is that these walls could be knocked down by political hammers, as children knock down toy blocks they have built into walls.

[2] *International Economic Relations,* p. 177.

of expanding foreign trade can be approached. The Secretary of Agriculture has made the following statements:

"A truly practical readjustment of our own tariff policy would involve the careful examination of every product produced in the United States or imported, and the determination of just which of our monopolistic or inefficient industries we are willing to expose to real foreign competition."[1] (*America Must Choose*, pp. 28-29.)

". . . It would seem, therefore, that international planning must include a complete survey, item by item, of all the products that enter into our annual output, and a conscious decision as to which kind of products we might receive in large quantities from abroad, in time of peace, without jeopardizing those industries which we absolutely require in time of war." (p. 18)

"Coming finally to consider a planned middle course in world trade, it would be sensible for us to pause a moment and more closely define our terms. There can be in practice today no such thing as an unmixed nationalist policy, or an unmixed internationalism. In using the term nationalism in this presentation of the American dilemma, I have meant simply to indicate the world trend toward a complete nationalist self-containment. By use of the term internationalism I have meant the opposite trend, toward wider and larger trade, the world over." (p. 26)

What are the implications of such statements? The simplest method of "readjustment" of course would be horizontal reduction of rates between two countries. But the sole recommendation of this procedure is simplicity. Tariff duties are of two kinds—specific and *ad valorem;* a horizontal reduction would have a different meaning with specific and *ad valorem* rates. Protectionists have often enough made the blunder of trying to use horizontal increases as rule; usually the rule was not adhered to, because wire-pulling and log-

[1] This must bring a smile to the faces of old free-trade Democrats like Thomas Walker Page. Just which are the monopolies already marked for attack is not clear, though we may infer that aluminum ware and photographic supplies are particularly under suspicion.

rolling prevent such a rule from being put into practice.[1] When the planned tariff changes, of which we hear so much, come to be drafted for country after country, they will not show horizontal reductions of rates: the reductions will either be according to some sliding scale by classes; or the reductions will be strictly by commodities, without general rule but based only on special considerations. Yardsticks are here illusory.

A sliding scale, by classes, enjoys a certain repute. In some countries, sliding scales and rates apply to different groups, based on various classifications. It is conceivable that tariff reduction might be offered on a sliding scale to correspond with proportion of import to domestic production of the particular article. Not long ago Owen D. Young suggested that American imports be divided into three groups: raw materials, duty-free; luxuries, with varying but high rates; and the large mass of dutiable articles into which American labor in town and country enters largely and which should have varying rates of really protective duty. The high rates in the group of luxuries would be primarily for revenue; the rates in the main group of staple goods would be protective in respect of presumed "costs of production." More elaborate schemes of classification and division have been suggested, by trade associations, reformers, and interested parties, to which little importance is to be attached because the political decisions cannot be based on such classifications.

Lionel Robbins in *The Great Depression* has laid down certain principles which seem to apply to the quotations above.

[1] Judging by the experiences of other countries, a conflict is bound to develop between our farmers who wish to admit imported goods to pay for the half-billion dollars added exports of farm products and our American investors who wish the same goods to pay for service charges on their foreign investments.

". . . A democratic community, at any rate, will attempt to organize production to meet the preferences of consumers. It will not value branches of production as such. It will value them for the various individual satisfactions which they make possible." (p. 148)

". . . A plan which was based upon the preferences of consumers would seek so to distribute its productive resources that the demand for all commodities was satisfied to the same level of urgency. . . .

"The requirement of a rational plan, as we have just seen, is that the factors of production (the land, capital and labour) should be so distributed between the various alternatives of production that no commodity which is produced has less value than the commodities which might have been produced had the factors of production been free for other purposes. . . . How is the planning authority to decide what distribution of resources satisfies this requirement?" (p. 150)

". . . The system would require the complete regimentation of individuals considered as producers. As consumers they could choose between the commodities available." (p. 155)

". . . The actual policy would be equivalent to something worse than high protectionism. . . . It would be a world of geographical syndicalism." (p. 158)

All classifications are based on grounds more or less specious. If the criteria are external, the classification will have little meaning; there will be wire-pulling and log-rolling to get particular commodities into, or out of, a class. If the criteria of classification are internal, the grouping again means little and the dispute in each case is resolved into an individual item. Under these circumstances, it would seem preferable, if a vainglorious attempt is to be made to demolish windmills, to take them as they come and not according to classes.

In short, it will certainly be found with each country that there is no other method than to consider each case on its individual merits or demerits, supported by friends and opposed by enemies, according to some rating (natural or artificial, economic or plausible) as essential, less essential, or non-essential in the American economy. It would resemble a "battle royal." A number of questions would enter into the technical classification of an article as necessary, semi-necessary, semi-dispensable, dispensable, luxurious, and "exotic." Whether the raw material were indigenous or imported would be germane. The age of the industry would have some bearing; also, whether monopolized. The location and political complexion of the capitalists and workers would have influence. The location, political complexion, and purchasing power of the consumers would need to be looked into, but would probably be glossed with adjectives. In some cases, suspension or partial shut-down of certain plants would involve other industries favorably or unfavorably; but in other instances no such collateral effects might be forthcoming. Even free traders admit that after a certain lapse of time the difficulties of readjustment may outweigh the advantages of a change in itself desirable; but the New Dealers are not so easily affrighted by difficulties of adjustments. It has usually been so much easier to put a duty on, or raise it, than to lower it or take it off. If we were living in a so-called "age of scarcity," a schedule of reductions might not appear so difficult; but in a so-called "age of surplus," where outlet is primary and capacity secondary, decisions to reduce are different and very difficult. In the case of agricultural products, the current systems of crop rotation, climatic influences, hazards, the dependence on mechanization and relations to submarginal land would be important points, among others. How would the various farm products participate in the added 500 million dollars of exports? Ever in the background would be lurking the shadows of substitution and replacement.

In the past half-century we have had five major campaigns of wire-pulling and log-rolling over tariffs: the McKinley and the Dingley tariffs of the 'nineties, the Underwood tariff of 1913, the Fordney tariff of 1922, and the Hawley-Smoot tariff of 1930. All the wire-pulling and log-rolling by politicians, capitalists, industrialists, and labor organizations would be repeated (perhaps only in miniature) in the discussion of every single commodity involved in the plan to lower the tariff in order to enlarge the imports of merchandise. Little wonder that the administration wanted changes to be made under Executive decision and not by Congressional action. But the problem remains the same between two countries as toward all countries.

The Secretary of Agriculture explicitly recognizes the difficulty:

> "A truly practical readjustment of our own tariff policy would involve the careful examination of every product produced in the United States or imported, and the determination of just which of our monopolistic or inefficient industries we are willing to expose to real foreign competition. This problem should be approached from the point of view of a long-time national plan which we are willing to follow for at least 20 or 30 years, even if some of our friends get hurt, and howl continuously to high heaven." (*America Must Choose,* pp. 28-29.)
>
> ". . . In such a struggle, all cannot be winners." (p. 29)
>
> "There will be actual pain, from dislocations in the business structure, and psychological pain from dislocations of traditional attitudes, and from denials of the traditional American opportunity to rule or misrule one's own business in one's own way, regardless of general consequences; whatever course we choose." (p. 30)

Bravely spoken, but naïvely. The position of the Secretary is essentially one of selected protection [1] and selected free

[1] The social planners evidently predicate the non-existence of infant industries in the historical sense. Presumably all of our industries were infants under the McKinley tariff. But the negotiators are certain to learn that if the infant-industry argument has any validity new infant industries arise in every decade.

trade, with planned lower tariffs as trend, at home and abroad.

RECIPROCAL TARIFF CHANGES OF FOREIGN COUNTRIES

Our adjustments are merely one side of the picture; the foreign countries must also make reciprocal adjustments.

"It should be recognized that our surplus problems here in the United States, and the resulting necessity of keeping parts of our factories idle and withdrawing acreage, or of widening foreign markets, or of doing these things in combination, is really part of a world surplus problem. This country has more industrial as well as more agricultural capacity than it needs for home consumption. Surplus capacity in industry shows up mainly in unemployment, rather than in a persistent accumulation of commodities; but in all branches of our economic life there is an identical tendency for production to outrun consumption. Other nations have just the same trouble, as we know from the prevalence of unemployment and dole systems throughout the world." (*America Must Choose,* p. 30.)

There is the rub of another color, to use a mixed Hibernianism. The word "bilateral" in commercial reciprocity treaties purports to designate, but really hides, the difficulty. When we select an American industry to be contracted, in order to increase imports of merchandise, in effect by treaty we select in a foreign country an industry to be expanded; and we may indeed have to select countries in which such expansion is to occur. Anyone having experience in international economic conferences recognizes the tenuousness and deviousness of such collective negotiations. Negotiations between two countries would appear to have more directness, it is true; but they suffer from indecision necessarily present on each side, due to the fact that there are several or many (or *n*th) parties to be kept in mind. That is, one bilateral negotiation is contingent on several others, in effect if not in drafting. *A* will make commercial adjustments by treaty with *B*, but this action by *B* is contingent on another treaty between *B* and *C*, just as *A's* action with *B* is contingent on another action of *A* with *C*. Bilateral treaties in the sense of the present movement must be so developed on our part as to adapt them to corresponding treaties with many countries; thereafter they must be adapted to the treaties between exporting countries; and finally, these must be induced to have their treaties with importing countries adapted to ours. The bilateral trade agreements involve and imply a regimentation of producers and consumers in this country, a planned economy in so far as this is to be secured through control of exports and imports. Clearly, this also is to be assumed for the foreign side.[1]

Secretary Wallace seems to have deep faith in bilateral trade negotiations. There are indeed a number of successful ones (depending on what is "success" and to whom it accrues), as in the case of the Runciman-Roca treaty, from which the United Kingdom emerged, with "the smile on the face of the tiger." But there are grounds for believing that the successful bilateral treaties cited abroad have been the best selections. We have as yet no experience. It seems likely, certainly possible, that when we undertake simultaneously to conduct bilateral treaties with many countries, and they do so with one another, the net outcome for each will be about the same as would be expected in an international economic conference. Bilateral trade treaties may fairly be called the bicker-and-dicker method of trade promotion. Success of negotiations will depend on what the countries are prepared to offer and accept; if we offer added markets, name the goods we desire, and hold out the lure of a growing negative

[1] Is it perhaps proposed to curtail exports (for example, automobiles) to a country unless that country imports additional cotton from us? It is one thing to import more manufactures in order subsequently to export more farm products; it is quite a different thing to export less manufactures unless foreign countries first accept more farm products.

balance of American merchandise trade in return for a foreign outlet for a certain amount of cotton, wheat, lard, and tobacco (Californians will not forget raisins and prunes), we shall probably get rid of these products, but at a price paid in our country by the urban population and farmers not engaged in growing the four crops mentioned. It was said of Sir John Blount that he entered business interviews with a Bible in one hand and a prospectus in the other, but neither hand knew what the other was doing. In a respectful comparison, it may be said of Secretary Wallace that he approaches a bilateral commercial treaty with a Bible in one hand and agricultural exports in the other; *and* each hand knows what the other is doing.

Quotas. In the recent experience of the world, the most promising (acquisitive) method is that of allocation of quotas. Quotas, of course, must be negotiated by the Executive, not passed by the Congress or Parliament. The method of quotas is brutal but positive. Quotas take diverse forms: quotas may be in specific amounts, in stipulated percentages, in *ad valorem* units—each from the side of the deliverer and of the taker. We select the list of commodities whose exports we wish to expand, let us say according to the "planned middle course" of Secretary Wallace, to the extent of some added 500 million dollars in farm products. We fix the planned surpluses to be disposed of—the quantities of wheat, cotton, lard and cured pork, tobacco, raisins, prunes, apples, and such other farm products as may in the interval have climbed the political ladder to the dignity of "crops demanding export relief" at "decent" prices. In a round-table conference, held in a star chamber, the 500 million added dollars will be split among these commodities, using either current prices or the "decent" prices to which Secretary Wallace looks forward. Then the appropriate department of the government (or horse-trading agency) exploring the world to seek customers takes up the negotiation on a more or less barter basis. Illustrations are as follows: Finland will pledge herself to take so much lard and wheat if we take so much newsprint and other paper. France will take so much tobacco if we take so much wine. Germany will take so much lard if we take so much potash. Japan will take so much wheat and tobacco if we take so much raw silk and textile tissues. China will take so much wheat if we take so much tung oil and human hair. Italy will take so much wheat if we take so much olive oil. Norway will take so much wheat and lard if we take so much dried fish and nitrate. The United Kingdom will take so much wheat and bacon if we take so much steel. Perhaps Australia and California will swap raisins during the reversed seasons. To some countries we have little to offer—for example, South Africa and Australia have little use for our agricultural products in exchange for their wool. Negotiations may become difficult, even when making benevolent presents. If the countries with which we are negotiating happen to sell to us more than they buy from us and have thus a natural balance of dollar exchange (there are 45 such countries), bartering will be made more easy. But if they happen to sell us less than they buy from us (there are 66 such countries), bartering will be very difficult. Much of course depends on how "decent" are the prices we are prepared to pay for the goods obtained in return. With some countries, the negotiations will resemble shipwrecked men swapping jackknives on a desert island; with other countries, the negotiations will resemble flat-dwellers taking in one another's washing; with others, it will look like a tenderfoot entering a faro game in a mining camp; but with still others, the negotiations will be between high-minded and competent civil servants intent on bilateral equity. If, as, and when we have succeeded in thus disposing of an added amount of agricultural products to the extent desired, we can then lower the tariff rate on the specified commodities which are to be accepted in return for them, the "planned inflow of foreign goods." That is, the allocation by quotas comes first and the tariff changes are sequential.

One must resist the temptation to enlarge on individual illustrations of anomalies. Holland affords an excellent, if almost ludicrous example of the incongruities sometimes inherent in bilateral trade treaties. In recent years Americans have gone into the raising of bulbs, to the injury of Dutch producers whose soil and climate are peculiarly adapted to this specialty. More recently, Holland has gone in for wheat raising, to which her soil is not well adapted. Suppose, now, in a trade agreement (it being conceded that we do not need to quarantine Dutch bulbs and Holland does not need to quarantine American wheat) we agree to take X amounts of her bulbs and she agrees to take X amounts of our wheat. Only a few countries can offer us bulbs, but many countries can offer Holland wheat, and these countries have no use for bulbs. Suppose, now, Argentina, having no use for Dutch bulbs, still offers Holland wheat at 20 cents a bushel below the American price. Is America to subsidize the exporters of wheat, or is Holland to subsidize the consumers of wheat? A neat illustration of the method of bilateral negotiations is to be seen in the relations of the United Kingdom and Australia. The United Kingdom, in effect, declines to accord to Australia the free entrance of beef granted to that dominion in the Ottawa Agreement, while on her side Australia declines to grant to British textiles the favorable terms of admission due her under the same Ottawa Agreement. If mother country and dominion cannot get together under an Empire preference, what chance to get together is there for two countries with different languages, histories, traditions, and resources? Our chemical industry was a direct product of the war and then represented a sign of American independence; is it now to be called exotic or monopolistic? Is lard to be swapped for chemicals?

Finally, the negotiations will depend, perhaps to a crucial extent, on whether loans as well as commodities are represented. If the borrowers and lenders of the net-debtor and net-creditor countries are permitted to take part, then the negotiations will inevitably become more difficult—since, to use a bull, the shadow of the invisible items of trade will darken the outlines of the visible items. Just now bondholders here are under a cloud, and must not disturb reciprocal changes of goods. But later, borrowers in net-debtor countries and lenders in net-creditor countries will try to "horn in" on the negotiations. As a matter of course, nothing else could be expected.[1] The individual borrowers, as well as the governments, in the net-debtor countries do not share the peculiar political stigma which for the time being attaches to the lenders in one particular net-creditor country, namely the United States. The borrowers in the net-debtor countries have obligations to other net-creditor countries quite as important as, or more so than, their obligations to us. We may feel now inclined to disregard long-term invisible items in the bilateral treaty negotiations and confine the agreement solely to visible items. But we may be sure the other net-creditor countries will not take this position. And it strikes us as equally certain that the net-debtor countries will find no incentive to divorce the visible from the invisible items in their international accounts. The bonds will be brothers of the quotas.

In the plan proposed, it seems to be taken for granted

[1] Sooner or later, countries feel forced to choose between visible and invisible claims. For example, Argentina has for the time being chosen to declare that the imports of a foreign country must provide sufficient exchange to cover Argentine obligations to that country before exchange can be used to cover exports from that country to Argentina.

that initial tariff changes will automatically start a train of secondary adaptations which will result in the increase in added imports contemplated. As we view the post-war history of international trade, this hope is illusory. Most European countries have learned this and now place their reliance on positive quotas, rather than on automatic and competitive adjustments following tariff changes. The policy of the United Kingdom within the Empire, as well as without, is now based on quotas. Certainly, if the other major countries adopt quotas, we must follow; if the other major countries were placing their reliance on tariff changes, then we could follow. But for us to place our reliance on tariff changes, while other countries place their reliance on quotas, is simply to invite open failure in the effort to dispose of our surplus crops. Only time, trial and error, can tell whether these surpluses are to be disposed of by quotas; but certainly this seems now to be the only positive method. In a sense, quotas are a polite name for barter; the treaty is but the envelope.

At this point enters the reform philosophy of the New Deal. As described above, the bilateral trade agreements could be negotiated by any "hard-boiled" Old Dealer. Indeed, the bilateral treaties between other countries have been negotiated by Old Dealers, with the sharpness of traditional trade practice. But the philosophy of the New Deal lays down two new provisions: first, the development must contribute not merely to enlargement of American exports but also to the predicated balance in this country between town and country, between regions and between classes, within agriculture and within industry; second, the New Dealers in our negotiations must seek out New Dealers in the foreign delegations and endeavor to have the trade agreements contribute in those countries to the same reform, the predicated balance between town and country, between regions and between classes. The purpose of the trade agreements is to secure "proper balance between American exports and imports." We take it the term "proper balance" implies further a proper balance between the imports and exports of the other party to the reciprocal treaty. To this end, it may become necessary to raise as well as to lower tariffs. Within a country we plan a fairer division of the national dividend; between countries we plan a fairer division of the total outturn of goods and services, by means of bilateral trade agreements.

How are these objectives to be simultaneously sought without continuous compromises between more or less vested interests in the countries concerned? The social planners assume that where competition fails to bring about decision, or arrives at inequitable decisions, planning would make prompt and equitable decisions. It is one thing to reduce tariffs in order to stimulate imports to correct an abnormal balance of international trade; it is a different thing to use increased imports to achieve an internal economic balance; these may not be antagonistic and may indeed be complementary, but they are not identical. In negotiation of trade treaties we must avoid the tactical assumption that international politics can be replaced by international economics. It is difficult within a country for economics to replace politics; it is much more difficult to do so between countries. Our bilateral treaties are to promote the cooperatively good life in this country and also the same ideal in the other countries. This of course may look to an outsider like interference into the private affairs of foreign countries. On this New Deal philosophy no capitalistic state could negotiate a trade treaty with Soviet Russia. Secretary Wallace regards the desire of all countries at all times to export more goods than they import as a consequence in each country of "maldistribution of income." Since it is the major purpose of the New Deal to correct maldistribution of income in this country, our bilateral trade agreements must be designed to accomplish this also for foreign countries, as well as for ourselves. A project of governmentally planned balanced economy would seem to imply something similar in a foreign country, if commerce between the two is to remain active. A planned economy in one country and a competitive economy in another would tend towards economic nationalism in the second country, since the results of planned economy in the first country would have the effect of indirect subsidy of exports. The obligation so to conduct trade agreements is not only implicit in the philosophy of the New Deal but is indeed both implied and expressly stated by Secretary Wallace.[1] There has always been a general understanding among diplomats that treaty makers should not take advantage of the negotiators of other countries; but a positive program of reform in the foreign country is new in the theory of commercial treaties. The bilateral agreements we have made do not seem to have given us abroad much reputation as a good neighbor. In a leader in *The Economist* of December 1, 1934 (pp. 1022-23), stands the following:

> ". . . Negotiations for reciprocal tariff concessions have been conducted with a number of States, and with some of them, notably Cuba, treaties have been concluded. But the President has applied to these negotiations the principles of the Yankee horse-trader rather than those of the good neighbour. . . . The New Deal, so far from making the United States a 'good neighbour' in the economic sense, has hitherto made her an even worse neighbour than in the 'twenties."

But to ascribe the tactics to the President personally is not fair.

[1] According to the Secretary, international trade is a manifestation of religion. In one of the sentimental expressions in *America Must Choose* which remind one of Uncle Henry's Bible lessons in *Wallace's Farmer,* it is suggested that realization of the international idea of trade, in the spiritual sense of the term, would represent a fulfilment of the "vision of Isaiah"—an opinion on trade that doubtless will be generally acclaimed by the descendants of the prophets.

NUMBER AND SCOPE OF TREATIES

The number of bilateral treaties presents an intriguing inquiry. The major countries must be covered, but all political units need not be included. One hundred and eleven countries have their foreign commerce reported in *Foreign Commerce and Navigation of the United States,* issued by the Department of Commerce. Of these one hundred and eleven trading countries, forty-five sell to the United States more than they buy from us, and sixty-six buy from us more than they sell to us. Of these one hundred and eleven trading countries, sixty-six were registered in membership at the World Economic Conference in 1933. Even this number, however, is far too large to be included in a comprehensive scheme of bilateral treaties; the list can be reduced to thirty-seven, including the United States.

One by one, these thirty-six other countries can be shown to be more or less indispensable to the United States, directly or indirectly, in their trading relations with us and with one another; all need to be included in order to make the bilateral treaties effective. In North America are Canada, Cuba, and Mexico. In South America are Argentina, Brazil, Chile, Colombia, Peru, and Uruguay. In Europe are Belgium, Czechoslovakia, Denmark, Finland, France, Germany, Hungary, Italy, Netherlands, Norway, Poland, Portugal, Rumania, Russia, Spain, Sweden, Switzerland, Turkey, the United Kingdom, and Yugoslavia. In Asia are British India, China, and Japan. In Oceania are Australia and New Zealand. In Africa are Egypt and the Union of South Africa. Of these countries, to twenty-one we sell more than we buy from them; to fifteen we sell less than we buy from them. Of the thirty-seven countries, six are net-creditor countries, the rest are net-debtor countries. The trading dilemma of the other net-creditor countries is of one order; the trading dilemma of the many net-debtor countries is of a different order. Of the net-debtor countries, the trading dilemma of those with a natural balance of dollar exchange is of one order; that of those with a natural deficit of dollar exchange is of another order. Each of these thirty-seven countries would need to contract a bilateral treaty with the other thirty-six, according to the hypothesis consistently advanced by Secretary Wallace. The maximum of such treaties within the thirty-seven countries would be over six hundred treaties, —certainly an appalling total, which would serve to eliminate unemployment in diplomatic services for years. The net effect of these hundreds of commercial treaties would be in the direction of that number of direct trade channelizations; equation of accounts through multangular trade would thereafter become much more difficult. Many will smile at this number and regard the computation as premeditated satire; but if one will try to reduce the number, the gaps will promptly become apparent. Of all the planned organizations ever conceived in the international sense, this would be the most stupendous. And yet Secretary Wallace remarks:

"The method of reciprocal trade, . . . makes no sales without providing opportunities for the buyers to pay the bill." (*America Must Choose,* p. 20.)

". . . It is easy for foreign trade experts to talk about triangular and polyangular trade and thus avoid the necessity of forming clear-cut trade deals with a given country. But if we are going to trend toward internationalism, it seems to me that the only safe way to handle it is to conclude both loans and trade deals with foreign countries as nearly as possible on a bi-lateral basis and not get involved in the confusing complexities of triangular and polyangular trade with which the economists like to mess up our minds." (p. 28)

To this gratuitous "slam" at the economists it is warranted to make the rejoinder that it is not the economists who "mess up" the mind of the Secretary of Agriculture, but the events of a century of active world trade between the Napoleonic Wars and the World War. Perhaps, however, the Secretary agrees with Henry Ford that "history is the bunk."

We have called bilateral trade negotiations the bicker-and-dicker method. Even after discussions and technical decisions are taken out of Congress and transferred to committees of the State Department detailed for negotiations of bilateral commercial treaties, the difficulties are thereby reduced but not evaded. Consider that a committee room is a small forum and not a star chamber: all that will have been changed is the substitution of a small forum for a large forum. But the wire-pulling and log-rolling will operate intensively on a small committee, just as it would operate extensively on a large Congress. The experiences with the Board of Trade in Great Britain since the war, in the adjudication of special tariff questions submitted to it under the tariff regulation of that country, do not lend assurance to the view that committees under the State Department would be able to act solely as trained civil servants, technical specialists, competent statisticians, and prophets of history. Negotiation of bilateral commercial treaties as a Cabinet function, or exclusive task of the State Department directly under the Executive, even with a distinguished Secretary Hull, is not a fool-proof substitute for foolish Congressional action; it may turn out to be little more than the substitution of a silent forum for a noisy one. Nevertheless, it is the only way to negotiate commercial treaties.

In any event, the inherent defect of bilateral negotiation will be continuously felt, even if our policy dispenses with the principle of most-favored-nation treatment. Still larger will be the difficulties if we try to maintain the spirit and letter of unconditional or even conditional most-favored-nation treatment. Bilateral treaties deal with direct trade and imply a channelization of import and export movements. A series of bilateral treaties will tend to resemble one of the detective stories in which each of the many chapters is written by an author who has not seen the other chapters. Adequate adaptation of bilateral treaties to one another will be found so difficult as to be almost impracticable, as is already coming to be the experience within Europe. And yet coordination is predicated. The purpose of the policy is to enlarge foreign trade; but the experience of a century teaches that expanding commerce depends not on stimulation of direct trade but on the growth of multangular trade.[1]

Are the negotiating countries supposed to use the leverage of a natural balance of exchange? Brazil has a heavy natural balance of dollar exchange; ought this to be claimed by the United States as preferentially applicable to imports from this country?[2] Great Britain virtually did so in the treaty with Argentina. But if, in all the bilateral treaties, each country in such advantageous position utilized the naturally favorable balance of exchange as a leverage to enforce movement of goods, we would find our country at a net disadvantage if we had an active balance of merchandise trade. Since we factually have a passive balance of merchandise trade, negotiations will be favored by that circumstance. Such a system needs no bilateral treaties, but makes the consumers of a country the virtual denominators of its export trade. Historically considered, to use a natural balance of exchange as an instrument for future pressure on trade deserves to be ranked as a form of diplomatic coercion. Such

[1] Excellent statements on direct and multangular trade are to be found in *International Economic Relations*, pp. 72-85, and in the report of A. H. Hansen, *ibid.*, pp. 146-57 and 164-73.

[2] It cannot fail to become manifest in our southern states that while the treaty with Brazil favors the expansion of export of manganese from that country to ours, there is nothing designed to arrest the expansion of growing of cotton in Brazil, to the ultimate injury of our future export trade in cotton.

pressure may become a "racket." An interesting suggestion is to be found in *International Economic Relations:*

". . . Indeed it would be sufficient in the case of many countries if we offered tariff concessions in return for an agreement with the other country that a certain large fixed proportion of dollar exchange would be allocated to the purchase of American goods, leaving it to the foreign country's importers to settle for themselves what American goods. . . . The foreign country would determine for itself how it would let the American goods in, whether by lowering certain tariffs, by assigning quotas to America, by abrogating embargoes, or what not. . . . We would be interfering less in the internal affairs of another power and we would not be interfering with triangular trade as much as we would if we insisted on straight barter." (p. 84)

In one place Secretary Wallace remarks:

". . . Even foreign loans might involve a certain amount of planning. . . . Rather consciously (?) Great Britain placed its loans with a long-time program of imports and an exchange of goods in view." (*America Must Choose,* p. 2; question mark ours.)

Are we to understand that Secretary Wallace contemplates the direct control of the individual private lender in one country and the individual private borrower in another, by the two governments, in the attempt to make the new invisible items fit into a predicated balance of merchandise trade of the two countries? Are we to understand that the Secretary contemplates not merely the possible use of embargo on foreign loans, but also embargo on construction in foreign countries of subsidiary plants of American manufacturers, and of public utilities and other service industries? Yet he would be supported in this by the experienced Basil P. Blackett, who remarks that "laissez-faire in international lending will clearly not work either in theory or in practice in this twentieth-century world." [1]

[1] *Planned Money* (New York, D. Appleton & Co., 1933), p. 167.

A question of consistency arises: should the net-creditor or net-debtor relation of one country to another impose on their channelized trade a corresponding balance of merchandise trade? Canada is a heavy net-debtor to the United States; should we accord to Canada a positive balance of merchandise trade with us? The United States is a net-debtor to Great Britain; should Great Britain accord to us a positive balance of merchandise trade with her? If we insist that the countries creditor to us shall take their payments directly in goods, are we willing for the countries debtor to us to make their payments directly in goods? A little statistical browsing through trade reports will make it clear that it is difficult enough for reciprocal trade to be channelized as mere exchanges of goods for goods, without attempting also to channelize debt or investment payments being made with goods. Quite certainly, debt and investment payments can hardly be effected except through multilateral trade. A country like Canada cannot pay her service charges to this country [1] through direct trade, but only through multilateral trade; Brazil, on the contrary, can easily pay her obligations to us through direct trade.

"Horse-trading" is confined to goods a country can dispense with; it can hardly include necessaries. It could hardly be a trading concession on our part to promise to take so much coffee from Brazil, so much silk from Japan, so much jute from India, or so much nickel from Canada —we would take these goods in any event because

[1] Foreign investments of Canadian nationals now stand close to two billion dollars, of which over half are in the United States. American investments in Canada stand close to four billion dollars. Therefore, the United States is net creditor to Canada to the extent of some three billion dollars, on which Canadians owe us annually for interest and dividends around 150 million dollars. Nevertheless, our balance of merchandise trade with Canada is active—in 1931 to the extent of 130 million dollars, in 1933 only 26 million dollars. Under these circumstances, and considering the similarity in resources in southern Canada and northern United States, it will not be surprising to learn that the United States and Canada find themselves unable to arrange a bilateral trade agreement.

we need them. In effect, one cannot swap needs against choices.

Also, the observing reader of *America Must Choose* will note on careful perusal that it presents but inadequate recognition of the importance of invisible items in influencing the movement of visible items in world trade. Put in another way, the reader is left to infer that if tariffs were lowered and other regulatory impedimenta to imports removed, foreign trade would revive significantly in consequence of mere relations of supply and demand. The reader is not warned that such reciprocal exchanges of goods would be contingent also, perhaps even controlled for the most part, for an indefinite term of years on monetary policies and variable exchange relations. In short, the presentation of the Secretary of Agriculture does not seem adequately to recognize that the reaction between producers' surpluses and consumers' choices may be determined by monetary as well as by commodity influences.[1]

As is revealed in *America Must Choose,* the Secretary of Agriculture retains an almost naïve interpretation of the importance of comparative advantage. In the industrial revolution comparative advantage represented the possession of coal and iron by the countries lying along the English Channel and the North Sea, exploited by the scientific genius of the Anglo-Saxon mind. The more recent phenomenon of dispersion of urban industry represents a rewriting of the doctrine of comparative advantage. It may indeed be remarked of the views of the Secretary of Agriculture, as was remarked of the Bradbury Committee of 1924 by J. M.

[1] In *Agriculture's Interest in America's World Trade,* issued in January 1935 by the Division of Information of the AAA, presenting "questions and answers on a vital aspect of America's future," with a foreword by Secretary Wallace, are fifty-five specific questions and answers, not one of which deals with internal devaluation and revaluation of currencies, depreciation of currencies abroad, and disequilibrium in foreign exchange rates as factors influencing foreign commerce.

Keynes, that the prevailing views assumed a mobility of labor and a competitive economy which no longer existed. The acts of trading are based upon that conception of the profit economy which regards a preponderating partition of the dividend of exchange as the natural objective of commerce. The Secretary of Agriculture may find it fitting to throw over the relations of farm and factory a spiritual mantle of cooperation; when once such a mantle has become an accustomed garment in domestic relations, it will be time to try it in international relations.

We regard such negotiations, in the number and amplitude necessary, as politically impracticable. Decades were required to secure general assent to most-favored-nation treatment. The internal political power and discipline necessary for such external negotiations does not exist in the large majority of these countries. There is no adequate mechanism of enforcement. A few recalcitrant countries can nullify the effect of a series of bilateral treaties otherwise successfully consummated. For years the French delegates have presented similar omnibus proposals to international conferences; but there was no indication that those delegates could put those proposals through their own Chamber of Deputies. In his apparent confidence that the Cabinets of other governments may be ranked with the Cabinet of which he is a member, Secretary Wallace shows his personal unfamiliarity with foreign affairs. It is to be kept in mind that in most countries the tactics and strategy of political obstruction are superior to those of advancement.

In *New Frontiers,* however, Secretary Wallace reveals what appears to be a beginning lack of confidence in the future of tariff bargaining. This is indicated in the following:

". . . I am wondering if it will be possible for the President to push his tariff bargaining so rapidly that foreign purchasing power will be sufficiently enlarged five or ten years hence to enable us to do away completely with agricultural control. . . . I fear, as I look at the nations which formerly took most of our agricultural products, that they may never again buy as much from us as they did before the war, during the war and immediately after the war.

"I look at Germany and Italy which are now mature debtor nations, and realize that because of this fact, it is much more necessary for them now to grow a large percentage of their own food than they did before the war. Many of our former good customers now have the problem of learning to act as a debtor nation must act, just as we have the problem of learning to act as a creditor nation must act. A debtor nation must sooner or later export more than it imports, and the problem is to discover just which of goods formerly imported can now be produced at home." (pp. 78-79)

". . . The hard fact is that so many of the nations of Europe are now in debt, and in the long run, debtor nations find it impossible to import goods as freely as creditor nations can." (pp. 81-82)

Secretary Wallace is elsewhere most meticulous in pointing out the difficulties and at times sounds a very pessimistic note on prospect of the operation; if he were a politician, one would suspect him of preparing a so-called "alibi." At the same time, *New Frontiers* is not an emendation of *America Must Choose*.

The number of special trade arrangements contracted during recent years between two countries is really astonishing. Something like thirty-five foreign countries have formal control of formal exchange, and most of the others have informal control invoked on occasions. It is understood that over four hundred special arrangements between countries are in operation, including barters, exchange ratios, clearing arrangements, quotas, special tariffs, and various forms of commercial treaties. Most countries have become convinced that for the time being they must control imports and/or exports of goods or choose between artificially pegged foreign exchange rates or artificially pegged internal prices. Once under way in the movement, a country tends to use all of these, on occasions, in relations to individual countries.

MOST-FAVORED-NATION TREATMENT

In the *Final Report* of the World Economic Conference held in Geneva in May 1927 stands the following recommendation:

"(1) The Conference therefore considers that the mutual grant of unconditional most-favoured-nation treatment as regards Customs duties and conditions of trading is an essential condition of the free and healthy development of commerce between States, and that it is highly desirable in the interest of stability and security for trade that this treatment should be guaranteed for a sufficient period by means of commercial treaties.

"(2) While recognising that each State must judge in what cases and to what extent this fundamental guarantee should be embodied in any particular treaty, the Conference strongly recommends that the scope and form of the most-favoured-nation clause should be of the widest and most liberal character and that it should not be weakened or narrowed either by express provisions or by interpretation. . . .

"The Conference has further considered the question of the best means of ensuring that full effect be given to the stipulations of commercial treaties. While recognising that, in the main, confidence must be reposed in the good faith of the contracting parties to fulfil their engagements, it is also clear that the possibility of recourse to a suitable arbitral or judicial procedure may often furnish the means of avoiding or settling difficulties whether of interpretation or of application." [1]

It is to no purpose to sketch the development of this principle of international trade.[2] It is based largely upon three considerations:

[1] League of Nations, *The World Economic Conference, Geneva, May 1927, Final Report,* C. E. I. 44 (Geneva, League of Nations, 1927), pp. 34-35.

[2] Over fifty commercial treaties contain provision for most-favored-nation treatment, conditional or unconditional.

(1) The broad equity of commerce is advanced by having general trade privileges open to all and allowing special privileges to none. There is both a positive and negative side to the case of special privilege. The positive side implies a special favor; the negative side means discrimination. Gradually the trading countries of the world have come to recognize that the development of commerce, as well as the interests of peace, are advanced by the principle of equity—the withdrawal of favoritism and the abolition of discrimination.

(2) A tariff is an objective and practicable system so long as the *ad valorem* and specific rates apply to all imports. Otherwise, different c.i.f. duty-paid prices appear on the domestic market of the importing country. When domestic producers have to meet different prices on comparable goods coming in from different countries, the normal relation of costs and prices is disturbed. The producers of certain regions may be favored, those of other regions injured. If the different import rates are reflected in final prices, some consumers are favored and others disfavored. In short, computable import prices depend upon unvarying tariff rates on identical commodities from different countries. The policy of most-favored-nation treatment has had the effect of securing uniformity between countries and has held tariff wars in leash. This policy must now be scrapped, if the bilateral treaties are to get anywhere on their way.[1] But the result between some countries is certain to be the opposite of that desired. Quotas are inherently provocative.

(3) From the exporting side, dumping and subsidy are the inevitable secondary results of unequal tariff rates in

[1] For example, the denunciation by Germany of the commercial treaty with the United States (which will terminate the present trade arrangement between the two countries in October 1935, unless modified by some new agreement in the interim) was based on objection to the most-favored-nation treatment clause. It is understood the clause is to be released.

importing countries. These either replace, intensify, or weaken the uneven import-duty rates, as the case may be. In the final analysis, the same unclarity emerges on the export side that is evolved through unequal duties on the import side.

In the broad sense, most-favored-nation treatment is a prerequisite to that equilibrium in the trade between countries in which costs, prices, and movements of goods and services interact to the advantage of both sides. In the forty-eight states of our country we have absolute most-favored-nation treatment; differences in prices depend upon types and qualities of goods and varying costs of transportation and distribution. The principle of most-favored-nation treatment in international commerce is essentially the ideal of applying between the countries of the world the same equality in the market which exists within the United States.[1]

The distinctions now held abroad in political circles between so-called conditional and so-called unconditional most-favored-nation treatment are for the most part fictitious or evasive.[2] The convenient notion that merchandise trade

[1] The following is an excerpt from a speech of Francis B. Sayre, Assistant Secretary of State, at the Round Table of World Trade and Merchant Marine, Chamber of Commerce of the United States, Washington, April 29 to May 2:

"The difficulty is that every preference granted exclusively to a single nation constitutes a discrimination against the trade of over fifty other nations. There can be no preference without discrimination. Any policy of trading in exclusive preferences means by its very terms and in its essence a policy of widespread discriminations. And discriminations lead inescapably to retaliations. Retaliations lead to trade warfare and the building up of new and still higher trade barriers. No nation desiring a permanent increase of trade can afford to adopt a policy of bargaining for preferences.

"Equality of treatment to all, tested and proved by three-quarters of a century of experience, constitutes the very cornerstone of American commercial policy, and is the only possible basis for the expansion and development of triangular trade upon which American commerce vitally depends."

[2] The United States followed a conditional most-favored-nation treatment from the beginning until 1922, when we adopted the unconditional most-favored-nation treatment.

between countries based on "exchange clearing arrangements" is in conformity with most-favored-nation treatment strikes us as sophistry.

It is understood to be the policy of our government to maintain the integrity of the letter of the treaties granting most-favored-nation treatment to other countries. Certainly from the Department of State, presided over by Secretary Hull, will emerge no trade agreement which covertly or indirectly nullifies most-favored-nation agreement.[1] We fancy, however, that the doctrine is not so sacred in the Department of Agriculture. Presumably the letter of the policy is clear; conceivably, however, there is latitude in interpretation. For example, consider the importation of sugar. The treaty with Cuba grants to the island preferential duties in return for preferences extended to American products entering the island. Presumably any country extending the same preferences to us would receive the same preferences extended to Cuba. At the same time we have a special law passed by Congress, the Jones-Costigan Act, which vests in the Secretary of Agriculture the power to allocate imports of sugar. As we construe this act, it is conceivable that a country like Java might offer sugar duty-paid and have the importation rejected as contrary to the allocation of import sugars to stipulated sources established formally by the Secretary of Agriculture. Whether this stands in front of the door of violation of the spirit of most-favored-nation treatment or actually on the threshold, we are unprepared to say.

This much, however, is quite clear: if our country respects the spirit of most-favored-nation treatment in the drafting and execution of bilateral trade agreements, this

[1] The drafts of the proposed bilateral treaties with Belgium and Brazil secure reciprocal tariff reductions, with maintenance of most-favored-nation treatment, without quotas or barters. This is sound classical doctrine, but it is not the New Deal in foreign commerce "by a long shot." These agreements are very different from most of the recent trade agreements between countries in Europe.

will tend to make nugatory the operations of these treaties. In the long run, the United States cannot follow most-favored-nation treatment on our side of the bilateral trade agreements, while the other contracting parties violate it on the other side. In the treaty with Brazil, which may be taken as representative of the policy of the State Department, is a reciprocal affirmation of unconditional most-favored-nation treatment and supplementary safeguards against impairment thereof through quotas, internal taxes, or exchange controls. In this treaty Secretary Hull has evidently taken the most explicit pains to avoid the rackets now going on within bilateral treaties. It may be safely affirmed that few countries in the world could sign such an agreement and continue in their present trading practices. Nor do we believe that the ideas of Secretary Wallace on bilateral trade objectives can be fitted into the formula adopted by Secretary Hull in the Brazil treaty. Treaties like those with Belgium and Brazil will facilitate exchanges of goods, but will not serve to increase the passive balance of merchandise trade as stipulated in New Deal doctrine. Evidently the two main theories of foreign trade are being brought to an issue.[1]

REMOVAL OF EXTRA-TARIFF OBSTACLES TO TRADE

On behalf of the plan of bilateral trade agreements, it is urged that in such negotiations the various special and abnormal impediments to trade are readily approachable and directly removable. That is, both countries in a bilateral negotiation would agree to drop these vicious practices. This answer holds for isolated cases. But more generally, the answer cannot hold, because country *A* might be glad to demolish such obstacles if country *B* did the same, but cannot do so unless country *C* ceases discriminations against coun-

[1] In the proclamation of the President issued on April first it is made clear that our application of most-favored-nation treatment depends on the regulations of the other side in each case.

try *A,* and country *B* cannot do so unless country *D* ceases discriminations against country *B.* In other words, a few countries cannot build down these obstacles unless most of the other countries do. This has been the difficulty in Europe; there seems to be no place to start the tearing-down process. The whole gamut of dumping, subsidy, and discrimination resists piecemeal solution. This was the statement so frequently made at the World Economic Conferences of 1927 and 1933: that all countries would need to agree to drop these practices and do so simultaneously and demonstrably; otherwise, no single country, here or there, could afford to undertake the reform. Under these circumstances, there is no good ground to assume that when the thirty-seven countries contained in our list conduct their negotiations for bilateral trade agreements, they will proceed piecemeal to abolish the numerous and varied extra-tariff obstacles to trade.

But this does not mean these obstacles are to endure. We urge the view that these extra-tariff obstacles have arisen, first, because tariffs are ineffective, and secondly, because of depreciation of currency, control of foreign exchange, and the general disequilibrium of visible and invisible commerce. These extra-tariff obstacles are primarily defensive. With recovery of stable currency relations throughout the world, it is to be expected that these devices will disappear by mere lapsing and will not need to be repealed either by bilateral negotiations or in general international economic conferences.

If, contrary to expectations, recovery should be long deferred, we shall presumably be driven to adopt defensive devices against those of others. We have already anti-dumping provisions. We may be driven to import licenses and to export subsidies. It would be an historical misfortune to be forced to such measures, since this would greatly fortify precedent. To avoid this contingency is one additional reason for early stabilization of currency and exchange.[1]

SUMMARY

The five planks of the foreign trade platform of the New Deal are restated. Preliminary to the analysis of the proposed mechanism of bilateral trade agreements, the history of the development of multangular foreign commerce is sketched. It is pointed out that the pronounced expansion of commerce before the war was due to the advantages of multangular trading. The proposal to develop bilateral trading is therefore really a reversion. It is pointed out that the volume of multilateral trade, correctly construed and appraised, is significantly larger than is currently appreciated.

Attention is drawn to the fact that the trading countries of the world ought to be segregated according to several different classifications. There are net-creditor and net-debtor countries. Countries have active or passive balances of merchandise trade. There are tropical lands and temperate lands. There are states with and without colonies. Commerce may be separated by continents or regions. For each country there is a list of countries with which exports of goods are greater than imports, and another list with which imports are greater than exports. Each bilateral treaty will constitute a special case.

Emphasis is laid on the point that apart from Canada (which is a peculiar but not a difficult case), in all instances except Europe we receive enough goods from each continent to pay for our exports to that continent and for service charges on American investments in that continent. It is in

[1] As of June 1, reciprocal bilateral trade treaties have been signed (not ratified) with Cuba, Haiti, Brazil, Belgium, and Sweden. These grant lowerings of some tariff rates and eliminations of others. It is understood that lowered rates are to be applicable to other countries with which we may later make reciprocal treaties, and in this sense we maintain unconditional most-favored-nation treatment with non-discriminating countries.

Europe where the chief difficulty is located—namely, we sell to Europe far more than we buy from her, which leaves less than nothing with which to pay the heavy service charges due us on loans to and investments in Europe. It may be conjectured that if our loans to and investments in Europe were scattered over the other continents, our passive balance of merchandise trade would naturally suffice to cover service charges on foreign loans and investments to the extent of perhaps 10 billion dollars, probably more than we own.

It is categorically stated that the prerequisites to recovery of foreign trade are in their order, (a) restoration of monetary relations and exchange processes, (b) removal of various obstacles outside of tariff duties, and (c) lowering of tariff rates. The question is then raised why the United States, instead of revising the tariff downward, transferred to the President the authority for making bilateral trade agreements. Economic, social, and political reasons were given for this far-reaching change in American policy.

The method of reducing tariff rates is briefly considered, with insistence that comparative costs of production cannot be relied upon for guidance. The Secretary of Agriculture is quoted to the effect that we shall need to survey item by item all goods now included in the imports and exports, selecting those believed to be most important. A quotation is drawn from Lionel Robbins which brings to the fore the particular interests of consumers. It is emphasized that each bilateral treaty will be a special case, with enforced contraction or encouraged expansion of particular industries at home and abroad.

Emphasis is laid on the fact that the scheme of bilateral trade agreements implies on the part of foreign countries the same objectives envisaged in our New Deal. In other words, a New Deal at home implies a New Deal abroad. The view is urged that tariff rates alone will not prove controlling, presumably quotas and allocations will need to be employed as supplementary measures. Numerous illustrations of bilateral dickering and bickering are given in forecast.

A survey of the countries of the world to which the tactics of bilateral agreements seem applicable brings out a list of no less than thirty-seven. Presumably the United States would need to contract at least thirty-six bilateral trade agreements. To be effective, most of the other countries contracting trade agreements with the United States would need to contract them with one another. Numerous illustrations are given of this requirement. The maximum number between the thirty-seven countries would be over six hundred trade treaties. The world would be concerned therefore with a community of bilateral trade agreements. Secretary Wallace has uttered significant misgivings as to the outcome of such a scheme. In the view of the writer, the community of bilateral trade agreements will be found to be an impractical and unattainable form of the society of nations, because there is no real community of interests.

Emphasis is laid on the high status of most-favored-nation treatment before the war, throughout the world and especially in the United States. The view is advanced that the bilateral trade treaties will be found incompatible certainly with the spirit and often with the letter of most-favored-nation treatment. Most-favored-nation treatment has been widely violated in existing bilateral trade agreements. Either most-favored-nation treatment must be given up openly, or the extensive projected system of bilateral treaties will destroy that principle of international equity.

Finally, it is urged that the removal of extra-tariff obstacles to foreign commerce is more important than the lowering of tariff rates. Most of these obstacles are defensive rather than protective in the ordinary sense. With revaluation of currency and restabilization of foreign exchanges, these defensive extra-tariff obstacles would be quickly abandoned in a natural reaction within the trading countries.

CHAPTER X

CONSIDERATIONS ON THE SIDE OF FOREIGN COUNTRIES

THE United States—with due consideration of our size, native resources, wealth, and political prestige—is still only one side of our international commerce. Other countries must be converted to the proposed movement—taught internationalism in spirit to a far greater extent than has been accomplished in fifteen years by the League of Nations. Little countries have autonomies of decision and powers of obstruction quite out of proportion to area and population. If the "planned middle course" is to succeed, we must lead where we have previously followed in recalcitrant fashion. Conversely to the nationalists who would contrive domestic agreements to keep us out of foreign entanglements, Secretary Wallace would contrive foreign agreements to keep us out of domestic entanglements. What are the views and interests, hopes and fears, of foreign countries on the proposed world-wide reorganization of our commerce? How would foreign countries view a plan which included buying an additional billion dollars' worth of their goods and selling them an additional half-billion dollars' worth of our farm products?

At the peak of prosperity a few years ago the reported foreign commerce of the world was equivalent to 70 billion gold dollars. At the low point of the depression it had fallen to 25 billion gold dollars. The commerce is now slowly rising. The decline was both in amounts and in prices; the recovery is in amounts, but also both in real prices and in changed values of money. All countries did not suffer proportionately in the decline. With recovery, all countries will not prosper proportionately. It is the general expectation that with the higher prices coming into influence, the restored world trade ought to equal shortly the equivalent of 40 billion gold dollars. Of this we seem soon to feel that a fifth belongs to us. If we secure 8 billion dollars' foreign trade, then a passive balance of a billion dollars and an added export of farm products of a half-billion dollars do not look so impossible from our side. But foreign countries, while applauding our hopeful estimate of recovery of gross world trade, are not so enthusiastic over our getting a fifth of it. Nations fight to retain trade when commerce is declining; they fight also to regain trade when commerce is recovering.

The country is here confronted with a broad question of policy. The New Deal sponsors a reorganization of society in the interest of equity between economic forces and social elements. We may, on the one hand, declare frankly that this is an internal reform which does not extend beyond our boundaries, that we have no interest in a corresponding reform in foreign countries. Or, we may declare that we have an interest, both in principle and in practice, in promoting in other countries the reform regarded as all-important in our own. Our decision as to attitude is not merely a dialectical exercise; without question, our tactics and objectives in a trade treaty will depend to some extent upon it. If Secretary Wallace speaks for the New Dealers, it is to be acknowledged that an ethical obligation rests on our country to recognize in other countries the political elements and technical circumstances which in those countries make for the new balance. When the "Sermon on the Mount" replaces the "law of the jungle" in the United States, the United States in dealing with other countries will need to favor those who support the Sermon on the Mount and oppose those who wish to retain the law of the jungle.[1]

The practical importance of the question is easily shown in countries which have undergone radical changes of government. Under the Nazi government the official German attitude on policy of foreign-debt payment is different from the attitude that would have been shown by the pre-war imperial government or was displayed by the government of the republic, which has been replaced by the totalitarian state. A definite change of attitude is to be discerned in the foreign policy of the corporate state of Italy; and also even in Great Britain, since a so-called national cabinet is not forced to defend its policy at a general election. The extent to which one ought to employ social convictions to influence foreign policy was perhaps the major cause of the break between Stalin and Trotsky: Trotsky sought continuously to regard all foreign countries as open fields for communistic revolution, while the more practical Stalin insisted on the present policy, in matters of trade, of having the Soviet government treat with capitalistic governments with mutual acceptance of "hands off" in the internal affairs of the other party. When the New Dealers come to negotiate commercial agreements, are they to seek out New Dealers in the foreign countries, or complacently treat with Old Dealers in the foreign countries while they refuse to treat with Old Dealers in our own country?

THE OBSTACLES TO COMMERCE

Secretary Wallace recognizes that the proposed reform of international trade cannot be secured through active

[1] The designation of "law of the jungle," as description of competition in trade, is not original with the New Dealers. The writer recalls having read years ago a similar reference in a discussion of the Stevenson Plan for control of rubber, in the course of which a plantation owner defended the scheme as orderly marketing and said the small native rubber tappers followed the "law of the jungle."

policy on our part against a passive, or antagonistic attitude on the part of other countries. The foreign countries must also take active measures; a true cooperation, a desire for "balance," is really prerequisite. Between the active measures on our side and the active measures taken abroad should be a planned correlation.

". . . We know now from bitter experience that there is no such magic in *laissez-faire*. Absolutely free competition, conducted nationally or on a world scale, produces unendurable overconcentrations of goods and power. . . . We have come perforce to think in terms not of free production and trade, but of planned production and trade, within and between nations." (*America Must Choose,* p. 14.)

National planning, therefore, does not mean planning confined within a country; it implies continental planning, hemisphere planning, empire planning, colonial planning, world planning. The French delegates to the successive international economic conferences have (on paper) consistently advocated "planned agricultural cooperation between producing and consuming countries." A pertinent illustration is to be found in the realistic planning evolved in the program of Major Elliot, Minister of Agriculture in the United Kingdom.[1] Indeed, in a sense the planning

[1] British opinion points with glee or regret, as the case may be, to the circumstance that Major Walter Elliot, Minister of Agriculture, is farther along the road of agricultural planning than is editor Henry A. Wallace, Secretary of Agriculture. For 1935 British growers have subsidies on wheat, sugar beets, and cattle. There is a marketing scheme for domestic hogs, milk, hops, and potatoes. There is rationing of imports on pork, mutton, lamb, beef, and eggs—in some cases called "voluntary." In the case of most products, the design is to stimulate the domestic outturn; but in the case of potatoes there is acreage restriction and potatoes below a certain size cannot be sold for human food.

So far as may be judged at a distance, Minister Elliot seems to possess virtually the same powers, outside of licensing of processors, that have been sought in the amendments to the AAA pending before the 1935 Congress, though the scope of the so-called "voluntary" agreements is not definable at a distance. Because Great Britain is a heavy net-importer, the so-called agricultural planning includes stimulation of domestic production, regulation of imports, and marketing control of both domestic and imported

for Empire Preference has set the model for this country.[1]

What, now, must be the objectives in such an international cooperation in bilateral trade? It is as true of trade as it is of production that the new does not usually grow out of the old, but appears alongside it and eliminates it by competition. We have learned in the depression that every domestic contraction of production tends to lower exports and that every contraction of imports tends to lower domestic consumption. The surplus-producing countries are to be asked to agree to a program of reduction of surplus, probably with the use of quotas and possibly on the basis of fixed prices. Reciprocal thereto, the net-importing countries are to be asked to lower domestic production and adjust their subsequently enlarged import requirements to the programs of the exporting countries. In effect, and to a considerable extent explicitly, we must ask the net-importing countries to contract their agricultures and expand their imports of farm products; and we agree, in return, to contract our export of manufactures and to permit them to expand theirs to us. This all is to be arranged through planned bilateral reciprocal treaties, supplemented by coordinated general programs based on more or less comprehensive agreements between competing surplus-producing countries. This, we take it, is the gist of the position of Secretary Wallace. It would seem, however, to be implied that the trade trends sought to be corrected are of recent development, reversible in nature, and correctable through negotiation. It strikes us this is

---

products. Only in the case of sugar have we as yet any comparable control of a foodstuff of which we are a net-importer. It is noteworthy that the extensive activities of the British Minister of Agriculture have been elaborated in support of a class which constitutes less than 10 per cent of the population of the United Kingdom.

[1] Empire preference was taken to imply greater profits both to mother country and dominions; but it seems to have worked out rather as a contest over the partition of the unenlarged profits.

entirely too simple and optimistic an assumption. One major trouble with the trade of the world, as Loveday has well pointed out in relation to the commerce of Great Britain, is that with each decade the proportion of goods with elastic demand rises and the proportion with inelastic demand declines. Three points deserve special emphasis.

(a) The food-importing countries of Europe expanded (or intensified) their agricultures as direct consequences of the war, thereafter as indirect consequence of disorganization directly after the war, and finally as defensive expression of the doctrine of self-sufficiency, which expressed the desire for security in the national food supply. This expansion and intensification of agriculture in Europe has not been haphazard, for the most part; it has been technically well planned. Agriculture has been influenced by reclamation of soil, improved methods, selection of superior seed, control of destructive parasites, and use of cheap fertilizer. Animal husbandry has been intensified; farm implements are superior to those of two or three decades ago.

(b) Against this development is raised a more or less hypothetical objection that costs are higher than in some of the surplus-producing countries overseas. Direct costs, yes; but are the indirect costs so much higher? Into agriculture have gone the unemployed of the cities, whose industries have been contracted or closed down through failure of foreign markets. What effective argument have now the overseas surplus countries to apply to the farm policy of the deficiency countries of Europe? They are to be asked to give up newer technical achievements, to evacuate lands, to reverse their revised relation of country to city, to contract the rural population and augment that of the cities, to exchange a visible relative security for an invisible relative security. There is no inherent peace in Europe; but all suggestions to scale down domestic agricultures assume the permanence of outlook for peace. No one who has attended international economic conferences since the war can but regard such proposals to the importing European countries as hypothetical or Utopian.

It strikes us further that Secretary Wallace underestimates both the immediate and later effects on consumption habits in net-importing countries brought about by innumerable restrictions on imports. We regard the innumerable restrictions on imports in the net-importing countries, especially of Europe, as negative rather than positive, defensive rather than offensive. But they have their household effect: adaptations occur, substitutions are enforced, and consumers finally change their habits in consequence. It is therefore not lightly to be assumed that if, as, and when restrictions are suspended, American farmers will find again the old customers who were lost during the interval of restriction. The war restrictions on consumption had a permanent effect. Only when all such restrictions are lifted will it be possible to say how much of the effect is temporary and how much is permanent. But we may be sure that the apparent assumption of Secretary Wallace that the export trade of the United States would rebound perhaps to its original dimensions in agricultural products, as a spring rebounds when the clasp is loosened, would not be found verified by the outcome.

(c) A third important point lies in the loss of export outlets for products of European urban industry. The importing countries of Europe are to be asked to raise less foods and feeds and to import more of them, paying for these increased imports with assumed, or stipulated, increased exports of non-agricultural products. But this last assumption implies that the outside demands for such European non-agricultural exports will be immediately revived *en bloc*. Secretary Wallace does not stand alone in this good-natured assumption.

A Victorian comment from *The Economist* of October 6, 1934 (p. 629), would seem to suggest that the countries with granaries overseas may encounter a changed demand, due to the new philosophy.

"The People's Bread.—Last century by dint of the export of settlers and capital, Europe fashioned for itself granaries in the world overseas. There, on virtually no-rent lands and under extensive methods of cultivation, the world's finest wheat was sent to feed the growing industrial populations of Europe, who, in return, exported the latest products of industrialism. For both the overseas settlers and the European workers, the growing volume of international exchange meant a rising standard of living. To-day *nous avons changé tout cela*—with the help of apostles of the 'new economics.' "

This view is almost naïve in disregarding the occurrence and extent of dispersion of industries since the war. To what extent is the retreat towards agriculture in western Europe the consequence of loss of export markets resulting from dispersion of urban industries? During the century between the close of the Napoleonic Wars and the opening of the World War, the countries of western Europe were engaged in the introduction and dissemination of new goods and services, of which the exports to backward or undeveloped countries were repaid largely with primary materials. The regular receipt of these primary materials, easing the burden and raising the standard of living, permitted of a rapid increase in population in western Europe, of which each new increment was dependent upon foreign sources of supply of primary materials. With the beginning of this century, however, and especially since the World War, an extensive and continuing dispersion of urban industries has taken place. Therefore, the absolute volume of manufactures outside of western Europe rises, the proportion of supply of manufactures of these countries supplied by

Europe falls, and finally the absolute amount supplied by Europe declines, affecting industry by industry in country after country. With declining outlet for products of urban industry, western Europe loses purchasing power for primary materials from overseas. Certain of these primary materials are not produced in western Europe, and of these the import must be continued, both in the interest of the domestic standard of living and of the export trade, which is in large part an "improvement trade." But others of these primary materials are produced in Europe; there the loss of foreign markets for Europe's manufactures finds indirect expression in increase of output, to secure larger domestic production of such indigenous primary materials. Thus, decline in international trade has forced western Europe to intensify her agriculture. Also, it seems to us likely that the Secretary underestimates the strength of agricultural elements abroad, the conservative elements in a self-sufficient-minded country. Self-sufficiency, or at least a lessened dependence on foreign supplies, has been taught to the world in the bitter lessons of the war and of currency depreciation. It has a range of action as a protective device, politically and economically. Furthermore, in an important sense it has a pronounced fiscal function, in that the balance of the international account depends directly, and indeed in some cases crucially, on the limitation of imports of agricultural products. Under these circumstances, it is idle for foreigners to apply the theory or principle of comparative cost accounting. It is out of place technically and politically, and inappropriate also, for foreigners to apply a principle of cost accounting to their customers which they do not apply to themselves. Certainly any cost accounting which we apply to American agriculture contains numerous intangibles like "decent" prices. European agriculture, whose class in each country is the strongest conservative group and which is now in addition the defender of the currency, is in position to dictate political terms in negotiations.

THE EXPANDING LIST OF COMPETING EXPORT STATES

It seems to us that Secretary Wallace underestimates the effect of the dispersion of industries going on in the world since the war and certain to continue. This dispersion of industries is of several kinds and orders of magnitude. The heavy industries of the United States and western Europe have found it to their advantage, as individual entrepreneurs, to sell factory equipment to less advanced countries. This equipment, set up in the countries of destination, constitutes a dispersion of industry. The extent of such dispersion may be guessed at in several ways: by production in the countries in which these plants have been set up; by lowered imports into those countries; and by increased exports out of these newly industrialized countries. An excellent, if somewhat exaggerated example is furnished by Japan.[1] In this form, the capital transaction represents purchase of the equipment by the entrepreneur in the importing country; the equipment may be purchased on time and therefore constitutes a foreign debt, but otherwise the dispersion is essentially an internal development.

[1] A pertinent illustration of dispersal of specialized industry is to be found in the textile plants of Japan, where high productivity on modern, semi-automatic machines makes for low labor costs which are endurable in a country with low living standards. The humiliating conflict between the United Kingdom, India, and Japan over the competitive textile trade is an extreme though not exaggerated example of what is to be expected along other lines. Export of manufacturing plants from Occidental to Oriental countries is an instance of what Spengler calls "the betrayal of technical science." As an illuminating illustration of the effect of dispersion of industry is further to be adduced the fact that the plight of raw silk growers in Japan is due quite as much to the manufacture of rayon in Japan as to competition with rayon in the countries which import silk heavily. The old Japanese proverb that their "welfare hangs by a silken thread" is now cynically changed to read "rayon" instead of "silken." When one traces the successive invasions of China, Egypt, Australia, and Canada by Japanese textiles, the implications for the British Empire of the dispersion of textile plants from the United Kingdom to Asia become manifest.

Another form of dispersion consists in a formal loan for the purpose of establishing the new enterprise in the expanding peripheral country. This is a common procedure. It differs from the first in the extent to which control lies in foreign rather than in domestic hands. Also, the term of indebtedness is longer and the nature of the obligation more formal.

Still another form of dispersion lies in the establishment of branch factories, foreign subsidiaries.[1] Such establishment of branch factories is favored, or even enforced, by tariff policies; Canada, for illustration, has the obvious policy of inducing, or compelling, Americans to establish branch factories instead of exporting finished goods into their country.

Dispersion of industries into foreign countries rests largely on four motives. In the first place, it is a natural evolution in the second stage of the industrial revolution, radiating from northwestern Europe to all parts of the world. A second reason lies in the establishment of industries outside of Europe which was directly provoked by the war, during which time distant countries were deprived of European goods. The third reason lies in the circumstance that the capital-goods industry of Europe and of the United States, overexpanded during the war, has since sought relief in foreign markets by export of capital goods and manufacturing equipment of all kinds. The fourth form of dispersion of industry is found in the widespread establishment of subsidiary plants in foreign countries, just referred to. Foreign branch factories are as much a common part of the manufacturing industries of the countries of western Europe as of

[1] A book by Frank A. Southard on *American Industry in Europe,* published in 1930 by Houghton Mifflin Company, gives a good idea of one small group of dispersed industries. In a sense, the building abroad of subsidiaries of American industries is a form of flight of capital; but more often it is flight from high costs or toward low costs.

those of the United States. One must not assume that branch factories merely replace exports from the parent factories. Tariffs, patents, and lower costs have also influenced the erection of branch factories, or even domestic factories, in the foreign countries concerned.

The dispersion of industries is obviously not reversible. Also, it is to be expected that the new industries scattered throughout the world will not confine themselves to domestic markets but will also seek export outlets. It is thus explained why international trade has been tending towards greater interchange of manufactured goods and less of the traditional exchange of manufactures for raw materials. Chauvinists sometimes urge that export of capital equipment should be prohibited, and indeed it was prohibited in many countries a century ago. Such a suggestion implies that the capital equipment could be secured by the importing country from only one exporting country. This is rarely the case. If it be true, as reported, that American bankers have loaned money to Brazilians to buy cotton-ginning machinery in this country, to be taken to Brazil to advance their cotton agriculture and textile industry, the answer to the objection would be that if Americans did not make the sale, the machinery-makers of other countries would do so. Russia, with increasing outturn of new gold, finds herself in position to buy increasing amounts of capital goods to equip factories, whose products will replace consumers' goods previously imported. Can the countries furnishing the machinery to Brazil and Russia thereafter endeavor to induce them to desist by using epithets like "self-sufficient"?

Now, the development of such dispersion of industries has the inevitable tendency to make changes in the visible and invisible trade equation. Since these dispersions are in the so-called capital-goods industries as well as in the industries of consumption goods, this means in consequence that the exports of the United States will decline relatively. Therefore our so-called passive balance of merchandise trade, which is the consistent position of a net-creditor country, will tend to enlarge as the industries of the net-creditor countries are dispersed to net-debtor countries over the world. Erection of subsidiary plants abroad by American manufacturers lowers the figure for credits in our international account, just what our New Dealers desire. Of recent developments, the transfer of cigar factories from Cuba to the United States reduces the debit side of our international account, just the opposite of what is being sought by the New Deal plan; importation of refined sugar from Cuba has the effect being sought.

What are contained in the reported 7 billions of "direct" foreign investments of Americans? Largely dispersion of American industries.[1] What are the extensive textile factories of Japan and India and of several South American countries? Dispersion of western European textile industries. Striking enough, indeed, has been the success of these newer urban industries in countries that were industrially backward only a few years ago. Many of these dispersed industries in previously backward countries are served by workers with low standards of living and long work hours; this, with efficient modern machinery, makes for low production costs. The development of semi-automatic machinery obviously favors such dispersion of industry, since there is no color line among operatives of semi-automatic machinery.

Japan, Russia, and India show how the land lies. The recently industrialized countries have no obvious incentive to yield their competitive position. Europe will not reduce her agriculture unless guaranteed the restoration of the corresponding markets for manufactures. The United States, Canada, Argentina, Australia, and South Africa will hardly

[1] The values of these direct investments consist quite as much of profits plowed back as of capital originally exported.

agree to give Europe priority in import of manufactures in return for added exports of farm products. The European development of agriculture is hinged on far more than a reciprocal relation to the United States; it is the relief picture of the dispersion of urban industry from Europe to the newer countries of the world. To suggest that these newer countries will give up their new industrialism is to fly in the face of old experience and new facts. The United States does not hold the ace, nor Europe the trump.

Finally, it needs to be emphasized that the backward net-debtor countries, only recently (partially) industrialized by dispersion of industries from western Europe and the United States, with their competitive goods must undersell within the net-creditor countries so long as the net-debtor countries are paying service charges on their borrowings. Only by re-lending abroad can the net-creditor countries keep out the goods of the recently industrialized net-debtor countries, disregarding, of course, tariffs, etc. This general reasoning must apply also to agricultural products. So long as net-debtor countries are paying service charges to us, we must expect their competitive farm products to undersell ours in our (unprotected) home market or in equally open or restricted foreign markets. The implications of this experience of trade seem to have escaped many of the proponents of the revival of export of agricultural products from the United States, a net-creditor.

INCREASE OF IMPORTS OF NON-COMPETITIVE GOODS

More or less tenuously incorporated into the prolonged discussions of payment of war debts was the naïve hope that these might be paid with "non-competitive" goods. Of these there are two groups: raw materials not indigenous to the payment-receiving countries; and "exotic" articles not made, though sometimes imitated, in the payment-receiving countries. In a word, what may be called the top and the bottom of the import list are here somewhat paradoxically conjoined.

There are several reasons why little is to be expected in any planned increase in importation of raw materials into the United States. (a) Such materials, with a few exceptions like copper and long-staple cotton, are already on the free list. (b) Import demand for such raw materials is conditioned on domestic demand for producers' goods and consumers' goods made from them, and on the subsequent export demand for such commodities. To import more raw material than enough to cover requirements would imply building up reserves in excess of merchandising stocks. Now, reserves of raw materials have indeed been built up in many countries since the war, but as result of unrestrained production and not through voluntary impounding by buyers. Most of these raw materials are imperishable and the cost of carrying reserves would be relatively low, outside of interest on capital; but most of them may be bought and sold in futures and therefore hedging obviates the necessity of carrying heavy stocks.

(c) Finally, we have the circumstance that even with raw materials not indigenously derived, the term "non-competitive" is relative rather than absolute. We do not produce silk, nickel, or tin, for example; therefore, no direct competition exists with domestic producers. But silk is a competitor of rayon, nickel is a semi-competitor of copper, tin is a competitor of zinc. When the range of substitution is fully explored, it is found that even for raw materials the term "non-competitive" needs to be significantly abridged.

Secretary Wallace has avoided this easy but misleading argument. In respect of "exotic" goods, however, he drops a hint which might perhaps be expanded into a larger expectation. Discussing the view that mechanization tends to wipe out regional differences and potentialities, the Secretary makes the following remark:

"I say, then, that in respect to raw materials and handicraft products, world exchangeability is as desirable now as it ever was; and I deny that mechanization wipes out national differences in skill and ingenuity." (*America Must Choose,* p. 13.)

The Secretary obviously refers to unique products of handicraft, objects of art, rare articles of whatever age, which embody the peculiar cultural characteristics of a people. How large is this class of goods?

Generously interpreted in the interest of increased imports, the list includes many highly prized and usually highly priced articles, which are either not made in this country at all, and not imitated at all or only imitated in an imperfect manner. The list includes furs, feathers, drugs, perfumes, gums, tapestries, laces, embroideries, table linen, ceramics, glassware, rugs, metal castings, sculpture, paintings, diamonds and other precious stones, deep-sea pearls, manuscripts, and curios. The list is long and contains an extraordinary variety of articles making an appeal to a limited clientele of the upper-income class. Such articles now tend to be duty-free if antique, i.e., made before a certain date. This could be waived, in the interest of enlarged import, and free entry made unconditional. Most of these luxuries, if native materials, are free in the original state but are dutiable if processed. This also could be waived in the interest of enlarged import and free entry made unconditional. Just how the importation of such articles is to be stimulated, as a planned policy, is hard to see, since the purchasing class stands less in need of incentive than of money.

Here, again, however, we encounter the circumstance that the term non-competitive is an exaggeration. Typical Oriental rugs, such as those imported from Persia and China, are not made in the United States; but imitations are made, and a high-grade copy may look better to the insular American than a low-grade original. The best foreign ceramics surpass ours; but the best American porcelains excel the poorest foreign pieces. Quite generally it may be said that over the entire field the American imitations of the highest grade are definitely competitive with the imported articles of the lowest grade, this of course applying to goods of modern manufacture. Substitution again also enters. We do not produce the virile beer steins and exquisite wineglasses made in Germany and Czechoslovakia; but we turn out tasteful containers from which the available beverages may be quaffed with equal gustatory satisfaction.

Finally, there is an element of style in such luxuries and, of course, antiquity carries prestige. Unquestionably the field is quite large, and if the effort were made consistently to facilitate imports by placing the articles on the free list, the gross sum of money involved in the import of this class of goods might be significantly enlarged. But for the most part, this could not be done through bilateral treaties. The number of countries involved is very large and the items are extraordinarily scattered. Most of the countries which turn out these peculiar and particular articles do not wish in return to receive cotton, wheat, and lard. Quite clearly if imports were to be favored and enlarged, the results would accrue through indirect rather than through direct trade.

According to the United States Tariff Commission, on the list of goods imported into this country 360 are non-competitive. There are some 940 items of which the imports have been less than 5 per cent of domestic production, and these may fairly be called semi-competitive. Then there is a long list of highly competitive goods. The added imports are not to be secured in the list of non-competitive goods, nor yet in the list of goods called semi-competitive; these added imports we must expect to be secured in goods that are highly competitive. Within this list must be made the selection of goods to be brought in to the direct injury of domestic producers, even though we try to soften the blow by calling the domestic production "exotic," "artificial," "high-cost," or even "monopolistic."

CONFLICTING INTERESTS OF MAJOR EXPORTERS

In all discussions of international agreements it seems to be taken for granted that competitors will subordinate their direct interests, bury their hatchets and under the influence of benevolent objectives reach cooperative agreements. But in fact, the natural obstacles to such agreements were never higher than now. This is easily illustrated in a survey of wheat, cotton, and lard in export trade.

Let us begin with *wheat*. In order to appreciate the difficulties of the major wheat-exporting countries, it is necessary to compare their expansions since the war. The following table contains the average acreage of the five years 1909-13, the highest and lowest acreages since 1920, the average acreage of the five years 1925-29, and the yearly acreages of the last five years, for the United States, Canada, Australia, Argentina, India, and Russia.

TABLE VI.—WHEAT ACREAGE OF PRINCIPAL WHEAT-EXPORTING COUNTRIES *

(Thousand acres)

Period or Year	*United States*	*Canada*	*Australia*	*Argentina*	*India*	*Russia*
Average 1909-13...	47,097	9,945	7,603	14,882	29,224	74,031
Average 1925-29...	58,286	23,104	12,797	19,019	31,544	70,959
1930	62,661	24,898	18,165	19,527	31,654	80,490
1931	57,103	26,355	14,741	16,028	32,189	92,066
1932	57,114	27,182	15,766	17,792	33,803	85,500
1933	47,910	25,991	14,965	18,041	32,970	82,138
1934	42,235	23,985	12,965†	17,198	36,062	88,877
Average 1930-34...	53,405	25,682	15,320	17,717	33,336	85,814
Highest since 1920 (inclusive).	64,566	27,182	18,165	22,426	36,062	92,066‡
Lowest since 1920 (inclusive).	42,235	18,232	9,072	13,219	25,784	54,362‡

* Based on data from U. S. Department of Agriculture, *Yearbook of Agriculture* and *International Yearbook of Agricultural Statistics*. The figures given are for harvested acreage.

† Sown acreage.

‡ Since 1924 (inclusive).

The striking feature of this table is the disproportionate expansion of wheat acreage in the United States and Canada. During the last decade, wheat acreage in many of the net-importing countries has increased, especially in Europe. This increase in wheat acreage in the net-wheat-importing countries has had the natural effect of reducing their import requirements. Said reduction in import requirements, coupled with the natural outturn of enlarged acreage in the surplus-producing countries, aided by a few bumper yields, resulted in an accumulation of carry-overs which for several years approximated a billion bushels. It has been proposed—as the objective of international wheat conferences beginning in the spring of 1933 and not yet concluded—that the wheat-surplus-producing countries shall submit to an acreage contraction, endeavoring to adjust export surplus to effective import demand. But what shall be the base line? Canada and the United States, the dominant countries (perhaps one should say the domineering countries) in the conference, apparently desire what amounts to a horizontal contraction. That is, Canada and the United States, whose acreages were greatly expanded, would take the same percentage contraction as Argentina and Australia, whose acreages were but moderately expanded. This suggestion is inequitable. If, on the other hand, the base line is the average acreage of 1909-14, the contraction to be imposed on the United States and Canada, in absolute figures of acreage, would be so much larger than that imposed on Argentina and Australia, as to make the proposition unacceptable to the wheat farmers of North America. It is significant that during 1930-34 the United States and Argentina reduced the average wheat acreage below that of 1925-29, the other four countries enlarged theirs. A compromise has been sought but has not been found; the solution lies a different way.

The next proposal, to evade this impasse by limiting exports on a quota basis, encounters a different but still insuperable difficulty. Judged by internal considerations based in each country on the circumstances of wheat growers, there is no common ground acceptable to wheat farmers in the surplus countries. Russia, which in the five years before the war exported an average of over 160 million bushels of wheat, is now asked to be content with a third of that, which makes the Soviet officials smile.[1] It is reported to be an adage among racketeers that division of losses occasions more murders than division of gains; this seems to be verified in the quota discussions in the international wheat conferences.[2]

On the other side of the picture, consider the conflicts between the European importing countries over the division of the acreage contractions to be imposed. Europe ex-Russia would be asked at least to produce 100 million bushels less, probably 200 million bushels, even perhaps 300 million bushels, that much less wheat than during the recent years—and to import that much more, mostly from overseas. How are these contractions to be allocated? On a population basis? On the basis of pre-war wheat acreage? On the basis of the highest wheat acreage? On the basis of the wheat acreage of the depression? Is each country to pledge itself to a stipulated per capita consumption of wheat? Picture the green-covered table around which are seated men like Elliot of Great Britain, Hermes of Germany, Gautier of France, Laur of Switzerland, Mariani of Italy, Colijn of Holland, Francqui of Belgium, and Rose of Poland. These delegates,

[1] If we accept the commonly held assumption that Russia will not again become a heavy exporter of wheat, then it becomes equally certain that Russia must develop the export of some other farm product to take the place of wheat as foreign purchasing power.

[2] It must look like a "racket" to find France, usually a net-importer, with an abnormal wheat surplus now asking for an export quota of 30 million bushels. Can one blame Argentina and Australia for feeling that this looks like a fifth ace up the sleeve?

as the writer knows from experience, are politically acute as well as technically intelligent; and they are stubborn. These delegates are asked to cut down wheat production and increase imports of wheat in proportion, in return for an intangible prospect of increase of industrial exports from their countries. When, now, these delegates submit the intangible prospect (but not a promise) to the industrialists of their respective countries, they are advised that the proposals are deficient in quantity and defective in quality. In no importing country can the industrialists and the agrarians get together on the acceptability of a proposition to contract wheat acreage and expand wheat imports and industrial exports; one side must yield, the other dominates. The failure of the 1933-35 international wheat conference is not accidental or incidental: it is inherent in the institution, no matter how planned.

Consider *lard,* and let us confine ourselves again to the importing countries of Europe. Lard is a fat of ordinary characteristics, which northern Europeans like because it has a meaty taste and a porky odor. But lard is on the defensive; the vegetable-oil substitutes are more highly refined, more uniform in behavior, and more attractive in appearance. In Europe the lard substitutes are not so highly developed; but margarines are manufactured in enormous volume. Technical advances have made it practicable to use almost any vegetable, animal, or marine fat in margarines and other processed cooking fats. We used to export well over a billion pounds of lard a year; it has fallen to little over half that. The per capita consumption of fat in Europe is higher today than it was before the war; but the proportion of American lard has fallen heavily.

Now appears our Secretary of Agriculture before the western European countries and asks them to restrain the breeding of hogs, to check the catching of marine animals and fish and the refining of their fats, to lower the import of tropical vegetable oils—and instead to take, let us say, a half-billion pounds more of American lard. Great Britain has colonies and dependencies which are heavy producers of oil seeds; she has an enormous margarine industry. There is a heavy production of butter in the dominions which must be sold to the mother country. Unless American lard is to be added to an already heavy per capita intake, the butter of New Zealand, the oil seeds of Africa, or the margarine syndicate must contract operations. And which one of the suppliers of competitive fats is to accept the retrenchment? What will we accept from the United Kingdom in return for 100 million pounds of lard a year? If British goods are to be sent over in return for lard, do we or the British select and stipulate the goods in payment?

Holland has colonies that produce oil seeds; so has Belgium, also France. None of these countries wish particularly to increase their per capita fat intakes; all are desirous of protecting animal industry at home and plant industry in the colonies. Sweden and Denmark can hardly be appealed to. Germany, however, needs fat and would be glad to exchange chemicals, steel, and textiles in return for it—but the American manufacturers of chemicals, steel, and textiles have other ideas. There is no market for lard in Spain and Italy, whose tastes run to olive oil, of which they are exporters. Central Europe—Czechoslovakia, Poland, and Hungary—are natural exporters of lard. Austria of course needs lard—that is, Vienna does; why did we not try to save the Kredit-Anstalt in order to find a market for lard? In short, the only prospects for revival of export of lard under any bilateral negotiations are in Germany and Austria—who have appetite but few means of payment.

Finally, consider *cotton*. For years our exports of cotton were outstanding in our international account. The highest export of cotton in any year since the war was 4,897 million pounds in 1927; the lowest was 2,743 million pounds in 1930. Our cotton acreage used to be more than half the cotton acreage of the world; our cotton crop was more than half the cotton crop of the world; we exported more than half of our crop. As late as the years 1930-31 our acreage and production were more than half those of the world. In 1931-32 our acreage had fallen below the line of half, though our crop still stood above it; our 1934 crop of cotton was considerably below half of the world crop.

Control of price and restrained marketing of coffee in Brazil stimulated the planting of coffee in countries outside of Brazil; now the Brazilian control of the world market has been lost and the other coffee-producing countries stand under the Brazilian umbrella. If we restrict cotton acreage —let us say, to below 30 million acres and the crop to 10 million bales—the day may arrive when American cotton is only a third of the cotton of the world. In the meantime we hope by negotiations to induce the cotton-importing countries to agree to take from us an added several million bales of cotton in return for exports of manufactures to the United States. The export of cotton is free, but possibly the sale would be controlled by governmental ownership. We can hardly hope simultaneously to sell more cotton and hold up our price. How shall we coax Japan to buy more cotton from the United States and less cotton from India? How can we hope to continue to sell annually to Japan raw cotton to the extent of more than a million bales if we restrict her export market for textiles by commercial treaties? Why should Brazil and Argentina buy cotton from this country instead of raising their own? Why should Lancashire import more American and less Empire cotton, unless we will buy the textiles made from it? Germany, of course, needs cotton, as do Czechoslovakia, Belgium, and Switzerland;

but they need it mostly as raw material for textiles to be re-exported. If we cannot accept their finished cotton goods, they have a lessened use for our raw cotton, unless other foreign countries will take their textiles in preference to cotton textiles exported from the United States. Is it practicable for us to reject the cotton textiles of these western European countries, and instead accept chemicals and articles of steel? The textile trade has the reputation of being the cutthroat trade of the world, and when American delegates sit in on a conference for the purpose of expanding raw cotton exports in return for imports of other manufactures than those from cotton, they will find themselves in the position of the slaughter of the innocents.

We hear a great deal of the "age of surplus" and the "age of scarcity." Trade negotiations are a part of the age of scarcity: the precedents, tactics, and limitations derive from the sellers' market. Now, suddenly, we endeavor, not in one line, but in many lines simultaneously, to negotiate exchanges in a buyers' market, with the tactics and experiences derived from a sellers' market. The dangers of price fall due to deflation have blinded us to the recognition of the dangers of price rise due to restriction. Each is asked to take more than he wants or can pay for. And we are to plan this in a world plastered with debt, practically without convertible currencies, and without clearing-houses for foreign exchange. In despair over elusive monetary tokens, we return to the forgotten practice of barter and hope to swap materials against materials, in terms of quotas; in effect trying to trade higher prices for higher prices. It starts out as a daydream; it will become a nightmare.

THE CURRENCIES OF TRADING COUNTRIES

The outstanding characteristic of foreign trade before the war was the extraordinary equilibrium throughout the world between currencies and exchange rates, prices and costs, and volumes of movement of goods and services. The total lack of such equilibrium is the outstanding characteristic of the disorganized foreign commerce of today. The violent transition of Germany from a net-creditor position of some 7 billion dollars to a net-debtor position to almost the same extent, and the abnormal transition of the United States from a net-debtor position of some 3 billion dollars to a net-creditor position of some 10 billion dollars, constitute the high points of revolution in the history of international finance, veritably the "war after the war."

The pressure to balance the international trade account bears more heavily on net-debtor than on net-creditor countries (though the creditors hold themselves greatly abused), which accounts in part for the rigid exchange controls in the net-debtor countries. Depreciation of currencies has the temporary effect of subsidizing exports, though at an inherent loss to the internal economy of the exporting country.[1] Fluctuations in currency tend to have a net effect resembling deflation. In every net-debtor country stands the choice between more import of goods and more payment on foreign debt; in every net-creditor country stands the choice between more export of goods and more receipts on foreign debt. There is an important influence on our imports and exports of goods exerted by the relative position of the dollar in relation to other currencies. If the dollar is relatively dear, this tends to depress our exports and favor imports; if the dollar is relatively cheap, this tends to favor our exports and depress imports. We observe here one form of so-called exchange dumping. When our New Dealers accepted the policy of enlarging the debits of the international account in contrast with the credits, this implied that a relatively dear dollar would favor this change. That is, when we seek an

[1] There are however glaring exceptions to the usual and expected experiences. For example, in 1934 the imports of goods into gold-standard Holland were depressed far more than exports of goods.

enlarged passive balance of merchandise trade, our dollar ought to be kept high in order to make this country a dear place for foreign purchases, and simultaneously to make the outside world a cheap place for American purchases. Instead, we revalued downward and in 1934 increased the active balance of merchandise trade.

In monetary policies the different countries in the world today belong to one of three groups. We have first the "gold bloc," which includes only France, Germany, Poland, the Netherlands, Switzerland, and Italy. In Italy and Germany gold is strictly under control; in the other four countries gold is under implied control, i.e., outflow would be restrained if imminent in large amount. The countries of the "gold bloc" have what might be called a semi-gold standard. These countries may still be forced off gold. The second group consists of the United States and Great Britain and the countries whose currency policies are more or less closely allied with theirs, including especially the so-called sterling-area. Perhaps the United States may be said to be on a pseudo-gold standard and Great Britain on a managed sterling exchange standard.[1] Finally, we have a large group of coun-

[1] In *New Frontiers* on page 93 stands the following comment: "When the British increased the price of their gold, they at once carried with them a large number of smaller countries and, after two and a half years, the United States." British opinion rejects the implication that the action of Great Britain "carried" the United States off the gold standard. It is the British view that *Great Britain was forced off the gold standard,* on both national and international grounds, whereas *the United States chose to leave the gold standard* on national grounds. At the time of our departure from the gold standard, the country was net-creditor long-term, net-creditor short-term, had an active balance of merchandise trade, and more or less all over the world individual debtors were denied the right to purchase dollar exchange in order to transfer payments due to our nationals. Under these circumstances it is British opinion that the United States chose to leave the gold standard in order to raise the internal price level. Moderate British opinion is illustrated in the following sentence taken from a leader in *The Economist* of December 1, 1934 (p. 1022):

> ". . . The depreciation of the dollar, initiated by the Inflation Amendment, egged on by the remarkable policy of purchasing gold at ever-rising prices, and crystallised by the 40 per cent devaluation, was one of the clearest cases of deliberate economic aggression in the history of currencies."

tries whose inconvertible paper currencies are determined by, and stand more or less helpless before, variable internal considerations. Between these three groups reigns disequilibrium; a definitive upswing of international trade, which might be justified by the trend of recovery from the business depression, is clearly restrained by the obvious transfer difficulties.

The disequilibrium in the world is clearly revealed by the continuing decline of prices of goods in terms of gold. During the last fiscal year, the price index of the British Board of Trade declined a further five points, in terms of gold, while rising three points in terms of shillings. The gold price of wheat on the British market stood close to 40 cents in 1934. Under these circumstances, it is illusory to expect that the fairly close concordances between dollar-price of gold and sterling-price of gold, which are expressive of equalization operations on each side, can be relied upon by traders as a form of stabilization. Prices in foreign countries, exchange rates, costs of shipping and associated services, and tariff rates in importing countries, remain not merely unstabilized but subject to artificial and unforeseeable variations, which do not reflect the traditional influence of costs on prices.[1]

The extraordinary relations in currencies of countries cannot be too often re-emphasized. Only a half-dozen countries have fixed parities for currency units. The gold standard for the so-called gold bloc is maintained only through sufferance. The majority of currencies are overvalued or undervalued in foreign countries; and when internal revaluations occur, as they must, countries will be tempted to compromise between true revaluation and true stabilization of foreign exchange rates. Depreciations of currencies not only influ-

[1] For an excellent appraisal see the Sixth Richard Cobden Lecture, delivered in May 1934 by Gustav Cassel.

ence prices of goods, they also modify foreign obligations. Under these circumstances in foreign commerce there is no foreseeable relation between cost in one country and final selling price abroad.

It is out of place to suggest that the so-called gold standard of the pre-war trading period should be restored.[1] With the fullest appreciation of the injury to foreign trade inflicted by depreciation of currencies, the appropriate and practicable remedy clearly does not lie in a restoration of the traditional gold standard. The main requirement of recovery in this respect is some mechanism which permits payments between individual and groups in different countries to exercise the same effects on prices as would be exercised by similar payments within countries.[2] That is, payments between countries must again be placed on the same footing as payments within countries. In *International Economic Relations* is found the following pertinent observation:

". . . More important even than international cooperation and coordination of national policies is the restoration of that degree of flexibility in domestic price structures and income structures without which orderly adjustments under the gold standard system are impossible. The most genuine spirit of international coopera-

[1] Cf. T. E. Gregory, *The Future of the Gold Standard* (London, Methuen, 1934). J. H. Williams, "Monetary Stabilization from an International Point of View," *American Economic Review*, March 1935, Supplement, XXV, 157-63.

[2] ". . . If recovery is more advanced in one country than another, it is difficult to argue that any point chosen in the light of the situation at that moment is likely to prove an equilibrium point. If we are to find an equilibrium point, we must assume a more or less parallel state of affairs in the two countries. . . . First, it is important to make what use one can of such rough-and-ready calculations as are available; second, there should be a willingness to experiment with a *de facto* stabilization for a considerable time before any more permanent arrangements come into force; and, third, account should be taken of the comparative position in each country in so far as internal movements of prices and costs are likely to develop, and of the relative burdens of the debt structures."—Royal Institute of International Affairs, *The Future of Monetary Policy* (Oxford, Oxford University Press, 1935), pp. 136-37.

tion and of willingness to obey in domestic policies the fundamental rules of the gold standard system cannot prevail against pressures of unemployment and persisting dislocations within domestic price structures." (p. 90)

This observation applies not merely to the gold standard but to any managed system of international exchange. The world must face the decision of selecting the form of managed (gold?) standard which in international trade is to replace the automatic gold standard which was so successfully operated before the war. It is not merely a question of reciprocal stabilization of currencies, whose values are formally based on domestic considerations, even if the currencies of all trading countries were set free. The conflicting short-term interests of debts and goods seem to many to make some form of (temporary) planned international system inevitable.[1]

The future of stabilization of currencies in the world depends on the United States to an extent which few Americans appreciate. A currency must be stable within a country before it can hope to maintain abroad a stable relation to the currency of another country. Currency stabilization within a country represents mainly a balance between debtors and creditors and between volume of money and volume of wealth. In the past when restabilization had become necessary, this has been achieved through painful trial and error; formal revaluation of the currency occurred after the fact—thus, the revaluation of the French franc in 1927 was merely the recognition *de jure* of what had occurred *de facto*. There is a wing of monetary theorists who believe that revaluation can be computed; the revaluation of the American gold dollar was an expression of this view. Practically all countries of the world face revaluation of their currencies: in most

[1] A sympathetic presentation of a planned international monetary system is to be found in *Planned Money* by Basil P. Blackett (New York, D. Appleton & Co., 1933).

cases on internal grounds, but in some cases on external grounds relating to foreign trade. Also, according to the philosophy of the New Deal, we must recognize in every country an equitable revaluation of currency and seek stabilizations which express just that. Let us assume that Great Britain and the United States both reduce by one-half the gold content of the dollar and sterling and stabilize on that basis at the accustomed ratio. Are these revaluations internally equitable in each of these countries? If so, are these revaluations correspondingly equitable to the prospective and equitable revaluations of the currencies of numerous other countries? Merely to state this question is to indicate that never in the history of the world has such a strain been placed upon commercial computation, and upon the application of monetary theory to trade practice. Incidentally remarked, we may be sure the started revaluation by Great Britain and the United States would elsewhere be regarded unanimously as excessive and adopted for the purpose of favoring the foreign trades of the two outstanding countries in international commerce.[1]

[1] If one were to judge by the relations of dollar to sterling during recent months, it might be assumed that a *de facto* stabilization had been secured —or indeed, it might be intimated facetiously that the dollar had joined the sterling area. This state of affairs may have been accidental; it may have been incidental to current movements of visible and invisible items in trade; it may have been a fortuitous coincidence of independent policies of those in control of the stabilization funds in the two countries; or it may have been due to coordination or cooperation without commitment. Eventually we may learn to what extent during this interval the stabilization funds of the two countries suffered losses or enjoyed gains. The radio address of the Secretary of the Treasury of April 13, 1935, gave formal notice to the world that our government stands ready to join in appropriate measures of stabilization of currencies. Despite the somewhat provocative tone of the address, foreign countries will consider themselves informed that our government is prepared to meet the issue with foreign governments on the implied condition that the past is to be forgiven and forgotten and that in the negotiations all countries "start from scratch," presumably according to new rules of the game. One fears that the foreign experts will be unable to discern, and will expect to be advised, just what experiences and achievements we have acquired during the past two years, whose lack it was in the summer of 1933 that led our government then to decline even formal conversations on stabilization.

THE CRUCIAL DIFFICULTIES OF FOREIGN COUNTRIES

". . . I cannot too sharply emphasize my conviction that internationalism must be even more carefully planned than a program of economic nationalism." (*America Must Choose,* p. 2.)

"Few people realize that it takes just as much planning to follow a plan of internationalism by exchange of goods, not promises, as it does the path of nationalism." (p. 28)

These words of Secretary Wallace bear, from the context, largely on tariff planning so far as bilateral foreign treaties are concerned. It is implied, in the persuasive general argument, that in tariff agreements lie the best prospects for international planning in the immediate future.

A large question of perspective is here involved. Secretary Wallace does not seem to see the foreign monetary forest for the foreign tariff trees. This inadvertent distortion of perspective applies both to the relative importance of the two groups of factors and to their historical evolution. In our country, the new faith in the effect of reducing import tariff rates is of the same order and inscrutable nature as the old faith in raising them. Perhaps the Hawley-Smoot tariff might be called an offensive tariff, since it will hardly be contended that it was enacted primarily to protect our country against unusual, untoward, and abnormal imports from abroad; there was some dumping of foreign goods into our country prior to 1930, but not enough to explain the Hawley-Smoot tariff. But for the most part abroad, the increasing height of tariff walls, and still more the numerous direct and indirect obstructions to the entrance of foreign goods into a long list of important trading countries, were responses of a defensive nature. The distinction is of crucial importance in discussions, and has been recognized by such an implicit free-trader as Lionel Robbins.

". . . We have examined already the effects of tariffs. But if we are to retain a sense of proportion, it must be realized that, in these recent developments, tariffs have been a relatively minor obstacle. It is the exchange restrictions, the quota regulations, the import prohibitions, which have done the greater damage. And it should be added, it is the persistence of such measures which offer the greater obstacle to recovery. Given stability of tariff conditions, however high the rates, the currents of trade may be expected eventually to become adapted to the new situation. The existence of a tariff is not inimical to the achievement of trade equilibrium—although no doubt the equilibrium which may be achieved in this way may be judged by commonly accepted standards to be inferior to that which could have been achieved in its absence. But with these other measures it is different. We have examined already how exchange restriction prevents the restoration of equilibrium. The same thing is true, although for different reasons, of the quotas. When the volume of goods that is permitted to pass the customs' barriers is rigidly fixed and cannot fluctuate with price or exchange fluctuations, then the entire mechanism of international equilibration, be it by way of gold flows or of exchange movements, is thrown completely out of gear. It is sometimes thought that it can be replaced by a series of barter trade agreements. But this is a pure delusion, based on the mistaken belief that equilibrium in the balance of trade between one country and the rest of the world implies equality of exports and imports between it and any other single country. As soon as it is realized that this is only the case by pure accident, the hope of reconstructing trade equilibrium by a series of bilateral agreements is seen to be quite without foundation. The concept of barter equilibrium is applicable only to exchange between two groups." (Lionel Robbins, *The Great Depression*, pp. 114-16.)

The high tariffs of today are shields, not spears: foolish shields perhaps, but still not vainglorious spears. When statesmen approach the practical problem of facilitating entrance of goods into countries now resisting them, this must be done with an understanding of the real basis of their resistance. For three years now a "World Economic Survey" has been issued annually by the Economic Intelligence Service of the League of Nations. With all appropriate condemnation of high tariffs, the larger immediate importance of monetary relations, and the influences of disequilibrium, are properly emphasized.

In practically every country of importance in the world are five pressing problems: (a) position and stability of the currency, (b) the national budget, (c) the price level, (d) the debt burden, and (e) the state of public confidence. The order is not the same in all countries, but practically everywhere these problems coexist. In some countries these problems emerged directly after the conclusion of peace; in others, directly after the price decline of 1920-21; in others, during the years of the "New Era" in the United States, which the disorganized foreign countries then regarded so cynically. With the march of the depression (now generally coming to be called The Great Depression) practically all countries were seized with internal economic conflicts. In October 1934, of the sixty-six countries in attendance (on paper) at the last International Economic Conference and of which only six are net-creditor countries, only seven countries possessed currencies with fixed parities, and were without exchange restrictions imposed directly or indirectly on imports. Of these it may be fairly remarked that their "fixed parities" are fair-weather parities, and it is not ungenerous to infer that even in these countries a "little control" has been on occasions indirectly and confidently exercised. The state of mind of the currencies of countries, if one may employ this expression, was never so confused as at the present time. Costs have been sacrificed to fictitious security, exchange stability to fancied stability of the internal price level, budgets to unemployment relief, and liquidation of excessive debt to appeasement of public clamor; behind stands the public psychology in defense of the improved standard of living so recently acquired.

Now these five major pressing problems are not theoretical

considerations; they are internally obvious, practical dilemmas or impasses. Much of the impulse for "self-sufficiency," most of the "economic nationalism" has derived from these pressing problems. In short, the much-berated "economic nationalism" and "self-sufficiency" were not forms of imperialism, petty in the case of a small country and grandiose in the case of a large state. They are not delusions of political grandeur. Pending solution of these internal problems, defense trenches had to be thrown up at the frontiers: the first trench was higher tariffs to keep out imports, the second trench was restrictions extending beyond tariffs, the third trench was exchange control. President Roosevelt threw up such a trench before the World Economic Conference. Thus construed, the post-war high tariffs abroad, which the Secretary of Agriculture decries so persistently, were the effect of the depression and not its cause. Competition between depreciated currencies has been worse than was competition between producers selling in international trade. Of course the tariffs in themselves intensified the depression, just as exchange control intensified the fiscal problem it had been set up to alleviate. But in the order of origin and of importance, tariffs were secondary and not primary.

Tariff rates mean little so long as the debit and credit relations in invisible items are not stabilized or foreseeable. When the disparities between uncontrollable price levels and uncontrollable external exchange rates lie outside the control of high tariffs, then by common experience these fall into the domain of arbitrary control by public officials. It is all too easy to berate creditor and debtor countries for their different types and acts of economic nationalism, overlooking the fact that a currency policy appropriate for a creditor country in the world of economic disequilibrium is inappropriate to a debtor country. And disequilibrium is the background of the internal and external conflict.

There is comfort as well as correctness in this view. If

the lessons of history are to be trusted, defense will subside when the offense is withdrawn. When the pressing problems, in country after country, are alleviated or solved, the obstacles of international trade will be retired, the extra tariff impediments will disappear, and import tariff rates will shrink to lower, perhaps even to low, levels. Recovery will not merely imply, it will enforce, a shift from nationalism to internationalism. High tariffs will be cured by recovery from the depression, not the depression cured by the lowering of high tariffs.

SUMMARY

We ascribe to the foreign countries contracting bilateral trade agreements with us the same desire and need we experience for internal balance between town and country; we must seek international cooperation instead of international competition, in a planned exchange of goods between countries, under the New Deal. This doctrine, however, runs counter to impulses towards self-sufficiency and is not felt abroad to be adapted to their consumers' needs and to their loss of export outlets for manufactures. Western Europe will not reduce agriculture unless guaranteed restoration of export outlets for urban industries.

The number of states exporting manufactures is steadily growing in consequence of dispersion of industries. This important newer development is explained and appraised. As a result of such dispersion of industries, we must expect our export of manufactures to decline relatively, later even perhaps absolutely. We can hardly hope to increase significantly our import of non-competitive goods. Decline in export of manufactures will tend to promote the passive balance of merchandise trade predicated by Secretary Wallace.

The major competitors of the United States in export of farm products are concentrated in a few countries. Wheat, lard, and cotton are used in illustration. These competitors are mostly newer countries, net-debtor countries, which will seek to take advantage of decline in European agriculture. Their inhabitants will find it difficult to see reasons for yielding to us.

Necessity of reform and stabilization of currencies is emphasized. With gold prices of agricultural staples very low, currency disequilibrium distorts prices and costs in international commerce. An indispensable prerequisite to recovery is installation of a sensitive system of equation of international merchandise accounts.

Foreign countries have several major difficulties—depreciation and instability of currencies, unbalanced budgets, low price levels, high debt burdens, and lack of public confidence. High import tariffs and extra-tariff obstacles to trade are mostly secondary and defensive. When these major defects are corrected, obstacles to movement of goods between countries will subside automatically.[1]

[1] As of June 15, it now seems probable, indeed inevitable, that sooner or later, directly or indirectly, in one way or another, the countries of the European Gold Bloc will go off gold and devaluate their currencies, devaluate their currencies and remain on a limited gold standard, or leave gold and tie their revalued currencies to sterling. This will be done to alleviate the suffering of deflation, restore trade, check flight of gold and capital, and revive confidence. If, as, and when such a development occurs, it ought to facilitate negotiations looking toward the establishment of new ratios of currencies and subsequent restabilization of exchange rates.

CHAPTER XI

ORGANIZATION INVOLVED IN THE THREE PLANS

BERTRAND RUSSELL closes *Freedom versus Organization* with the following sentence:

". . . It is not by pacifist sentiment, but by world-wide economic organization, that civilized mankind is to be saved from collective suicide." [1]

Probably no two men now in public life in the English-speaking countries have more different minds, and origins, than Bertrand Russell and Henry A. Wallace; but they are agreed in this forecast. Doubtless they would disagree on the type, scope, and technique of the organization required to save the world. Russell presumably inclines to an oligarchy of specialists, while Secretary Wallace relies on cooperation within a democracy. Secretary Wallace has clearly revealed in general terms the scope of organization which he feels will be necessary to put the "planned middle course" into operation. The following quotations from *America Must Choose* illustrate the point of view of Secretary Wallace:

". . . Tariff adjustments involve planning just as certainly as internal adjustments do." (pp. 1-2)

". . . What tariffs to lower? What goods to accept? How readjust our own farming operations and industrial operations to the planned inflow of foreign goods?" (p. 2)

". . . I cannot too sharply emphasize my conviction that internationalism must be even more carefully planned than a program of economic nationalism." (p. 2)

[1] *Freedom versus Organization, 1814-1914* (New York, W. W. Norton & Co., 1934), p. 451.

"Of course, there are a few of our manufacturing industries which would require readjustment if we continue to follow the national plan exclusively, but for the most part the burden of the adjustments will fall on agriculture.

"International planning, on the other hand, would throw the greater burden of adjustment on factories rather than on farms." (p. 8)

". . . the fact remains that the pain and distress of nationalist readjustment, and a retreat from world markets would bear down far more heavily on agriculture than on industry." (p. 10)

"If we finally go all the way toward nationalism, it may be necessary to have compulsory control of marketing, licensing of plowed land, and base and surplus quotas for every farmer for every product for each month in the year. We may have to have government control of all surpluses, and a far greater degree of public ownership than we have now. It may be necessary to make a public utility out of agriculture. . . . Every plowed field would have its permit sticking up on its post." (p. 11)

"This will involve a radical reduction in tariffs. That might seriously hurt certain industries, and a few kinds of agricultural businesses, such as sugar-beet-growing and flax-growing. It might also cause pain for a while to wool-growers, and to farmers who supply material for various edible oils. I think we ought to face that fact. If we are going to lower tariffs radically, there may have to be some definite planning whereby certain industries or businesses will have to be retired. The government might have to help furnish means for the orderly retirement of such businesses, and even select those which are thus to be retired. . . . It would seem, therefore, that international planning must include a complete survey, item by item, of all the products that enter into our annual output, and a conscious decision as to which kind of products we might receive in large quantities from abroad, in time of peace, without jeopardizing those industries which we absolutely require in time of war." (p. 18)

"Few people realize that it takes just as much planning to follow a plan of internationalism by exchange of goods, not promises, as it does the path of nationalism. . . .

"A truly practical readjustment of our own tariff policy would involve the careful examination of every product produced in the

United States or imported, and the determination of just which of our monopolistic or inefficient industries we are willing to expose to real foreign competition." (pp. 28-29)

It is next pertinent to inquire to what prospective extent the organization under "nationalism," under "internationalism," and under the "planned middle course" respectively, would be different, in type, extent, and technique.

Under a forthright *nationalism* it would be necessary to take out of crop land at least 50 million acres of good land or some 100 million acres of poor land; to regiment all regions, all crops, and all farmers to greater or lesser extent; to establish an extensive system of payments to recompense farmers for contraction of acreage; to control, modify, and possibly execute the steps of distribution of farm products; to impose processing taxes in order that consumers should be made to contribute to the government the sums paid out to farmers; to revise farm taxation to meet the contracted operations and the lessened outturn; to refund farm debt, in terms of principle and interest, to meet the contracted operations and the lessened outturn; to distribute and re-employ, in ways not yet foreseeable, the farm population that would be made redundant by contracted operations and lessened outturn; to allocate the domestic market between competing farm products; to control the importation of directly and indirectly competitive farm products, and to expand outturn of domestic products that might be used in substitution; and to endeavor in one form or another so to raise the price level of farm products or lower the price level of industrial products as to maintain the purchasing power of the farm dollar on a plane appropriate to the American standard of living.

Under a forthright *nationalism,* it would be necessary also to carry through fairly extensive but less thoroughgoing modifications in the operations, types, and outturn of industrial products. Inventions, new methods, obsolescence, and reorganization would need to be controlled under a planned program. These industrial products would represent our purchasing power for agricultural and industrial imports; and if the imports were to be selected and controlled on the basis of a planned scheme of requirements, it would be necessary to plan the exports also, possibly with the introduction of quotas of industrial exports and industrial imports. Embracing both town and country, an equitable re-balance of our economic life would be striven for.

Since under a forthright *nationalism* the country would avoid a passive balance of merchandise trade, the service charges on foreign loans could not be paid in dollars, and the earnings of direct investments abroad could not be transferred in dollars. These foreign investments of American nationals would perforce have to accumulate abroad; possibly the rights and obligations of American owners of the foreign balances and properties would in case of war, or even in time of peace, become the subject of diplomatic controversy. How to protect the foreign property right of American holders when their earnings could, by the very definition of the system, not be brought into the United States, would represent a large problem, compared with which the blocked marks and pesos are, for example, a small present problem. Further export of American capital would presumably not occur, and exports of merchandise would become more difficult. It would be found necessary to supplement high import tariff rates with additional impediments to importation, such as quotas, licenses, taxes, and the other devices now in use throughout the world.

If one will survey the existing experiences in "economic isolation" to be witnessed in numerous countries throughout the world, one will be brought to the realization that a plan of economic nationalism would require both intensive and extensive organization, for which we possess some precedents in our national experience (mostly during the war), but for most of which it would be necessary to create new implements and rules. The most relevant illustrations of such nationalistic organization are to be found in Russia and Italy, under different forms of government. A re-reading of Thuenen's *Isolierte Staat* [1] yields no guidance for modern economic nationalism.

Under a forthright *internationalism* (which would mean practically a tariff-for-revenue) the burden of adjustment would fall almost entirely on urban industry. No land would need to be withdrawn from crops; indeed, it is assumed that in certain regions and for certain crops the acreage in operation might expand. In a few directions, truly, imported farm products would compete severely with domestic products: high-grade Marquis wheat from Canada would displace lower-grade domestic hard wheat to a considerable extent; duty-free imported vegetable oils would compete drastically with cottonseed oil and lard, to some extent with butter; refrigerated meat from the Southern Hemisphere would displace American meat on the poorer tables of the industrial coastal cities; higher-grade imported wool would compete destructively with lower-grade domestic wool. But in such cases it is assumed that the prices paid by farmers for operative equipment and buildings and for household goods would be so greatly lowered, and the costs of production thus so much reduced, that lower selling prices would be acceptable with the larger volumes presumably to be expected.[2] In the very theory of internationalism it is implied that under this system Europe (ex-Russia) would cooperate to contract her agriculture and resume heavy importation

[1] *Der isolierte Staat in Beziehung auf Landwirtschaft und Nationalokonomie* (The Isolated State in Relation to Agriculture and National Economy).

[2] This contention is hardly advanced in a strongly affirmative manner.

from the United States. This could not be allowed merely to be expected as a matter of course; there would need to be international agreement to insure the scaling down of the agriculture of the net-importing countries, to correspond with the state of the agriculture of the United States. Just how, by negotiation and organization, the European landlords and peasants would be induced to cooperate in this contraction of their acreage and loss of their outturn, is not, unfortunately for the planned internationalism, to be found in the psychology of the peasants or in the records of international conferences since the war. Finally, the agricultures of the competing surplus states—Russia and the overseas extractive countries—would need to be held in leash, to be kept in line with the agricultures of Europe and the United States. Protection from dumping of cheap staples would still need to be prohibited.

On the side of urban industry very extensive adjustment would need to be made. Many American manufacturing plants would be closed, others would have their operations curtailed. We would need to accept probably two billion dollars' worth of added imports, mostly manufactures. It would be necessary to set up a schedule of priorities based on criteria in respect of labor, capital, and methods, for which we have no precedents outside of war. A scheme of permissible and prescribed substitution would have to be set up and enforced. Provision would need to be made for reimbursement of losses, in respect both of plants and securities. Extensive revision of taxation would need to be introduced, appropriate to the new redistribution and scaling down of industries. Superfluous urban labor would need to be distributed and re-employed; presumably the urban population would decline and the rural population rise, relatively. In short, a most extensive reorganization and regimentation of urban industry is implied, compared with which the controlled industry of the war was a blue-print and the NRA of the New Deal a bare alphabet. Just as in the case of farm products, it would be necessary, through cooperation, to secure the appropriate adjustments (if they could be forecasted) in urban industries in foreign countries, which would permit of a give-and-take in the enlargement of imports into the United States.[1]

Under a forthright *internationalism,* finally, the service charges on existing foreign investments would be paid with goods. We would acquire a heavy passive balance of merchandise trade. Presumably new foreign investment would be revived, the balance of merchandise trade would later be still more strongly passive, to the extent necessary to cover the payment of old and new service charges on foreign debt and to meet the increased export of farm products (possibly but not certainly) to be expected under this system. The plan of internationalism implies enlarged foreign trade; this would, according to New Dealers, need to be organized within the United States (balanced between town and country) and between this country and the principal importing and competing countries. And since these importing countries would need to organize their internal economies, just as we would need to organize ours, the bilateral organization would represent an extensive and unprecedented regimentation of the export and import industries in the countries active in foreign commerce. It goes without saying that a system of internationalism cannot be developed in the

[1] Incidentally remarked, there is a great deal of rather naïve expectation in regard to the position of agriculture under internationalism. It is not obvious why a country like Russia should be expected to contract her agriculture on external grounds. It is not safe to disregard the probability of production costs of agricultural products in some parts of the world being reduced to such low levels as to be inacceptable to American farmers no matter how low the prices on what they buy. In short, it is not to be assumed that under a tariff-for-revenue-only, the new relationship to be expected between prices received and paid by American farmers would be such as to make the purchasing power of our crops bring to the growers the standard of living to which they are accustomed.

absence of stable, or at least foreseeable and insurable, exchange rates; this would imply either the revival of a changed gold standard or of a managed international currency. Victorian economists hold that foreign trade would flow freely in the absence of regimentation and that new adjustments would emerge; but Secretary Wallace is afraid of it because "absolutely free competition . . . produces unendurable overconcentrations of goods and power."

Coming now to consider the organization required in the event of the adoption of the *"planned middle course,"* we observe that this partakes of the characteristics and opportunities, and of the difficulties and limitations, of both the *nationalist* and *internationalist* plans. It would entail much less contraction of agriculture than is enforced in the nationalist plan; it would entail much less adjustment of industry than is imposed in the internationalist plan. Yet from the standpoint of organization, considering that the difficulties of organization are essentially qualitative rather than quantitative, it is doubtful on either side whether the organization of the "planned middle course" would in either direction be so very much easier than the two extreme plans.

Consider agriculture. The *"planned middle course"* requires the contraction of crop land by 25 million acres of good land or 50 million acres of poor land. How much easier would it be to eliminate 25 million good acres than 50 million good acres, or 50 million poor acres than 100 million poor acres?[1] Contraction of crop land by 25 million good acres would to some extent entail regimentation in all regions, for all crops, and of all farmers; a system of payments to recompense farmers would have to be set up, smaller but politically perhaps quite as difficult. Distribution of farm products would need to be controlled; processing and compensa-

[1] In the report of the Land Planning Committee of the National Resources Board, it was proposed to retire seventy-five million acres of poor farm land in order to retire twenty million acres of poor land in crops.

tory taxes would need to be imposed. Farm debts and farm taxes would still require readjustment; the farm population would still be somewhat too large in some regions and require relocation; it would still be necessary to decide between competing domestic crops; it would still be necessary to raise the price level of farm products. In short, the problems and burdens of organization to readjust supply to demand would of course be smaller, but quite as intricate, and conceivably not much less difficult politically.

Industrial adjustments also, though smaller in scope, would be indispensable. Contractual relations with foreign countries through bilateral treaties, with or without quotas, would still be required, with the items under negotiation not so large, though almost as numerous and perhaps quite as intricate. The increased imports to be expected would be reduced from more than two to one billion dollars, according to our estimate. But the selection and allocation of the goods to be imported might be about as difficult in the lesser as in the larger volume. The changes in the tariff, the log-rolling and wire-pulling, would not be politically alleviated with a somewhat smaller objective, but might instead be augmented. The history of tariff wars does not suggest that these assume bitterness in proportion with the magnitude of the objective involved; they arise more as expression of the sensitiveness of the interests involved. Under a "planned middle course" the payment of service charges on foreign debt could hardly be guaranteed unless the passive account of merchandise trade is larger than assumed; nor would an increase in export of farm products proportional to the acreage contraction be assured. In the case of the "planned middle course," the objectives would be smaller, but the difficulties perhaps little less, and the disappointments possibly as large.

In short, it seems to us from the standpoint of organization that the *"planned middle course"* lacks in part the outstanding incentives and objectives of *nationalism* and *internationalism* respectively, while sharing their difficulties. In the outside world a plan of clear-cut nationalism or of clear-cut internationalism would make an appeal to different countries on their respective merits, whereas a "planned middle course" might appeal to neither side and would possibly displease both. "Nationalism" and "internationalism" are esteemed to be clear-cut; the "planned middle course" is likely to be regarded as a compromise without definitive features or attractions.

The Secretary uses the expression "precisely halfway between these two extremes." Precisely halfway between 0 million acres and 50 million acres. Surely the word "precisely" is here nothing but a none-too-plausible adverb: no one can draw such a line "halfway." So long as there is an issue between high tariff and tariff for revenue, a technical argument would be possible. But when the free-trade advocates agree to a "moderate" protection in order to avoid readjustments, and the high-tariff advocates agree to a "lower" protection in order to check monopoly, then they meet on a middle ground of compromise and only waste words on relative and comparative production costs. The compromise on relative production costs and comparative advantage was, is, and will continue to be a straddle, since these cannot be defined in theory and reproduced in practice. By the same token, any planned middle course involves a dialectical straddle.

Finally, the inherent weakness of the "planned middle course" is fully revealed when one comes to realize that it is primarily, indeed one may say only, a tariff policy, with adjustments and organization appropriate thereto. It takes little account of monetary circumstances. But the plain truth is that in the world today, and for the foreseeable future, monetary policies, under- and overvaluation of currencies, uncontrollabilities of exchange rates, and controls of transfers are of far greater influence than tariff rates on the inbound and outbound commerce of the nations active in international trade.[1] Secretary Wallace does not make his plan of tariff compromise contingent on preliminary monetary stabilization between trading nations. Following monetary stabilization, the nationalist and the internationalist plan respectively would appear in an entirely different light from a plan without monetary stabilization. The attempt to determine the trade of the United States by bilateral negotiations on tariffs, with organization by the contracting parties appropriate thereto, is beginning at the small end of the problem. The cart is in front of the horse. No trader knows the future value of the dollar in terms of other currencies. Secretary Wallace seems to think that the major cause of the depression, so far as it involves our agriculture, lies in high tariffs; this is just as biased as the wider view in Victorian circles that the major cause of the world depression lay in tariff walls. The present absurd tariffs are largely the result of the depression, but the previous tariffs were not the cause of the depression.

A general observation may fittingly conclude this section. Those who, like Secretary Wallace, believe that *laissez-faire* is the cause of economic disorganization ("absolutely free competition, conducted nationally or on a world scale, produces unendurable overconcentrations of goods and power") and those who, like Bertrand Russell, see in it the roots of imperialism in the widest sense, agree that the

[1] In July 1933 President Roosevelt informed the World Economic Conference in London that it was not possible to plan a stabilization of exchange rates until our country had effected an internal revaluation of the currency. This was a sound position. It applies now to international planning. It is not possible to plan internationally until after a country has planned domestically and proved the plan in trial and error. Secretary Wallace is trying to plan internationally before he has planned domestically to a successful outcome.

remedy is planned organization. The larger and more widespread a problem, the more organization required. What is lacking in this ultimate wisdom is inability to realize the magnitude of the coordination of forces involved in the stipulated organization. *This lies within the collective capacity of mankind only when the contracting countries have the internal political powers to execute the essential foreign coordinations.* There is today, unfortunately, no indication that any considerable proportion of the governments of the thirty-seven states named above possess the prerequisite political power or technical capacity. To revert to the earlier phraseology—if we grant the good intentions, and assume the intelligence, we still see no precedent for the mechanism and no adequate evidence of the discipline.

The question is often asked, what is the difference between the New Deal and Socialism? The difference is one of method, not of objective. Socialism implies ownership of the means of production, with subsequent equitable partition of the dividend. The New Deal implies control and regimentation of the means of production, ownership being left ostensibly in private hands, with subsequent equitable partition of the dividend. Under Socialism, which really means state ownership, there is unification of ownership and operation. Under the New Deal, ostensibly there is private ownership, with operation according to a planned system under the authority of the state. Thus interpreted, the New Deal stands much closer to Fascism than to Communism. It differs from Fascism in that this is an oligarchy at the top of the corporate state while the New Deal is designed to operate through cooperation of individuals within a democracy. The New Deal shares the inherent weakness of democracy, contrasted with the inherent strength of an oligarchy, in respect to technical mechanism and concentration of discipline. It differs from Communism in the discipline needed and possessed. The organization implied in the New Deal is far beyond anything previously undertaken in our country, both in scope and detail.[1] It is in few ways simpler than the organization in Communism and Fascism.

SUMMARY

Despite obvious misgivings, Secretary Wallace argues for the "planned middle course" on the ground that the adjustments and requisite organization would be simpler than those required for the extreme plans of "nationalism" and "internationalism." It is not certain that the essential difficulties would be significantly different. The adjustments necessary in agriculture and industry would be somewhat smaller and technically somewhat simpler; but the political difficulties would probably not be significantly less. The "planned middle course" lacks the outstanding objectives and the incentives of "nationalism" and "internationalism," but still partakes of their worst difficulties. The method of the planned middle course is mostly tariff reduction—certainly an old prescription for a relatively new disease. Concluding observations are devoted to a comparison between the New Deal, Socialism, Communism, and Fascism.

[1] In the light of the recent decision of the Supreme Court, would it be constitutional for an official in Washington to allocate arbitrary amounts of an import or an export quota to one state and different amounts to another state?

CHAPTER XII

SUMMARIZED CRITICISM

THE "planned middle course" of Secretary Wallace has three major objectives: (a) the removal of 25 million acres from tillage; (b) the increase of agricultural exports above the otherwise level to the extent of a half-billion dollars; and (c) the increase of non-agricultural imports over the otherwise level to the extent of a billion dollars. These planned extensions of foreign trade are to be attained through bilateral trade agreements with a large number of countries. These treaty negotiations are already under way with many countries.

The objectives of the New Deal, as presented in the "planned middle course," are for the most part not new; but the procedures are for the most part for this country both new and unique. Throughout the previous chapters we have had frequent occasion to question this, to qualify that, and to refute the other. Here we wish to focus some of the objections into summarized criticisms. It will be advantageous first to make a résumé of the most relevant points.

(1) The important trading countries of the world exceed fifty in number; let us use thirty-seven in illustration. It is implied to have our country adopt thirty-six bilateral commercial treaties. Under each of these treaties the trade movements of the United States must tend more than at present towards a passive balance of merchandise trade. Each of these thirty-six treaties ought to be coordinated with the other thirty-five, expressing a consistent policy of stimu-

lation of certain agricultural exports and repression of export of certain manufactures from the United States, with increase mainly of non-agricultural imports into this country from the thirty-six foreign countries.

(2) Of these thirty-seven countries, only six are net-creditor countries, the remainder are net-debtor countries. In each of these bilateral treaties account must be taken of this relationship. Since under a forthright system of bilateral treaties, international commerce will tend to be channelized and multangular trade reduced, it follows that a different strategy in negotiation would need to be applied to those countries which sell to us more than they buy from us, than would be applicable to those which buy from us more than they sell to us. Clearly, the objective in respect to a passive balance of merchandise trade in the account of the United States will demand a different treatment, depending on net-creditor and net-debtor status and also on active or passive position of trade of the contracting countries with this country.

(3) Among the countries of the world, the United States is unique in being at once a heavy actual and potential exporter of agricultural products, industrial raw materials, and semi-finished and finished manufactures all the way from industrial equipment to final consumers' goods. The United States thus occupies the anomalous position of being a net-creditor country with a strong urge towards active export which is inherent in our resources, technical equipment, and natural genius. Germany, as a net-debtor country, is in a position quite as anomalous as that of the United States, since Germany by virtue of her resources, technical equipment, and natural genius should be a net-creditor country.

(4) At present five of the thirty-seven countries are nominally on the gold standard; a group of the countries are on the (managed) sterling standard; the rest of the coun-

tries are on inconvertible national standards. In most countries the problem of currency is for the moment the mainspring of tariff policy. It is clear that the countries of the gold bloc must reflate their price levels, perhaps devalue their currencies. Such reflation of the price levels within the European gold countries, however, must be done through some policy agreement with the countries that have abandoned gold and thus secured a measure of elevation of the price level. Two things are sought: a stimulation of enterprise through improvement in the price levels and a restoration of the flexibility of foreign exchanges upon the newer levels. Until such a coordination is secured in Europe, no defensive tariff walls will be lowered. For each of these treaties it will be urged that the present situation constitutes an emergency. Was a fitter stage ever set for a Machiavelli?

(5) Certain of our bilateral treaties will be contracted with important net-importing countries which in the past have been heavy importers of agricultural products from the United States, on whom in the future reliance must be placed (if at all) for the revival of this export trade. These are principally the industrial countries of Europe. These countries must be induced to contract their agricultures and instead to import from the United States. Reciprocally, we must contract certain manufacturing plants and import goods from them instead, which possibly implies enlargement of their manufacturing plants or establishment of new ones. These countries would probably need to be pledged to accept certain quotas of farm products from this country against which we would pledge our acceptance of certain quotas of manufactures. In particular these countries ought to pledge themselves to grant to the United States not merely quotas but probably also proportions of their total imports of farm products, as protection against the possibly cheaper import prices from competitive exporting countries. Secretary Wal-

lace hopes these increases in imports and exports can be secured through bilateral lowering of tariff rates, but certainly there will need also to be stipulations to insure the regimentation involved.

(6) Among these bilateral treaties will be many with countries which like ourselves produce large exportable surpluses of farm products. The list includes Canada, Cuba, Argentina, Australia, New Zealand, South Africa, Russia, Denmark, and Holland. The bilateral treaties with these competitive exporting countries would need to contemplate some provision for a division of the import markets. In order to enjoy quotas or allocations in Europe, we must recognize quotas to our competitors. In order to carry through bilateral treaties with our competitors in export of farm products, we shall need to bear in mind the reciprocal negotiations between our country and the principal net-importing countries: the right hand dealing with Canada will need to know what the left hand is doing in dealing with the United Kingdom; and so forth. It would seem to be imperative that our bilateral treaties with these extractive countries should include the complete list (including those of central Europe), since obviously one wheat exporter not under treaty could make the wheat agreements of others inoperable. This implies that a set of wheat treaties would replace the futile wheat conferences.

(7) It is presumably implied that when we contract bilateral trade treaties with thirty-six countries, these countries will find themselves prepared, or compelled, most of them at least, to contract bilateral trade agreements with one another. If each one of thirty-seven countries were to make a bilateral trade treaty with each of the other thirty-six, this would amount to approximately six hundred bilateral treaties. The number is impressive enough, from any point of view. The order might become a matter of jockeying,

since it would be of advantage to negotiate late rather than early. The technical difficulties, considering the limitation of trained staffs in most countries, are appalling. Sooner or later such a program might be completed—probably by the time the world has passed through this depression, gone through another boom, and landed in another depression.

(8) Certain treaties would deal especially with peculiar problems, such as those of non-competitive goods trading against highly competitive goods. How much American cotton would Japan pledge herself to take from us instead of from India, in return for added imports of raw silk from Japan into the United States? What have we to offer Egypt, Brazil, and India to induce them to plow up part of their enlarging cotton acreage? These are examples. This subgroup of treaties would present most intricate dilemmas.

(9) None of these treaties could be enforced in the absence of concordant or adaptable monetary policies, stable national currencies, balanced budgets, and foreseeable foreign exchange rates. The United States could not expect important countries of the world to agree to enter into contractual disposition of goods and services without some system of equilibrium in foreign exchange relations and in equation of current balances, such as existed before the war. One of two viewpoints might be anticipated: the negotiating countries might prefer to declare that they could make no commitments abroad until they had set their domestic monetary houses in order (as we disclosed in London in 1933); or they might profess a willingness to make commitments in respect of merchandise trade, with full appreciation of the prospect that such commitments might ruin the producer classes of their countries and subject the consumer classes to untoward effects. If we judge the temper of the world correctly, most of the nations would decline to bind themselves to contracts in respect to movements of commodities, so long

as the machinery and facilities of international trade in monetary terms are in virtual chaos.

(10) There must be some provision for appeal, adjudication, and enforcement. Most treaties contain provision for a tribunal to which disputes may be referred. There is no reason to anticipate that bilateral commercial treaties will find automatic execution. The history of the recently rephrased commercial treaty with Germany is an illustration in point. If each pair of countries is to have a tribunal for appeal and decision on disputed points, the number of such tribunals will only be less feared than the number of separate bilateral treaties.

(11) The scheme of bilateral trade agreements as planned by Secretary Wallace presumably represents the extension of the New Deal into foreign commerce. It is proposed so to formulate the bilateral treaties as to contribute in the United States to a better balance between city and country and a more equitable distribution of the national income. It is implied correspondingly that in the negotiation of these bilateral treaties endeavor shall be made to introduce the policies of the New Deal into foreign countries, to bring about a better balance between town and country and a more equitable distribution of the national dividend. Implied, therefore, is a bilateral regimentation of industry and agriculture. This will be a new form of missionary activity. In the past, trade followed the missionaries; here the missionaries follow trade.

These observations apply to the "planned middle course" of Secretary Wallace quite as they would apply to a planned internationalism, which he has sketched. Even if the world continued along the path of economic nationalism, the circumstances to which we had adverted under paragraph (9) would still remain; but there is little question that negotiations towards a workable international monetary exchange policy would be less difficult, because less eccentric, in the case of economic nationalism than in the case of economic internationalism. Let us now proceed to the relevant criticisms.

With respect to the program of *contraction of acreage,*[1] little objection is to be raised in principle, nor are the details severely to be criticised. It is to be agreed that our agriculture was overextended by the war. Also, the agricultures of many of our competitors in world markets were overextended by the war. Even before the onset of the depression, there was a lack of foreign purchasing power in terms of money, which has been exaggerated by the depression; with recovery from the depression, a deficiency of such purchasing power is still to be anticipated. Therefore, since the rate of growth of our population is tapering off, contraction of acreage in crops seems inevitable. This holds even if the stipulated increase in export of American farm products were to be secured. Whether the figures of 25 million good acres or 50 million poor acres are somewhat too large or too small is not a point of criticism. In theory, it would be better to remove 50 million acres of submarginal land—land that has one or more of several defects of soil or climate—restore these scattered areas to the public domain and return them to grass, brush, or forest, as seems most appropriate. As a practical measure, however, it seems more likely that the land would be taken out of the acreage now devoted to wheat, corn, and cotton, for the most part. Technically trained men are available to plan such a contraction of acreage. The secondary problem of surplus due to increased productivity with improved methods on the contracted acre-

[1] "Studies of our land requirements which take into consideration the available land areas, the probable growth of population, the trend in consumption, technical progress in agriculture, and foreign-trade prospects indicate that the present need is not agricultural expansion but contraction."—Arthur M. Hyde, Secretary of Agriculture, "The Year in Agriculture," *Agriculture Yearbook,* 1931, p. 40.

age would not arise for a few years. The allocation of the stipulated additional export of farm products would be more difficult politically than technically. In short, the acreage adjustment phase of the "planned middle course," while bristling with difficulties of a minor nature, is not seriously to be criticised on general national grounds. The regimentation of agriculture on the contracted basis is more open to criticism than is the acreage contraction itself.

The compensatory part of the "planned middle course," the *adjustment* on the side of *urban industry,* is much more open to criticism. To plan an increase of non-agricultural imports equivalent in value to a billion dollars, and sequentially to curtail the operations of urban industries to the extent of the equivalent of a billion dollars, would necessitate selections between goods and services, between regions, and between industries, on a scope never before undertaken and for which precedents do not exist. The selections on the domestic side would necessarily involve considerations of availability of resources, of processes, of obsolescence and new equipment, and of costs of production. In the selection of the added non-agricultural imports the same considerations would apply. An intensive and extensive regimentation is implied. Such adjustments would inevitably provoke technical adaptations and defensive reactions on the part of consumers. We do not believe factual material exists, at home or abroad, to enable social planners to arrive expeditiously at convincing and equitable decisions. That such a regimentation of urban industry would lead immediately to the courts is perhaps more a fact than a criticism. In our judgment, the New Dealers grossly overestimate both the planning talent at our command and the factual information in our possession. We venture to make the challenge that a review of the acts of the War Industries Boards in the belligerent countries during the World War will fully confirm this criticism. As we stated above, we feel that in respect to contraction of agriculture, reasonably efficient adjustments could be arrived at technically; but with respect to the contemplated adjustments in urban industry, the decisions would be largely guesswork. And guesswork is the fault now laid at the door of private initiative.

We regard the *order of procedure* as inverted, or, better perhaps, perverted. The mechanism of tariff reduction is exaggerated out of all historical proportion. The order of procedure ought to be (a) revaluation of currencies and stabilization of foreign exchanges, with restoration of an efficient system for clearance of accounts in international trade; (b) elimination of extra-tariff obstacles to foreign commerce, including all of the devices outside of import duties—licenses, permits, taxes, certificates, subsidies, quotas, regulations of use, embargoes, and whatever else there may be—that is, to restore the situation as it existed before the war, when tariff duties were practically the only device tending to restrain imports of goods; (c) lowering of import duties either by spontaneous action of individual countries or through agreements between countries. Let these be briefly considered in the same order.

(a) *Revaluation of currencies and stabilization of foreign exchanges.* It has presumably to be recognized that gold is no longer money, in the old sense, whatever its future status as a monetary commodity. Money within a country is credit based on bank deposits. How to interrelate the credit in one country with the credit of another country is the transfer problem of foreign trade. International commerce is an aggregation of goods and services that represent promises to deliver on one side and promises to pay on the other. The expeditious clearing of these promises is dependable upon foreseeable, or insurable, rates of exchange of the moneys of the buying and selling sides. Whenever such clearances are channelized, the balances at all times must tend to be high; whenever these clearances are centralized, the balances remaining on any day tend to be small. Such balances in the past were sometimes covered with a shipment of gold, but clearly might as well be covered by overdrafts. It is upon the restoration of such stabilization between values of currencies that the recovery of world trade depends. Such restoration does not imply the return of movements of gold; if our scope of management is not far enough advanced to get past that stumbling block, then the recovery of the processes of international exchange of goods and services will be deferred. The goods and services are continuously emerging, with foreseeable seasonal variations; the mechanism of transfer of titles and of possession to these goods and services has ceased to function on the scale of outturn of the goods and services. This restoration is the first problem in international commerce. The price level, the tariff level, are secondary.

The long-term question is larger than the settlement of exchange rates, more than application of purchasing power parities. At present the risks of doing business in foreign countries are heavy. The currencies are unstable within the countries; for the protection of currencies and of national budgets, imports of goods are restrained. Differences in prices in different countries do not react on costs, or costs on prices, as they must if flexibility of commerce is to be facilitated. Between countries, prices and costs have little relation to volumes of production and consumption. A comprehensive undertaking, first to revalue currencies within countries and then to allow these parities to seek their relations in open markets with the parities of other countries, is the first requisite. Out of such trial and error will emerge in each country the information as to the real value of the currency which is now lacking. Also, there must be a basis of convertibility which can be insured or hedged, on the foreseeability of which importers and exporters can depend. This means the restoration of that flexibility and facility, so conspicuous before the war, which made payments between countries almost as easy and riskless as within countries. This involves amplification of the use of bankers' acceptances; further, this implies a method and place of clearing regularly the accounts of such trading countries as are to some extent out of balance. There will need to be some control over extremes, for a time at least; but within moderate and specified ranges the free adjustment of parities must be permitted and encouraged.

To say this is not to argue for restoration of any stated form of the gold standard or for the acceptance of any system of managed standard. This is not to decide between cooperation of central banks or a Bank of International Settlements. It does not imply gold standard or credit standard, automatic or managed. It means an agreed and accepted procedure. It is merely to argue for restoration of the flexible equilibrium, the ebb-and-flow of the tide of international transactions described earlier as characteristic of the highest development of foreign trade just before the World War. The processes of exchange in the monetary sense, the processes of distribution in the transfer sense, the processes of equation in the price sense, these must be restored before recovery can be expected. Currencies must be given their true internal values: some are overvalued abroad, others are undervalued abroad, and these malpositions must be corrected to obviate the perversive influences on imports and exports.

The policy of monetary reform involves initially only the acceptance of concordant policy by a few of the leading countries. In the very nature of the negotiations a few countries can get together on a monetary policy far more easily than a large number of countries can get together on a tariff policy. Just as a group of countries followed the United Kingdom in the use of sterling when that country left gold, so a far larger group would at once follow the leadership of the key countries in a reform of monetary policy. This leadership, in the nature of things, must lie within the net-creditor countries. It does not imply subordination of the United States to Great Britain, nor the converse. It implies simply a definitive, though possibly adjustable, valuation of the currencies of the strategic countries whose currencies have now no virtually fixed parities, viz., Great Britain, Japan, and the United States. Until these countries make up their minds what the pound sterling, the yen, and the dollar are worth internally and on that basis proceed to an acknowledged parity between them externally, there is no possibility of cohesion of the other actively trading countries of the world in any plan. Once dollar, yen, and pound sterling are flexibly and openly exchangeable, on free markets, then equilibrium with flexibility will be restored in the marts of world trade. The policy of Great Britain means the policy of the British Commonwealth of Nations. All of the European countries off the gold standard will follow Great Britain. The policy of the United States practically implies the policy of the large number of countries which sell to us more than they buy from us. The countries of the gold bloc, led by France, may be trusted to adjust themselves to any established international position. Germany and Italy will follow, by logical persuasion or automatic economic compulsion. A monetary agreement between a half-dozen countries (really only four, the United States, Great Britain, France, and Japan), is not only more adaptable than trade agreements between thirty countries; it is the direct approach to the fundamental problem, of which high tariffs are merely a bad symptom.

It ought to be kept in mind that in the revaluation of currencies and subsequent stabilization of foreign exchanges long-term considerations should take precedence over temporary exigencies, even if these resemble emergencies. Every effort ought to be made to make the revaluations and stabilizations enduring. This is no place for the display of *force majeure;* equity is most important. If, for illustration, it should be decided to revalue the dollar and the pound sterling in terms of gold at half of their pars and then by agreement to maintain between them over a period of time the normal ratio of 4.86 to 1, this would not be equitable on several grounds. It strikes us as absurd, in view of the resources, debts, and volumes of money in the two countries, to state that the real value of the dollar is no higher relatively than the real value of the pound sterling. The objective in revaluation of currencies and restabilization of foreign exchanges ought to be to have the *de facto* status recognized *de jure.* The objective ought not to be a changing of import and export relations to the advantage of some countries and the disadvantage of others. Put it another way, revaluation of currencies and restabilization of foreign exchanges should be permissive of trade, not mandatory to trade. It would be a tragic blunder if the major countries of the world should make the mistake made by Great Britain in 1925, namely, revaluation of the currency on the wrong basis.

(b) *Elimination of extra-tariff trade obstacles.* It is to be re-emphasized that these perversive devices are not of the same order and origin as import tariff rates, and do not represent the last stage of "astronomical" import duties. These are defensive devices for the real or fancied protection of a country from the effects of depreciated currency and disorganized foreign exchange. They have for the most part different motives from high tariff rates; quotas and embargoes have essentially little in common with high tariff rates. Many of the countries of Europe could abolish their import tariff schedules and control the inbound movements of foreign goods entirely by these devices. Once currencies are revalued and foreign exchanges restabilized, once the normal modes of transfers of payments between countries are restored, once the purchase and sale of goods and services between countries resemble what they are between states in our country, then these extra-tariff obstacles will have lost their *raison d'être*. Many of them will cease by the very terms of their enactment, just as an anti-dumping penalty lapses when dumping ceases. Beyond this, once the real or fancied need for the defense disappears, the trenches will be abandoned. The world recognizes the abnormality of these devices, and they will be marked for cancellation on all sides when currencies are again stable and the exchanges equitable. Bilateral trade negotiations are not the appropriate method of eliminating extra-tariff obstacles to commerce: whatever promise such agreements hold to the contracting parties will lie in the field of tariff duties.

(c) *Lowering of tariff rates.* In the "planned middle course" of Secretary Wallace the additional export of farm products above the otherwise level is to be sought through lowering of tariff duties in the importing countries (presumably with the assistance of quotas), and the increase of non-agricultural imports into our country above the otherwise level is to be sought through lowering of tariff duties (presumably with the assistance of quotas); these reciprocal concessions would be fixed in bilateral trade agreements. Before exposing the inherent limitations of the bilateral agreements, it is important to face squarely the question of most-favored-nation treatment, adopted by our country in 1922.

The United States has not yet crossed the Rubicon of

most-favored-nation treatment versus special national concession. Bilateral trade agreements, negotiated to obtain special concessions, have tended to cause friction between nations; whenever such concessions are not generalized to all countries, they are likely to disturb established currents of international trade. An outlet gained in one country may be lost in others and imports may be favored from countries not best adapted to the product in question. In particular, bilateral trade, channelized by agreement, checks multangular trade, which, at the peak of our foreign commerce, probably approached half of the total. The argument for bilateral agreements outside of unconditional most-favored-nation treatment fails to dislodge the lesson of experience in favor of concessions generalized within most-favored-nation treatment. Classical economists certainly, and realists in general, are agreed that in reciprocal trade treaties the broadening of the channels of trade should take precedence over securing of special advantages; broad general concessions instead of narrow individual advantages should be the adopted principle of such negotiations. The conventional and traditional bilateral trade treaties have not given to invisible items that freedom of play which quite certainly will be demanded by debtor countries in the future; the new kind offers no better promise. To endeavor through bilateral treaties to attain anything approximating a balance of trade in goods between two countries, would seriously disrupt commercially established trade relations, forcing goods into direct channels which more properly should circulate through multangular channels. It seems probable that with channelized trade the average length of ocean haul would be increased. We regard as fallacious any planned development of foreign trade that promotes direct trade and discourages multangular trade. It is not to be questioned that the systematic promotion of direct trade through bilateral treaties cannot favor gross expansion of foreign commerce as much as promotion of multangular trade, which, in its very nature, does not prejudice direct trade, since multangular trading includes direct trading while stipulated direct trading excludes multangular trading. Also, it requires no argument to show that channelized direct trade is bound to increase the difficulties of net-debtor countries in making payments due on their borrowings. There is indeed involved what may be called fair play between direct and multangular foreign trade. The history of fulfilment of commercial treaties is not reassuring; as a group, they are decorated with the sub-order of "chastity, second-class." Only lately, the German government denounced the commercial treaty with the United States, and in general commercial treaties are denounceable after a fashion not permitted with more formal treaties. If, now, the bilateral treaties are to be non-denounceable, this will imply a somewhat different formulation. But nations change their minds on trade questions more easily and more often than on military questions. With return of prosperity, other countries, it may be predicted, will abrogate their direct trade agreements and return to multilateral commerce.

Apart from most-favored-nation treatment, it seems to us obviously impossible to get tariff rates lower by any form of agreement (bilateral or in conference) so long as currencies are depreciated and not revalued, foreign exchanges are unstable and unforeseeable, and prices between countries do not comport themselves with prices within countries. So long as importing countries, especially net-debtor countries, cannot balance their national budgets and cannot square their international accounts, it is impossible to ask them to lower their import tariffs, unless the soliciting countries are in position to guarantee acceptance of stipulated enlargements of exports from the countries in question.

This, in hypothesis, seems to be implied in the scheme of bilateral trade agreements between the principal countries. But this expectation, we insist, cannot be realized through direct channelized trade but only through multangular trade; and the otherwise development of multangular trade represents precisely the failure of the project of stimulating direct trade through bilateral agreements.

To lower tariffs without reestablishing the processes of trade would be to accomplish next to nothing. Devaluations of currencies have the effect of raising tariff rates; when currencies are revalued again, all tariff rates will require readjustment. To re-establish the processes of trade would be to make the lowering of tariffs through bilateral negotiations in large part superfluous. The high tariffs have been principally defensive, safeguards against the disorganization resulting from loss of equilibrium in the processes of trade. Once the processes of trade are re-established, the defensive need subsides; then high tariffs, and other impediments to imports, will tend to decline of their own weight. When the traders of different countries are once more free to trade with no more than foreseeable risks, with the tools of exchange again in their hands, traders' influence in each country will be found active in support of political agitation to lower tariffs and remove other obstacles to trade. The so-called "self-sufficiency," the "economic nationalism," which arose partly because international trade had become too risky to be continued, will subside by common consent when international trade has become again so practicable as to be remunerative. In our view the preference for direct over multilateral trade is a short-sighted mistake; quotas will turn out to be a restraint of commerce at the best and a boomerang at the worst; the departure from most-favored-nation treatment will prove to be the abandonment of a principle for an expedient; and the exaggeration of tariff rates over currency values will turn out to be an inversion of the perspective.

Limitations of planning. We have finally again to insist on the inherent limitations of the method. In the absence of experience and precedent, it is gratuitous to expect social planners in any country to possess the technical skill necessary to carry through expeditious and efficient bilateral trade negotations. The experts in the trades could not do it, and the planners outside the trades cannot do it. The factual material is not available—the data on costs and bulk lines, substitutes, limitations of capital, labor, and primary material, and standards of living in the competing countries. For the purpose under consideration the doctrine of comparative advantage is a paper hypothesis and would be of little assistance if it were a practical form of analysis. In short, what the mechanism of bilateral trade agreements is intended to do, it would not accomplish. The contracting parties would be negotiating on the basis of guesses, and the outcome would be determined largely by conjecture and conjunction. The negotiations might turn out to be largely a trading of higher prices for higher prices. In the physical sciences it is not only permissible, but indeed obligatory, for the student not to know what to think until the experiments are performed. This may some day become inevitable also in the social sciences, but at present no politician expects such rigid requirement to be met.

This all is on the assumption of absence of political influence. This of course is not at all to be assumed, just the opposite in fact. Most of the commercial treaties of the past have been tinged with political influence in support of vested interests or in opposition to new developments. The history of the steel cartels furnishes eloquent evidence. The trade agreements under the Empire preference policy of the British

Commonwealth of Nations are openly ridiculed on both sides.

Of course, we shall be told that the New Dealers in all countries will change all this. In every country the "Sermon on the Mount" is to replace the "law of the jungle." It will be urged that during the next few years the New Dealers in all countries will not only discover and define equity between all individuals and groups, but will discover and perfect a method of analysis of production, trade, and consumption which will provide the factual material for putting the ideals into practice. Unfortunately, the time element cannot be disregarded. The levels of intelligence, social and technical, vary widely in different countries. The laws and customs differ greatly from country to country. Racial characteristics and skin colors cannot be disregarded. Some countries have highly perfected industries, trading and banking organizations, others are more or less backward. Within a small circle the problem of planning appears simple; as the horizon extends, the perspective becomes inscrutable. By deferment of continuity and tenuousness of immediate results, programs of practical so-called reform wear themselves out.

It is proper to subscribe to the doctrine, in no wise imminent in the New Deal, that a mature net-creditor country should have a passive balance of merchandise trade. For example, with restoration of foreign commerce, our credits in merchandise and associated services should equal 4 billion dollars and our debits in merchandise and associated services should equal 5 billion dollars. But this cannot be predicated irrespective of prices. Other things equal, American nationals have the right to be paid the service charges on their loans and investments abroad, and American farmers may be accorded the privilege of exporting an additional volume of produce—but only if the nation thereby receives goods not produced at home or goods producible abroad at lower prices than at home. In a going economy, Americans with foreign investments and American farmers have not the right to impose higher costs upon their fellow citizens; and if the predicated exports of farm products and the receipts of Americans on foreign investments are only receivable at higher costs, then the investments abroad and in American farms should be liquidated. As a bare fact, the net-creditor countries of Europe have been glad to have passive balances of merchandise trade because they received from abroad goods not produced at home or producible at home only at higher prices.

In summary, with reversion to the earlier phraseology, the "planned middle course," in particular the application to foreign trade, is based on the best of intentions; it has available a limited and imperfect technical intelligence, due to indeterminateness of social and economic forces; it employs a mechanism not proved by experience and showing many obvious defects; finally, there is no evidence that we possess the discipline to carry through the plan. A majority in Congress is not an evidence of national discipline. Without regard to the inherent differences between the New Deal, Communism, and Fascism, there is no indication that the New Deal has acquired the discipline which obviously exists in Russia and in Italy. Judged by the NRA and the numerous alphabetical institutions devoted to unemployment relief and public works programs (specifically excepting the AAA), it is fair to say that our country exhibits about the same inchoate discipline that exists in Germany under the Nazi movement. It is not the discipline of officers that counts most in a social reform, but that of the rear ranks. The discipline that comes of coercion does not extend into details as does the discipline that comes of conviction. With good intentions, a limited intelligence, a faulty mechanism, and a low-grade discipline, the projected "reform" of international trade will make slow progress. Most realists will conclude that a flourishing foreign trade is more easily reformed than a languishing one, and the first order of the day is primary recovery of foreign commerce. If we insist on reform, we may fail in recovery.

Social planners, here and abroad, seem to make the assumption that the social sciences are as exact as the physical sciences. The precautions adopted in planning in the physical sciences may therefore be reasonably applied to planning in the social sciences. Back of the computations are theories; but to be safe guides, these theories must be based on experimental knowledge. Where the experimental knowledge is inadequate, the theories become misleading as bases of practice. This is the misfortune of the present stage of social planning. The experimental knowledge, meaning by that precedent and reproducible experience, is not adequate to constitute a safe foundation for far-reaching reconstruction.

National planning is based on size and characteristics of population, physical resources, and geographical relations. International planning presupposes clear-cut national units. The purchasing power of a currency abroad depends upon its purchasing power at home; in a similar sense, a social plan for foreign countries depends upon social status at home. We are introducing new rules into the social game. Would it not be wise to test out the new rules at home before we sponsor them in foreign tournaments?

History teaches lessons, for reformers as well as for obstructionists. Social improvement proceeds mostly by short-term adjustments, which gradually expand into long-term reconstruction. Economic improvements originate mostly within countries, and extend gradually into foreign lands. There is little chance of combining a short-term adjustment with a long-term reconstruction. There is little chance of combining a national with an international improvement. One proceeds from the small to the large, from the simple to the complex. Secretary Wallace is too ambitious; he would socialize simultaneously the agricultures of the United States and of the world. And this would be attempted by trial and error abroad before the method is proved at home. In every "planned society" under modern conditions it has been found necessary to "plan" public opinion in support of the "Plan" by securing a "planned" control of speech, press, and communications. Shall this prove true of the New Deal? It is characteristic of this administration that when an experiment into an unexplored field fails to yield the results hoped for, it is changed into another form of attack. We predict that the "planned middle course" of Secretary Wallace will turn out to be impracticable and will be replaced by a different policy. The baton will pass to the hand of the Secretary of State. Despite the new popular views of Sombart, Elliot, Wallace, *et al.*, the world will turn from planned and managed foreign trade to simple rules, lower tariffs and most-favored-nation treatment. Here and abroad, imports and exports will again be determined by costs and qualities, by elasticities of supply and demand, not by selection of goods and services by political officials, elected or appointed.

INDEX

Acreage contraction, appraised, 281–282
Agricultural Prices, book by Henry A. Wallace, 2
Agricultural products, average export of, 31
Agriculture, adjustment by withdrawal of crop acreage, 47–48; balance between industry and, 205–207
Agriculture's Interest in American World Trade, 214 n.
America Must Choose, pamphlet by Secretary Wallace, 1, 2, 3, 5 n., 7; diagnosis, prognosis, and treatment in, 14–21; on adjustment of supply to demand, 31–32, 38, 50–51, 52, 81, 82; on unemployment of farmers, 86; on agricultural exports, 98; on surplus problem, 105, 199; on international debts, 122; on exports *vs.* imports, 129, 148, 194, 198; compared with League of Nations *World Economic Survey,* 150; on exchange of goods, 153; on increasing imports, 154; on planned export policy, 169–170; on fulfilment of Isaiah's vision, 207 n.; on method of reciprocal trade, 209, 212; on tariff planning, 256; on organization necessary for "planned middle course," 262–264
"American Agriculture and World Markets," article by Secretary Wallace, 1
Argentina, wheat exports of, 243, 244, 245 n.
Asia, U.S. trade with, 183
Australia, wheat exports of, 243, 244

Balances of Payments, League of Nations, 121 n., 130 n.
Bean, L. H., 81 n.
Belgium, reciprocal treaty with, 220 n.
Bismarck, on good intentions, 8
Blackett, Basil P., 212, 254 n.
Borsig, E. von, 108
Brazil, valorization of coffee in, 168; reciprocal treaty with, 220 n.
Budget, national, 258

Canada, American trade and investments in, 183, 184, 213 n.; wheat expansion in, 243, 244
Capital, pre-war export of, 117–121; post-war export of American, 121–127; short-term movements of, 128; export of, current position, 141; post-war short-term movements of, 142
Cassel, Gustav, 252 n.
Central America, U.S. trade with, 183
"Charted Course Towards Stable Prosperity, A," article by Secretary Wallace, 3
Chicago, comparative wheat price in, 111
Clark, F. M., 43 n.
Clark, J. M., 42 n., 44 n.
Coffee, valorization of, in Brazil, 168
Cole, G. D. H., 42 n.
"Constantly normal granary," 38, 76 n.
Consumers' goods, 39
"Co-operatively good life," 8
Corn acreage, contraction of, 74–75
Corn and Hog Surplus of the Corn Belt, reviewed by Henry A. Wallace, 3
Cost, comparative, as basis of tariff rate, 193
Cotton, difficulties of exporting, 247–249
Crop land. *See* Farm land, in crops
Currencies, of trading countries, 249–255; extraordinary relations in, 252; stabilization of, 254–255
Currency, depreciated, effect on tariff revision, 187–188; depreciation of,

source of trade obstacles, 222; depreciation of, effect on trade account, 250; position and stability of, 258; revaluations of, 283–287

Debt, pre-war, to foreigners, 120; burden of, 258
Debts, foreign, service charges on, 137; war, influence on trade, 172; foreign, payments on, *vs.* more imports, 250
Diet, acreage contraction through changes in, 79–81
Difficulties, crucial, of foreign countries, 256–260
Dumping, effect on tariff revision, 188; exchange, 250

Economic internationalism, Secretary Wallace on, 17–19
Economic nationalism, Secretary Wallace on, 17, 19
Economist, on American tariff concessions, 207; on "new economics," 233; on dollar depreciation, 251 n.
Elliot, Walter E., 10, 30
Ellis, H. S., 39 n.
Epstein, R. C., 43 n., 44 n.
Europe, wheat production of, 245–246; importation of lard in, 246–247
Expenditures, government, abroad, 136; abroad, encouragement of, 174
Export tax, 169
Exporters, major, conflicting interests of, 243–249
Exports, American wheat and hog, 110–111; goods, effect on, of capital export, 123–124; American goods, post-war, 129; qualifications to reports on, 130–131; services attached to, 136–137; gold, 140; capital, current position of, 141; lowering gross value of, 153; decreasing quantity of, 168–170; decreasing price of, 170–172; countries classified by, 182; quotas, 201–204; industrial, European loss of, 232–233; states competing in, expanding list of, 235–243
Extractive countries, contrasted with processing countries, 166–167

Factories, branch, abroad, 123, 236–237
Farm land, classification of, 56–60; submarginal, 60-62, 70–73; in crops, retirement of, 62–83, 84–85
Farm management, effect of acreage contraction on, 77–78
Farm population, 86–87; peculiar social values of, 88–90; must be contracted, 90–91; decline in market for its products, 92–94; and acreage reduction, 93–94
Farm products, declining market for, 92–94; desired level of export of, 98–102; foreign need of, 102–105; problems of surplus in, 105; "exotic," in Europe, 106; foreign need of American, 113–114
Federal Council of the Churches of Christ in America, 12
Federal Farm Board, 38
Feiler, A., 127 n.
Fibers, imports of, 156–157, 161–163
Food production, self-sufficiency in, 108–110
Foreign exchange, surplus or deficit of, 182; stable rate of, *vs.* stable price level, 193; balance of, effect on bilateral treaties, 211; stabilization of, 283–287
Foreign trade, commercial services in, 137; New Deal policy on, 178–179; direct and indirect, 179–182; American by regions, 183–184; State Dept. estimate of recovery of, 184–185; restriction of, 185; visible and invisible items in, 204, 214; peak and low point of, 226; New Deal and, 226–228; obstacles to, 228–235
Foreign policy, necessary factors for successful, 5

Germany, compared with Great Britain and U.S., 149; denunciation of commercial treaty with U.S., 218 n.; shift in debtor-creditor position, 250
Gold, import and export of, 140, 172–173; decline in price level, 252
Gold bloc, 251
Gold standard, U.S. pseudo, 251; restoration of, 253–255, 285
Goods, imports of, 159–160, 239–243
Great Britain, its balance of trade, 144–146; pre-war comparisons with Germany, 149; leads in com-

mercial services, 175; trade coordination with U.S., 191; sterling exchange standard of, 251
Gregory, T. E., 120, 253 n.

Hansen, A. H., 137 n., 145 n., 211 n.
Hog products, American export of, 110–111
Hoover, Herbert, Lincoln Day address as President, 6–7
"Horse-trading," and bilateral treaties, 213–214
Hull, Cordell, compared with Henry A. Wallace, 4–5; on U.S. recovery in world trade, 185

Ickes, Harold L., and Secretary Wallace, 25
Imports, increased, stipulated as necessary, 129–130; qualifications to reports on, 130–131; services attached to, 136–137; gold, 140, 172–173; to be expected under New Deal plan, 144–149; to be expected under nationalism, 146; to be expected under "planned middle course," 146–147; added, to cover loan and investment charges, 148; effect of added export of farm products on, 148–149; raising gross value of, 153; increasing quantity of, 154–160; increasing price of, 160–168; effect of tariff rate on, 192–193; quotas, 201–204; effect of restriction in, on consumption, 232; of noncompetitive goods, increase in, 239–243
India, industrialization of, 238 n.
Industries, infant, 198 n.
Industry, balance between agriculture and, 205–207; urban, dispersion of, 232–239; urban, adjustment of, 282–283
International Economic Relations, on exports, 26; on balance of trade, 53–54; on reciprocal trade agreements, 191; on tariff concessions, 212; on flexibility in domestic price and income structures, 253–254
International payments, balance of, defined, 115–116
International Wheat Conferences: (1933-35), 168; (1931), 190
Internationalism, in U.S., 266–268

Investment, types of foreign, 123; American foreign, 124–126
Investments, foreign, service charges on, 127, 137; abroad, American direct, 238

Japan, industrialization of, 235, 238
Jones, J. M., 192 n.
Jones-Costigan Act, 220

Keynes, John Maynard, 39, 143, 215
Kuznets, Simon, 44 n.

Lard, European market for, 246–247
Lending, American, abroad criticized, 124–125; boomerang effect of foreign, 126
Leven, Maurice, 44 n.
Lloyd George, David, 10
Loeb, Harold, and associates, 44 n.

McClure, Wallace, 5 n.
Malnutrition, 102–105
Margarines, European manufacture of, 246, 247
Marx, Karl, 12
Mercantilism, contrasted with passive balance of trade, 171–172
Merchandise trade, bare, balance of, 131–136; correct balance of, table, 139; desired shift in, illustrated, 147–148; balance of, summarized, 151–152; balance of, shifted from credit or debit side, 153; passive balance of, contrasted with mercantilism, 171–172; passive balance of, enlargement of, 175–177; active *vs.* passive balance of, 182
Metals, increasing imports of, 155–156; imports of, increasing prices of, 161
Mills, F. C., 43 n.
Mitchell, Wesley C., 39
Morgenthau, Secretary of the Treasury Henry, on stabilization, 255 n.
Most-favored-nation treatment, 188–189, 190, 191, 192, 217–221; in "planned middle course," 289–291
Moulton, Harold G., 39 n., 44 n.
Mun, Thomas, 115 n.

National Resources Board, report of Land Planning Committee, 51; survey of submarginal land, 76

National income, share of agriculture in, 92
Nationalism, in U.S., 264–266
Net creditor and net debtor countries, 175, 182; international trade accounts of, 250
New Deal, case of, against society, 11–30; foreign trade policy, 178–179, 205–207; compared with Socialism, Fascism, Communism, 273–274; extension into foreign commerce, 280
New Democracy, The, book by Secretary Ickes, 25
New Frontiers, book by Secretary Wallace, 3; on social changes for cooperative good life, 20–21; on beneficent forces of disintegration, 22–25; on adjustment of supply to demand, 38; seeks farmers' cooperation, 48; on adjustment of supply to demand, 52–53, 54; on retirement of crop land, 70–71; on "ever-normal granary," 76 n.; on tariff bargaining, 215–216; on British increases in gold price, 251
Nourse, E. G., 44 n.

Ohlin, Bertil, 121 n.
Ottawa Agreement, 203
Owen, Robert (1771–1858), 11

Page, Thomas Walker, 194 n.
Palyi, V. M., 42 n.
Paper, imports of, 163–164
Pavlovsky, George, 192 n.
Peek, George N., 5 n., 127 n.; reappraisal of our foreign investments, 126 n., 143 n.
Pius XI, Pope, 12
"Planned middle course," Secretary Wallace's presentation of, 17, 19–25; four objectives of, 27–28; summarized, 29; acreage contraction under, 83, 281–282; imports to be expected under, 146–147; weakness of, 269–272; résumé of, 275–280; adjustment of urban industry in, 282–283; lowering of tariff rates in, 288–291; summarized appraisal, 294–295
Planning, limitations of, 292–296
Population, classified, 86–87; slackening rate of increase, 92, 94; pressure of food supply on, 92–95, 97. *See also* Farm population
Price, stable, *vs.* stable foreign exchange rate, 193
Price level, 258
Processing countries, contrasted with extractive countries, 166–167
Public confidence, state of, 258
Public domain, return of land to, 72

Quotas, import and export, 201–204, 205

Rathenau, Walter, 13
Raw materials, importation of, 240
Remittances, immigrant, encouragement of, 174
Robbins, Lionel, on planning, 41, 42, 195–196; on obstacles to trade, 256–257
Roosevelt, President Franklin D., 10; on economic balance, 25; on stabilizing exchange rates, 272 n.
Royal Institute of International Affairs, 253 n.
Rubber, Stevenson Plan for control of, 168
Runciman-Roca treaty, 200
Russell, Bertrand, on economic nationalism, 7; on salvation from collective suicide, 262
Russia, industrialization of, 238

Sayre, Francis Bowes, 5 n.; on most-favored-nation treatment, 219 n.
Schumpeter, Joseph A., 39
Self-sufficiency, in food importing countries, 231–232; origin of, 258–260
Service charges, 137; currently due from abroad, 142–143
Services, in international commerce, 136–137; increasing use of foreigners', 173–175
Ships, use of foreign or American, 174
Smith, J. G., 192 n.
South America, U.S. trade with, 183; industrialization of, 238
Southard, F. A., 192 n., 236 n.
Stamp, Sir Josiah, 120
Sterling-area, 251
Subsidies, effect on tariff revision, 188
Sugar, imports of, 158–159, 165;

Cuba's restriction of exports, 168
Subnutrition, 102–105
Supply, adjustment to demand, 32–37, 45–46

Tariff, difficulties of revision, 187–191; method of reduction, 192–199; reciprocal adjustments in, 199–207; trade obstacles outside, removal of, 221–225, 287–288; high, effect on depression, 256–258, 259–260; reduction of, of secondary importance, 293
Thorp, Willard L., 150 n.
Travel, foreign, by Americans, encouragement of, 174
Treaties, fulfilment of, 8; bilateral, effect on tariff revision, 189–190, 191, 192; bilateral, difficulties of, 199–207; bilateral, number and scope of, 208–217; bilateral, policy of, 223–225; bilateral, dependence on monetary policy, 279–280; bilateral, method of enforcing, 280

Unemployment, effect on tariff revision, 187
United States, gold reserve of, 140; compared with Germany, 149; export status of, 182; foreign trade of, by regions, 183–184; departure from traditional tariff legislation, 186–192; Canadian investments in, 213 n.; shift in debtor-creditor position, 250; gold standard of, 251; nationalism in, 264–266; internationalism in, 266–268; "planned middle course" in, 269–272
U.S. Department of Commerce, *Balance of International Payments of the U.S.*, 131
U.S. Department of State, position on most-favored-nation treatment, 220–221

Values, essential, grading in domestic trade, 49

Wagner, Adolf, 108
Wallace, Henry A., record of, 1–4; compared with Cordell Hull, 4–5
Wallace's Farmer, 1, 3, 26
Warburton, Clark, 44 n.
West Indies, U.S. trade with, 183
Wheat, American export of, 110–111; American importation of, 111; difficulties of exporting countries, 243–246
Wheat growing, poleward migration of, 106–107
Williams, J. H., 253 n.
Wooton, Barba P., 42 n.
World Affairs Pamphlets, 1, 2
World Economic Conferences, 1927 and 1933, 190; 1927, *Final Report* on most-favored-nation treatment, 217
World Economic Survey, contrasted with *America Must Choose*, 150
Wheat acreage, contraction of, 73–74; of major exporting countries, 243